"*Where Justice and Mercy Meet* combines solid moral reflections on the death penalty with captivating stories of people caught up in this system. Both deeply interesting and educational, this book should reach a wide diversity of readers."

— Richard C. Dieter, Executive Director
Death Penalty Information Center
Washington, DC

"Schieber, Conway, and McCarthy have put together a true Catholic meditation on the death penalty. Their authors bring us into an immediate consideration of what the death penalty entails and shepherd us through a variety of considerations, including the evolving tradition of Catholicism that finally and inevitably brings us to oppose this form of punishment. What is most effective about this collection is just how mindful the editors are of the readers. They accompany us with introductions, narratives, testimonies, and questions such that we cannot eventually avoid the question about whether as Catholics we can in any way speak approvingly of this anti-life practice. A prophetic and necessary work for our time that will hopefully awaken us all to a very dark and hidden, and profoundly unchristian, practice. Well done!"

— James F. Keenan, SJ
Founders Professor in Theology
Boston College

Where Justice and Mercy Meet

Catholic Opposition to the Death Penalty

Edited by

Vicki Schieber, Trudy D. Conway,
and David Matzko McCarthy

LITURGICAL PRESS
Collegeville, Minnesota

www.litpress.org

Library of Congress Cataloging-in-Publication Data

Where justice and mercy meet : Catholic opposition to the death penalty / edited by Vicki Schieber, Trudy Conway, and David Matzko McCarthy.
        pages cm
     ISBN 978-0-8146-3508-7 — ISBN 978-0-8146-3533-9 (e-book) (print)
        1. Capital punishment—Religious aspects—Catholic Church.
     I. Schieber, Vicki.   II. Conway, Trudy.   III. McCarthy, David Matzko.

HV8698.W474   2013
261.8'3366—dc23   2012040762

We dedicate this book to murder victim family members
who focus on forgiveness and restorative justice
in response to their deep loss and suffering.
Your witness fills us with hope.

Contents

Foreword   xi
   Sr. Helen Prejean, CSJ

Acknowledgments   xv

Contributors   xix

Part I: The Death Penalty Today   1

   Chapter 1: Facing the Truth   3
      The Appearances and Realities of Lethal Injection   6
         Kim Philip Hansen
      Review and Looking Forward   13
      Questions for Discussion   14

   Chapter 2: Seeing Ourselves from an International Perspective   16
      An International Perspective on the Death Penalty   18
         Amanda Beal
      Review and Looking Forward   28
      Questions for Discussion   30

   Chapter 3: Trying to Get It Right   31
      Rethinking the Death Penalty   34
         Trudy D. Conway
      Review and Looking Forward   43
      Questions for Discussion   44

   Chapter 4: The Power of Stories   46
      Stirring Hearts and Minds   49
         Kurt Blaugher

Review and Looking Forward   55
Questions for Discussion   56

Part II: A Christian Rethinking of the Death Penalty   57

Chapter 5: Forgiveness and Healing   59
The Eucharist: Forgiveness and Personhood   61
Rodica Stoicoiu
Review and Looking Forward   67
Questions for Discussion   69

Chapter 6: Jesus Christ and Sacrifice   70
Jesus Christ as Scapegoat: Christology, Sacrifice,
and the Death Penalty   72
David Cloutier
Review and Looking Forward   81
Questions for Discussion   83

Chapter 7: Hebrew Scriptures—"an Eye for an Eye"   84
Biblical Principles: Mosaic Law   86
Richard Buck
Review and Looking Forward   95
Questions for Discussion   96

Chapter 8: The Bible and the Church   97
WWJD? Jesus, the Death Penalty, and US Catholics   99
Sr. Mary Katherine Birge, SSJ
Review and Looking Forward   107
Questions for Discussion   108

Part III: Church Teachings on Capital Punishment   111

Chapter 9: The Catholic Moral Tradition   113
The Ancient, Medieval, and Early Modern Views   115
E. Christian Brugger
Review and Looking Forward   124
Questions for Discussion   125

Chapter 10: The Church Today   126
The Church and Capital Punishment in the Modern Period   128
E. Christian Brugger
Review and Looking Forward   135
Questions for Discussion   136

Chapter 11: The *Catechism* in Historical Perspective   137
    The Catechetical Tradition   139
        Msgr. Stuart W. Swetland
    Review and Looking Forward   147
    Questions for Discussion   148

Chapter 12: The Death Penalty in the Catechetical Tradition   149
    The Gospel of Life   151
        Msgr. Stuart W. Swetland
    Review and Looking Forward   159
    Questions for Discussion   161

Part IV: The Least of These   163

Chapter 13: Money Matters   165
    The Economics of the Death Penalty   168
        Alejandro Cañadas and John Schwenkler
    Review and Looking Forward   176
    Questions for Discussion   178

Chapter 14: A Legacy of Race   179
    The Death Penalty and Race   181
        Timothy W. Wolfe
    Review and Looking Forward   192
    Questions for Discussion   193

Chapter 15: Vulnerabilities and Risks   194
    People with Disabilities and the Death Penalty   196
        *Thomas H. Powell, Robert Perske, Patricia A. Lester,
        and Dominique L. Nguyen*
    Review and Looking Forward   206
    Questions for Discussion   208

Chapter 16: A Matter of Discipleship   209
    The Heart of Our Faith   212
        Fr. James Donohue, CR
    Review and Looking Forward   221
    Questions for Discussion   222

Conclusion   223
        Vicki Schieber

Foreword

Sr. Helen Prejean

As a Catholic, is this, perhaps, the way you feel about this issue?

> You have *got* to be kidding! You *cannot* be saying that the Catholic Church now teaches that the death penalty is a pro-life issue on some kind of equal par with the quintessential pro-life issue of all time—abortion? Unborn children are absolutely innocent. They have dignity because they're coming straight from the hand of God, and they're vulnerable and defenseless and deserve a chance to live. As a Catholic, to be pro-life has always meant being against abortion. In fact, the two concepts, pro-life and anti-abortion, are practically synonymous. But murderers are in no way innocent. They are guilty as sin of horrendous acts against innocent people. They completely lost their human dignity when they callously killed their fellow human beings. They broke the law and showed no respect for human life, and we must deal with them as justice demands. They have done vile, unspeakable acts, and acts have consequences. You kill others; you give up your own life. Murderers deserve to die, and the families of their victims deserve simple justice. Victims' families are traumatized forever by murderers' heinous deeds against their loved ones. Why should murderers be allowed to live when the victims' families' loved ones lie buried forever in the ground? What about respecting the dignity of victims' families? I'm a practicing Catholic and pro-life to the core, and I say in good faith and a clean conscience that I believe in the death penalty. The Catholic Church has always taught, and continues to teach today, that those who murder and are a menace to society may be executed by the state. Protecting the lives of innocent citizens from callous murderers is pro-life, too. It is precisely because I am pro-life that I support the death penalty.

Welcome to the swirling waters of current Catholic discourse on the death penalty. Welcome to the pages of this amazing book. A unique endeavor, I must say, is this compendium of reflections created out of prayerful, faith-inspired discussions, research, courses, conferences, and conversations with authors like me by faculty and friends of Mount St. Mary's University. I know of no other book quite like this one. It is a joint project, two years in the making, that comes from the minds and hearts of a small but mighty Catholic community. Glancing at the table of contents you'll see that the death penalty issue is examined from every possible angle. In every essay, every chapter, you'll discover information you never knew before. I promise you that. I've learned things from this book that I never knew before, and I'm steeped up to my earlobes in this issue. I eat it for breakfast, and often, before I fall asleep it's the last of my waking thoughts. There's plenty to learn and reflect on because putting people to death legally in a country, oftentimes with religious justifications and legitimacy, is, to put it mildly, a moral issue with many, many ramifications.

Never fear that these pages are a one-sided polemic, aimed only at upholding the perpetrator's rights. The suffering of murder victims' families and their search for healing also receive ample expression in these pages. Is it true that the only way grieving families can experience justice, healing, and "closure" is by the deaths of those who killed their loved ones? Well, prepare your soul for the testimony of Vicki Schieber, whose daughter was murdered, and whose words will be the last in this book. And rightfully so. A vibrant Catholic, Vicki is a mother who has suffered the loss of her child in the most wrenching, anguished way imaginable. But, with Christ's healing grace, this valiant woman has come through the crucible of loss alive and believing and loving in the most generous way. It seems fitting and right that hers is the last voice we will have, ringing in our ears at the end of the book. And throughout the book you will learn Vicki is joined by other Catholics—like Marietta Jaeger and Antoinette Bosco—who respond to the murders of their family members in the spirit of the gospel.

What I love most about this book is that at its burning center is the most essential dialogue of all—the death penalty brought face-to-face with the Gospel of Jesus. As we confront the death penalty, this is the heart of the challenge for us Christians. The development of Catholic teaching that you'll see etched out in these pages arises out of this dialogue. The living tradition of the church is always emerging out of the dialogue we Catholics engage in head-on with the suffering world. In the Catholic section of this precious little tome, you'll hear about my personal dialogue with Pope John Paul II about the death penalty. Every word of my letter to him was forged out of the personal experience of watching human beings put to death in the electric chair or by lethal injection. It clarified forever for me the essential meaning of the Gospel of Jesus, and I found myself saying to the Holy Father: "Walking with this man to his death, the essence of the Gospel of Jesus becomes very clear: what are you for? compassion or vengeance? love or hate? life or death?" There's nothing like seeing the reality of state killing close-up to clarify what we really believe. All the political and cultural and legal rhetoric gets stripped away. That's why in my books, *Dead Man Walking* and *The Death of Innocents*, I have included the subtitle *An Eyewitness Account*.

So, welcome to the journey of delving into this book. I suggest you gather in community—even if it's just with two or three other people—as you descend into these pages. It traces a faith journey of the community of believers who wrote and compiled what you now hold in your hands, now waiting to be explored and prayed over by you. Who knows how you might emerge out of the other side of this journey? Do you believe in the Holy Spirit? I do. I believe the Holy Spirit guides us and nudges us (and sometimes drags us kicking and screaming) always toward greater and greater *Life*. Speaking of the Holy Spirit, this book does not necessarily need to be read in linear fashion, starting at the beginning and plowing through to the end (it might feel like *plowing* if you do that). Go immediately to the chapter that most attracts you, most draws you in, and start there. That's mainly how the Spirit of Love moves us—through attraction. So, feel free to delve into the book as the Spirit moves you.

The Holy Spirit and I have been journeying together on the death penalty issue for twenty-five years or so—in the presence of the Catholic community, which means everything to me. I keep learning. With God's grace, the energy keeps rising within me. It is with great joy that I collaborate with the faith community of Mount St. Mary's in putting this book into your hands. May its words stir you to greater Life. That is my hope for you. That is my prayer for you. Come, let us journey together.

Acknowledgments

This book is a testament to a number of goods valued by its editors and authors, in particular the goods of community, collaboration, interdisciplinary inquiry, and service. Over the past fifteen years, Mount St. Mary's University generously sponsored lectures, classes, conferences, projects, and seminars focusing on the issue of the death penalty. This focus is not surprising, for the Mount seeks to deepen students' understanding of their faith as practiced in just and compassionate engagement with the world. Often people lose interest in issues over time; our community's sustained interest in the topic of the death penalty speaks well of the Mount. The first death penalty speakers at the Mount were persons who cared deeply about this issue—relatives of murder victims who oppose the death penalty. The depth of their convictions and passionate work to end the death penalty made a lasting impression on our community and shaped our ongoing inquiry. Vicki Schieber, one of our editors, was one of our first speakers. Her stand against the death penalty in response to the tragic murder of her beloved daughter, Shannon, was a testament to her living the Gospel of Christ. Over the past decade, faculty, students, and speakers collaborated across disciplines in exploring the many facets of the current practice of the death penalty. We learned much from each other and for this, we are grateful.

In the summer of 2010, Karen Clifton, director of the Catholic Mobilizing Network to End the Use of the Death Penalty (CMN), and Vicki Schieber, one of its executive members, approached Trudy Conway, a member of the Mount's philosophy department, about contributing to the educational outreach initiatives of CMN. Knowing the collaborative spirit and creative work of the Mount's faculty, Trudy proposed that faculty work with David McCarthy of our theology department, Vicki Schieber, and herself in writing a book on Catholic teaching on the death penalty.

We also invited Christian Brugger, the author of *Capital Punishment and Roman Catholic Moral Tradition* and past participant in death penalty programming at the Mount, to join us in our work. Over the next two years, faculty from a range of disciplines participated in discussions with persons actively involved in repeal of the death penalty and ministry to death row inmates. We learned much from our discussions. The enthusiasm and insights of the authors throughout this project have been impressive. As active scholars and dedicated teachers, they sacrificed their time and effort in working with us on this project. We are deeply grateful to them for their excellent contributions to this book. They evidence the importance of collaborative, interdisciplinary inquiry distinctive of Catholic liberal arts education.

Sister Helen Prejean met with the editors and authors as the project began to take shape. Her keen insights guided the design of this book. She emphasized the importance of our inquiry taking off from the stark realities of the death penalty in the United States today and the role Catholic social teaching can play in bringing us to reflect on its moral dimensions. As discussed in chapter 4, Sr. Helen's *Dead Man Walking* was a catalyst precipitating Americans' caring about this issue. Based on her wise recommendation that we emphasize the human dimensions of the death penalty, we wove personal narratives throughout the book. Her guidance made this a better book.

On many levels this book is a testament to community. A faculty community shaped this book. A community of prison ministers influenced our reflections. A community of families of murder victims and condemned inmates brought us to understand the realities of the death penalty. A community of passionately committed abolitionists motivated our work. Because of the many relationships that shaped this work, our references to persons throughout the book use their first names. Our own collaborative work on the death penalty has been deeply enriched by what we have learned from these praiseworthy persons who do what Sr. Helen calls "soul-size work."

This book was made possible through the collaborative work of a philosopher, theologian, and former sociology professor/business professional and current death penalty activist. We have worked on this project as we jostled—sometimes with stress, other times with laughter—our busy and rich lives devoted to family, teaching, scholarship, advocacy, and local community. We appreciate the patience of our spouses, children, and grandchildren as we focused on this work. With enthusiasm and passion we worked on this worthwhile project and are always indebted to the support of two excellent secretaries, Katie Soter and Gloria Balsley.

The final chapter of this book refers to the "hopeful perseverance" of Dorothy Day. Teaching is definitely a vocation sustained by hope. We greatly appreciate the enthusiastic anticipation of this book expressed by our students. They are what drives, sustains, and makes joyful all our work. We look forward to having them join our conversations about this book. We hope it brings them and other readers to deepen their faith in its just and compassionate engagement with the world. We also hope our book furthers the good work of the Catholic Mobilizing Network to End the Use of the Death Penalty.

Vicki Schieber, Trudy D. Conway,
and David Matzko McCarthy
Editors

Contributors

Friends of Mount St. Mary's University

E. Christian Brugger holds the J. Francis Cardinal Stafford Chair of Moral Theology at St. John Vianney Theological Seminary in Denver. He speaks across the country, publishes, and teaches in the areas of bioethics, sexual ethics, and Catholic social teaching.

Robert Perske is an advocate for persons with intellectual disabilities in the criminal justice system and author of numerous books and articles on this subject. He has provided decades of service to defense attorneys and defendants with intellectual disabilities, primarily in murder and rape trials.

Vicki Schieber is a member of the organizational team of the Catholic Mobilizing Network to End the Use of the Death Penalty (CMN) and staffs CMN's internship and educational programming initiatives at the Mount.

Rodica Stoicoiu is a systematic theologian who specializes in the theology of the liturgy. She has taught at the undergraduate and graduate levels; her other areas of research include trinitarian and communal ecclesiology and work in the Roman Catholic/Orthodox dialogue.

Mount St. Mary's University

Amanda L. Beal is a professor in the political science department. Her research is predominantly in the area of social justice, especially welfare and development initiatives in Latin America and Europe. She teaches courses in international studies and in the core curriculum as a global cultures specialist.

Sr. Mary Katherine Birge, SSJ, is a Sister of St. Joseph of Springfield, Massachusetts, and a professor of theology at the Mount. Her areas of research and writing include the Synoptic Gospels, Pauline literature, and the Catholic Epistles (letters of James, Peter, John, and Jude). She teaches mainly Scripture courses in the core curriculum and for theology majors.

Kurt Blaugher is a professor of theatre in the Department of Visual and Performing Arts. He has directed over fifty productions at the Mount. His area of research is modern and contemporary American theatre. He teaches courses in performance and theatre history, as well as courses within the core curriculum.

Richard M. Buck is a professor in the philosophy department. His research and writing is in the areas of ethics, political philosophy, philosophy of law, and Jewish philosophy. He regularly teaches courses in political philosophy, philosophy of law, and the core curriculum.

Alejandro Cañadas is a professor of economics at the Mount. His research interests are development economics, behavioral economics, and neuroeconomics. He teaches macroeconomic courses at the Mount and integral neuroeconomics in the MA program in Integral Economic Development Management at the Catholic University of America.

David Cloutier is a professor of theology. He teaches and writes primarily in the areas of moral theology, sexual ethics, and Catholic social thought. He has written a textbook on Catholic sexual ethics, and his current research pertains to the morality of luxury consumption in today's society.

Trudy D. Conway is a professor of philosophy. Her areas of research and writing are contemporary philosophy, virtue ethics, and intercultural dialogue. She teaches courses in the core curriculum and on contemporary philosophy, virtue ethics, the death penalty, and intercultural dialogue.

Rev. James M. Donohue, CR, is a Resurrectionist priest and a professor of theology. His Resurrectionist community is based in Ontario, Canada. Father Jim presides and preaches at St. Bernadette Parish in Severn, Maryland. His research and writing focuses on the rites for the sick, the dying, and the deceased. He teaches ministry and pastoral education courses as well as courses in the core curriculum.

Kim P. Hansen is a professor of sociology. His research and writing focuses on religious diversity, professional subcultures, and the medicalization of death and dying. He teaches sociology of medicine, sociology of religion, sociology of the military, and social inequality.

Patricia A. Lester is a Mount graduate of the class of 2011 and is currently working for the Fellowship of Catholic University Students at the University of Connecticut.

David M. McCarthy is a professor in the theology department. He teaches in the core curriculum as well as courses on the *Catechism*, theology and film, moral theology, and Catholic social teaching.

Dominique L. Nguyen served as a presidential intern and is a member of the class of 2014.

Thomas H. Powell is president of Mount St. Mary's University and a former professor of special education. His scholarly research and writings focus on persons with intellectual disabilities, especially social interactions between children with disabilities and their siblings.

John Schwenkler is a professor of philosophy. His research is mainly in the philosophy and psychology of mind and action. He teaches courses in the core curriculum and in epistemology and philosophy of psychology.

Msgr. Stuart W. Swetland is the Archbishop Harry Flynn Professor of Christian Ethics at Mount St. Mary's. His research and writing are in the areas of moral theology, Christian social ethics, Catholic identity, and catechesis. He teaches courses in moral philosophy, theology, and the ethics of war and peace.

Timothy W. Wolfe is a professor in the sociology and criminal justice department. His research and writing are in the areas of race and the criminal justice system, as well as the sociology of jazz. He teaches mainly research methods, data analysis, and introductory sociology.

Part I

The Death Penalty Today

This book focuses on the Catholic position on the death penalty, especially as it is practiced in our contemporary American society. The opening chapters bring us directly into the reality of the death penalty in the United States today. Although the number of executions has declined in the last decade and the current method of execution has run into complications, executions keep occurring. Yet they occur in the middle of the night in restricted, deep recesses of prisons with only select prison personnel participating and few witnesses observing. They often receive only passing acknowledgment in local papers. For the most part our lives go on without awareness of their occurrence. The chapters of part I raise our awareness. The first two chapters ask us to consider the realities of the current method of execution (i.e., lethal injection) and the company we keep in continuing to perform executions at a high rate compared to other countries in the world. The third chapter introduces us to the long and conflicted American debate about the death penalty and to the moral and legal concerns that have brought the courts to tinker endlessly with this practice. Most Americans are not aware of these debates or the intricacies of their arguments. But films, dramatic performances, and the stories of victims' families have helped the public start to care and think about capital punishment. The fourth chapter explores the role of story: by showing the human faces of those affected by murder and the death penalty, the issue starts to matter to us.

❖

Chapter 1

Facing the Truth

Editors

This opening chapter asks us to deal with what actually occurs in execution chambers across our country. Kim Hansen, a professor of sociology, strips away illusions, bringing us to face the realities of what American citizens ask prison officers to do in their names. Starting this book with executions is risky. If we show that methods of execution are inhumane, then many readers might say, "Good. Murderers should suffer at least as much or more than the victims of their brutality." However, I, Vicki Schieber, can tell you that this claim is self-destructive. My daughter was raped and murdered in 1998, and still it is hard to write the words and remember the horror of it. My husband and I realized that seeking vengeance would not, as we were told, bring closure. Victims' families who pursue the death sentence suffer from high rates of divorce, unemployment, and poor health, and most never gain the promised closure of the execution itself. Instead, my husband and I chose to honor our daughter's memory through our work to abolish the death penalty. We have found capital punishment to be extremely arbitrary and biased, and often a threat to innocent individuals. When Shannon was murdered, we hardly knew what to think. We were devastated and wanted justice. We had a sense, however, that capital punishment was not right. Now, through our work against the death penalty, Shannon's memory is hopeful and healing for the world. Capital punishment could not be, for us, an expression of Shannon's intelligence, energy, love, and hope.

One of the other editors of this book, Trudy Conway, spent time between hope and hopelessness with a death row inmate as he awaited execution. Trudy will tell the story: I (Trudy) regularly visited a man who, all told, was on death row for twenty-two years. The time just before the execution is called the "deathwatch." Two or three officers stay with the prisoner to prevent suicide and to begin the highly detailed execution protocol. My attention was naturally focused on Vernon, the condemned man. I knew his worries about his grief-stricken family members, his faith-filled hope for a last-minute stay (which was granted at the last minute), his comfort to me as I lost hope, and his concern that he uphold his dignity as he endured the deathwatch. But in experiencing this deathwatch, I couldn't avoid also thinking about the correction officers. They had come to know the person they were now preparing to kill—to kill as part of a job and often against their own wishes. Wardens and religious advisers take the final walk to death with the condemned inmate. They know most closely the realities that Kim Hansen will describe in this chapter and the toll they take on human souls. Some witnesses say a bit of oneself dies during an execution.

The chapter unmasks the truth about executions by lethal injection. We try hard to convince ourselves that this most technologically advanced, clean, efficient method of killing is civilized and humane. But as we strip away the illusions, moving beyond appearances to realities, we discover it shares many of the features of previous methods—hanging, death squad shooting, electrocution, and gas asphyxiation—now viewed as barbaric and uncivilized. Kim is convinced that if ordinary people knew what really happened at executions, support for the death penalty would decline further. He sets out to have us face what others directly witness.

In *Dead Man Walking*, Sr. Helen Prejean describes the first execution she witnessed. She waited with Patrick Sonnier at Louisiana State Penitentiary's execution chamber in Angola. "A metal cap is placed on [Patrick's] head and an electrode is screwed in at the top and connected to a wire that comes from a box behind the chair. An electrode is fastened to his leg. A strap placed around his chin holds his head tightly to the back of the chair. He grimaces. He cannot speak anymore. A grayish green cloth is placed over his head. . . . Only the warden remains in the room now, only the warden and the man strapped into the chair. . . . I hear three clanks as the switch is pulled with pauses in between. Nineteen hundred volts, then let the body cool, then five hundred volts, pause again, then nineteen hundred volts. 'Christ, be with him, have mercy on him,' I pray silently."[1]

In another state, Donald Cabana, warden of Mississippi State Penitentiary, witnessed his last execution, this time by a seemingly more humane method—death by gas asphyxiation. Like other wardens, his main concern centered on all going smoothly according to strict protocol, without anything going wrong. Supportive of the death penalty throughout his

---

[1] Sr. Helen Prejean, *Dead Man Walking* (New York: Vintage, 1994), 93–94.

twenty-five years as a corrections officer, he began to question this ultimate punishment through the years of responsibility for overseeing it. In his book *Death at Midnight, the Confession of an Executioner*, he marked the execution of Connie Ray Stevens as a "personal moment of truth."[2] Cabana's account makes us face the reality he faced.

"Let's do it," Donald emphatically announced. Then "the lever dropped with a thunderous noise, sending its deadly payload of cyanide into the chemicals beneath the chair. The EKG monitor fluctuated wildly, its beeping growing louder and louder. With Edward Johnson's execution still fresh in my mind I knew only too well what to expect . . . [as] a cloud of poisonous gas began rising from the floor."[3] Donald had counseled Connie to take deep breaths to bring his death more swiftly. To his horror, Connie began to hold his breath, gripping the arms of the execution chair. Donald recognized this as the last act of a man desperate to live, even as he faced an inevitable death. Calling to God to make him breathe deeply, he witnessed the violent throes of his dying begin—his eyes rolling back into his head, a wild fear gripping his face, all his muscles straining, and his face twitching violently as liquids flowed from his mouth and eyes. After eight minutes as observers waited for the EKG machine to register his death, Connie's body went rigid one last time, appearing to take one loud guttural last breath. Officers in protective garb and face masks began to wash his body down with a garden hose. As he left the execution scene, Donald Cabana knew he would never again do this. And he knew that the public had to face what it asks public servants to do in the secret recesses of execution chambers across this country.

As he reflected on the execution of this twenty-seven-year-old man he had come to know well, he found himself thinking how insane this execution was, how this young man's life was worth saving, how they would be executing a man who no longer was the young, bitter, authority-defiant drug user arrested years ago, how he had accepted responsibility for his crime and posed no threat to his fellow inmates. His thoughts turned to the suffering of the victim and his family traceable to a young man's selfish act of greed in a robbery. But he found himself questioning whether the execution of this frightened, lonely, and deeply remorseful man would ever eradicate their pain. He questioned how this sordid business of executions was supposed to be the great equalizer, the restorer of justice. Moral awareness begins with naming things as they are, and the death certificate

---

[2] Donald Cabana, *Death at Midnight: The Confession of an Executioner* (Boston: Northeastern University Press, 1996), xi.

[3] Ibid., 188.

issued at executions clearly states the cause of death as "homicide." But can a legal homicide equalize or rectify an illegal homicide? Convinced that we, as members of society, should raise ourselves higher than the acts of murderers, Donald Cabana refused to participate in any more executions using any method. He concluded that if the public continues to seek vengeance through executions, let us at least witness and face what we called him to do.

In *The Death of Innocents: An Eyewitness Account of Wrongful Executions*, Sr. Helen Prejean's words hauntingly echo Donald Cabana's: "Citizens would consider the death penalty even more shocking if they could see it close up. But the death penalty is designed to make sure that doesn't happen."[4] Kim Hansen agrees that each of us needs to face the truth about executions, played out in the darkness of night to shield citizens from their awful realities. The following chapter forces us to see our American executions up close. Our further reflections on the death penalty have to begin with these stark realities.

The Appearances and Realities of Lethal Injection

Kim Philip Hansen

Executions don't really look like executions anymore. If you were to witness a typical one, you wouldn't see a gallows or a gas chamber, a firing squad or electric chair. Instead, you would see a bed or gurney, the kind they have in hospitals. The prisoner will be strapped to this bed, the way a mental patient might be strapped in to keep him from hurting himself. He'll be covered with a clean white sheet up to his waist, almost as if he's been tucked in. An intravenous (IV) line will be put into his arm by a nurse who wears white plastic gloves and swabs his arm with disinfectant first. It really looks like the nurse cares about the prisoner and wants to protect him from unnecessary embarrassment, pain, and infection. Maybe you'll recall the last time a nurse stuck you in the arm. In fact, it looks a lot as if he's there to give blood. There's a machine in the room that monitors his heart rate. The beeping sound it makes strengthens the impression that you're in a hospital. The nurse checks the IV line one last time, before someone behind a curtain presses a button that sends chemicals into the prisoner's arm. He seems to fall asleep very quickly, and nothing much

---

[4] Sr. Helen Prejean, *The Death of Innocents: An Eyewitness Account of Wrongful Executions* (New York: Vintage, 2006), 234.

seems to have changed except the machine monitoring his heart. You remember that this wasn't a hospital, but a prison, and that this was no medical treatment. The reason why you forgot that was that you were supposed to. Executions are made to look like medical procedures on purpose, because appearances matter.

We admire medicine in our culture. Doctors are respected in society and cast as heroes on TV. We grant them lots of authority—who else gets to see you naked or prick you with a needle? We marvel at the body of scientific knowledge they command, and associate science with things like progress and neutrality. We assume that doctors go into medicine because they want to help people, and look to them in our most vulnerable moments, hoping they will save our lives and the lives of those we love.[5] If a doctor found a man lying in a bed, his veins full of poison, we know that doctor would try to save the man's life, unless, of course, the doctor was participating in an execution.

Think about that for a second! When prisoners are executed by lethal injection, medical procedures and medical people are used to take life rather than save it. Why would we kill people in such a distorted way? The answer has to do with our culture's denial of death.[6] Before the United States modernized, most people lived on farms where animals were slaughtered all the time and almost everyone was born—and died—at home. Death was sad, but familiar. Now in the twenty-first century, we celebrate youth, dread growing old, and fear death. If doctors are usually heroes in our popular stories, the dead are usually angry and frightening villains: zombies, ghosts, and vampires.[7]

In spite of that, we modern Americans like to think of ourselves as more rational, more humane, and more advanced than we were in the past—more civilized! In the process, we developed ever more "civilized" and "humane" methods of execution.[8] Our Supreme Court, for example, has decided that executions can only be constitutional if they don't violate the

---

[5] See Paul Starr's *The Social Transformation of American Medicine: The Rise of a Sovereign Profession and the Making of a Vast Industry* (New York: Basic Books, 1982); and Elliot Friedson's *Profession of Medicine: A Study of the Sociology of Applied Knowledge* (Chicago: University of Chicago Press, 1970).

[6] See Philippe Ariès, *Western Attitudes toward Death: From the Middle Ages to the Present* (Baltimore: Johns Hopkins University Press, 1974).

[7] See Michael R. Leming and George D. Dickinson, *Understanding Dying, Death, and Bereavement* (Fort Worth: Harcourt Brace, 1940).

[8] See David Garland, *Peculiar Institution: America's Death Penalty in an Age of Abolition* (Cambridge, MA: Belknap, 2010).

Eighth Amendment's ban on punishments that are "cruel" or "unusual." So we switched from hanging to shooting to electrocuting to gassing, each method supposedly less cruel than the previous one, and each with its own difficulties in practice. Lethal injection is simply the latest attempt to find a method of execution that looks humane and doesn't upset witnesses.

The appearances of lethal injection are deceiving: it's not a humane procedure at all. To understand why, it's necessary to understand what it is that's being injected into the prisoner. A typical execution uses three different drugs, injected one after the other. The first drug used is sodium thiopental. It's an anesthetic that is supposed to make the prisoner unconscious. The second drug is pancuronium bromide (also called pavulon), which paralyzes the prisoner's muscles. Among the muscles pancuronium bromide paralyzes are the ones used for breathing, so the prisoner begins to suffocate. It also paralyzes the facial muscles, arms, and legs. So if lethal injection looks painless, it is because the second drug makes it impossible for the prisoner to wince, writhe, or cry out. The third and last drug given is potassium chloride, which makes the prisoner's heart stop beating.[9]

If everything goes according to procedure, the prisoner will theoretically be unconscious when the second two drugs are given, and will die quickly and without much pain. However, all kinds of things can and do go wrong. First of all, it can be hard to start a proper IV line. It can be tricky even with medical training and experience, and execution teams often lack both. Sometimes, the prisoner's vein will collapse when the needle is inserted. Finding a good vein is harder than usual if the prisoner is overweight, cold, a former intravenous drug user, or nervous—and who wouldn't be nervous at their own execution? Sometimes, the execution team will miss the vein entirely and inject into soft tissue, or they'll inject so that the poisons run the wrong way in the vein. Even with a good vein, the IV line running from the syringe into the prisoner's body may become pinched or clogged, or the vein may leak where the needle punctures it. One of the reasons this happens is that sodium thiopental comes in powder form and has to be mixed right before it's injected. If it sits still too long, it can begin to sediment, turning solid again. It can take a long time and several attempts to get all this right.[10]

When a man named Christopher Newton was executed in Ohio, it took ten attempts and almost two hours to establish an IV line that could deliver the drugs. He was even offered a bathroom break during his own

[9] See Elizabeth Weil, "The Needle and the Damage Done," *New York Times* (February 11, 2007).

[10] Ibid.

execution! And ten attempts? Can you imagine a firing squad having to shoot ten times? Or someone dropping through the gallows ten times before he actually hangs? Newton's wasn't the only lethal injection that was botched. It took about 90 minutes to kill Joseph Clark, and afterwards a doctor told British journalists that he'd been "tortured with needles for 45 minutes" as the execution team tried to find a good vein.[11]

Another concern is that the drugs may be used improperly. There are few guidelines about their exact doses and preparation, and the three drugs may mix with and dilute each other so that they don't work properly. If the pancuronium bromide dilutes the sodium thiopental, then the prisoner won't be unconscious and will feel the effects of the second two drugs. What would that be like? Pancuronium bromide stops your breathing, so it would feel just like being buried alive. Moreover, potassium chloride causes a burning feeling where it's injected—in fact, foot-long chemical burns have been found in the arms of prisoners who have had it shot into them. Remember, this would still look painless because the pancuronium bromide makes it impossible to express pain. Because of this middle drug, it's very hard to tell whether the prisoner is conscious and aware or not.

Contributing to problems with lethal injection is the often dubious expertise of the execution team. The very first lethal injection was botched when the warden in charge of executing Charles Brooks in Texas in 1982 mixed all three drugs together in the same syringe, which made them turn into a "thick, white sludge."[12] When one of the two doctors on hand checked on Brooks to pronounce death and found that he was still alive, he didn't try to save him in accordance with the Hippocratic Oath, but advised the execution team to give the drugs more time to work.[13]

The states of Missouri and California have also had serious problems. Although the medical specialty best trained to administer the drugs in the lethal injection cocktail and monitor the prisoner's status are anesthesiologists, Missouri relied on a surgeon with more than twenty malpractice lawsuits against him who admitted to making many mistakes because he was dyslexic. He defended his participation by giving examples of how bad a job execution teams might do without his supervision, because they often had no medical training and wouldn't have previously done any of

---

[11] "What's Wrong with Lethal Injection?" BBC (January 2008), www.bbc.co.uk/sn/tvradio/programmes/horizon/broadband/tx/executions/lethal_injection/.

[12] Weil, "The Needle and the Damage Done."

[13] See Atul Gawande, "When Law and Ethics Collide—Why Physicians Participate in Executions," *New England Journal of Medicine* 254 (2006):1221–29.

the necessary procedures. One Missouri execution team tried injecting the drug cocktail into a prisoner's thumb, another looked in a prisoner's arm for a vein that's actually in the leg, and yet another execution team did their work in the dark by flashlight.[14]

According to the *New York Times*, a judge examining nine members of California's execution team in a state procedure review found that they injected the cocktail into the prisoner from another room with poor lighting and IV bags were hung so high it was impossible to see if the drugs were flowing correctly. The team leader admitted he didn't know how many syringes to use in the procedure or how to tell how conscious the prisoner was, and one of the nurses admitted she had not studied the guidelines she got about how to mix the drugs because she just wanted to get her "job" done and not have to "know about it." Clearly, she didn't care to reflect on what she was really doing. The doctor who designed the three-drug injection protocol told the *Times* reporter that "it never occurred to me when we set this up that we'd have complete idiots administering the drugs."[15]

What these examples illustrate is that lethal injection is such a difficult procedure and that it often causes excruciating pain. When Angel Diaz was executed, he took thirty-four minutes to die and grimaced in pain for twenty-six of them. His autopsy revealed an eleven-inch chemical burn on one arm and a twelve-inch chemical burn on the other.[16] The judge mentioned earlier found out that six of the last eight prisoners killed in California could have been conscious when their diaphragms were paralyzed, meaning they would have felt like they were drowning—hardly a humane execution method—without being able to thrash about or struggle against it.

Lethal injection can't even be made to *look* humane unless physicians are involved, and many states now require that a doctor be present. However, the American Medical Association and almost all other medical professional associations, including those of nurses, have ethical codes that prohibit their members from participating in executions.[17] While medical personnel can believe what they want about the death penalty as private citizens, they cannot participate in them as medical practitioners without violating their professions' codes of ethics. Some of these codes are very

---

[14] Ibid.

[15] Weil, "The Needle and the Damage Done."

[16] Amnesty International, "Abolish the Death Penalty," www.amnesty.org/en/death-penalty.

[17] See John M. LeGraw and Michael A. Grodin's "Health Professionals and Lethal Injection Execution in the United States," *Human Rights Quarterly* 24:2 (2002): 382–423.

specific. The AMA prohibits its members from prescribing or preparing the drugs; choosing the injection site, starting the IV line, and injecting the cocktail; inspecting, testing, or doing maintenance on the equipment used; training or supervising the execution team; and monitoring the vital signs of the prisoner. Doctors aren't allowed to declare the prisoner's death, either, because if the prisoner is still alive they are professionally bound to try to save him, which would make for very awkward interactions with the execution team. The only thing a doctor is permitted to do is certify the prisoner's death after someone else has declared it.[18] The reason why the professional associations don't want their members participating in executions is that they recognize lethal injection to be a perversion of medicine that is directly contrary to healing and saving lives.[19]

Medical professional associations also want to defend the collective reputation of their members. Past abuses of medicine, including experiments on racial minorities in our own country that lasted well into the 1970s and Nazi doctors assisting in state-sanctioned killings in Germany during World War II, tarnished their reputation and continue to remind professionals of their duty to be altruistic and serve their patients, not the state.[20] As a result, medical personnel could get in trouble with their professional associations if they violate these codes. The American Public Health Association threatens sanctions against members that participate in executions. While the AMA doesn't have the authority to revoke licenses to practice medicine (because these are issued by states, not the AMA), the Georgia State Medical Board has been sued for not punishing doctors who violated medical ethics by assisting in executions. Doctors can also lose the trust of their patients and the respect of their communities if they participate in executions. One of the doctors, whose state medical license was challenged, found a sign on his clinic door saying "the killer doctor."[21]

It's difficult to find doctors willing to kill. Recently, Ohio couldn't find any, and when Missouri sent a letter to three hundred anesthesiologists

---

[18] American Medical Association Opinion 2.06, "Capital Punishment," www.ama-assn.org/ama/pub/physician-resources/medical-ethics/code-medical-ethics/opinion206.page.

[19] LeGraw and Grodin, "Health Professionals and Lethal Injection Execution."

[20] See David Rothman, *Strangers at the Bedside: A History of How Law and Bioethics Transformed Medical Decision Making* (New York: Basic Books, 1991); Robert Jay Lifton, *The Nazi Doctors: Medical Killing and the Psychology of Genocide* (New York: Basic Books, 1986); and James Jones, "The Tuskegee Syphilis Experiment," in *Perspectives in Medical Sociology*, ed. Phil Brown (Long Grove, IL: Waveland, 2008).

[21] Gawande, "When Law and Ethics Collide."

asking for help, the American Society of Anesthesiology sent a letter to its members warning them against volunteering. In California, two anesthesiologists who had volunteered backed out when they learned what exactly was expected of them, at which point a judge ruled that California's execution protocol was unconstitutional.[22] In North Carolina and Kentucky, too, executions have been delayed because officials got caught between the legal opinion that lethal injection is cruel and unusual without medical expertise and the principled refusal of health care professionals to violate their ethics.

It's not just that doctors willing to kill are becoming harder to find, even when offered large sums of money. The drugs needed are also increasingly in short supply. Sodium thiopental was only made by one company in the United States, Hospira, which published a letter protesting its use in executions in 2010. In the end, pressure from activists, the fact that it counted for less than 1 percent of their sales, and trouble getting necessary ingredients from one of its own suppliers (also under pressure from activists) led them to stop making sodium thiopental in early 2011. That decision, combined with the fact that sodium thiopental expires so that existing supplies gradually become useless, has caused a serious shortage, which has delayed several executions.

The states that use capital punishment responded by trying to get the drug from overseas, but that strategy was met with instant resistance. For a while, Hospira made sodium thiopental in Italy, wanting to sell it for legitimate medical uses, but stopped because they were afraid their employees would be prosecuted because they couldn't reassure the Italian government that it wouldn't end up being used for executions in American prisons. In Germany, pharmaceutical companies have agreed with government officials not to sell sodium thiopental to the United States, and the British government has shut down supplies from companies under its jurisdiction. Some states then ordered pentobarbital from a Danish company, intending to use this drug in place of sodium thiopental even though the manufacturer, Lundbeck A/S, was marketing it as a treatment for epilepsy. When Lundbeck found out from activists what was happening, they first asked the states not to use their product that way, then started rejecting orders from states that have the death penalty, and then required buyers in other states to sign agreements not to redistribute the drug without Lundbeck's approval. Unfortunately, they had already sold

---

[22] Ibid.

enough pentobarbital for dozens of executions, and eighteen people were killed using it by the middle of 2011.

What conclusions can we draw from this overview of lethal injection as an execution method? One is that the death penalty makes the United States look quite bad in the eyes of our friends and allies abroad. Another is that pressure on businesses can be very effective, so that there's no reason to feel as if signing a petition or making a phone call is futile. More importantly, resistance to having killing dressed up professionally and administered by individual health care practitioners shows us the importance of taking ethical stands. But most important of all, we see that lethal injection is inherently cruel. It covers up the appearance of pain even as pain is being inflicted, so there is nothing "humane" about it. If ordinary people knew what really happened in an execution chamber, support for the death penalty would decline. If that wasn't the case, there wouldn't be a need to disguise it in the first place. You can make a big difference by simply educating your peers, friends, and families.

Review and Looking Forward

Editors

Sister Helen Prejean opens *The Death of Innocents* with the words of Jimmy Glass, executed by the State of Louisiana in 1987: "the truth arrives disguised, therein the sorrow lies" (iv). We all know how challenging it can be to face the truth at times. We all know how we manage to resist facing it—avoiding situations that get under our skin, acting as if they don't concern or involve us, or distorting them so they seem more acceptable. Sister Helen often says, quoting Dorothy Day, that she seeks to comfort the afflicted and afflict the comfortable. Kim Hansen's chapter leaves us uncomfortable, even deeply troubled. A number of years ago, I (Trudy Conway) had a troubling conversation. My daughter Sedira confronted me in our kitchen, saying that she couldn't understand how I could oppose the death penalty, as I had as far as she could remember, and not do a thing to stop executions. She added that if all the people who opposed the death penalty *did* something about it, executions would cease sooner rather than later. She was right. Our government executes in our name with our tax dollars, so we have a responsibility to learn the truth about executions and respond based on our convictions. Ordinary citizens can't simply let themselves off the hook by saying "what do I know; what difference can I make?" Dorothy Day, Servant of God, recognized that we build a just society little by little.[23] Dorothy is known for her service to the poor and as cofounder, during the Depression era, of the Catholic Worker Movement. In the *Catholic Worker* issue of September 1957, she wrote, "One of the greatest evils of the day is the sense of futility. Young people say, 'What can one person do? What is the sense of our small effort?' They cannot see that we can only lay one brick at a time, take one step at a time; we can be responsible only for the one action of the present moment."[24]

Like the writings of Donald Cabana and Sr. Helen Prejean, Kim's chapter brings us to face the truth about executions occurring across our nation. He ends his chapter by stating that each of us can make a big difference by simply educating our peers, friends, and families. In a similar way Sr. Helen ends *The Death of Innocents* with a page of additional resources, including avenues for learning more about upcoming executions; state, national, and worldwide abolitionist organizations; and murder victims' family groups who oppose the death penalty. Addressing young people as they begin a journey with her into our courts and execution chambers, her preface expresses hope that such learning will impassion them—will set them on fire regarding this issue. We want to share this hope with our readers.

Questions for Discussion

1. In what important ways do you think execution by lethal injection is similar to and different from execution by hanging, death squad shooting, electrocution, and gas asphyxiation? Why do you think that we no longer use these former methods of execution? Why have we convinced ourselves that execution by lethal injection is more humane?

2. In his book *Death Work: A Study of the Modern Execution Process* (Wadsworth, 2005), Robert Johnson explores in great detail the ways we have executed people in the past and the way we do it now. He concludes the execution process today is "distinctly mechanical, impersonal and ultimately dehumanizing. . . . The death penalty is, at bottom, a tragic social institution that matches the tragedy of

[23] The title "Servant of God" designates that Dorothy Day's "cause" to be declared a saint is underway in the Catholic Church.

[24] Jim Forest, *All Is Grace: A Biography of Dorothy Day* (Maryknoll, NY: Orbis Books, 2011), 209.

violent crime with a punishment that is itself tragic and violent. We minimize or ignore the death penalty at our peril" (xv). Discuss how you understand his claims and what you think of them.

3. If we could refine the process of lethal injection so as to eliminate all suffering, would such punishment become civilized and humane?

Chapter 2

Seeing Ourselves from an International Perspective

Editors

Our contemporary global community is full of exemplary individuals and nations that have provided models of justice and hope. In responding to violence and injustice, South Africa provides an extraordinary example that inspires and motivates people throughout the world. In the aftermath of apartheid, the global community waited to see how South Africans would respond to those who committed the most horrific violations of human dignity and rights against their people. Rather than responding with vengeful retaliation to these acts of violence and dehumanization, the South African people sought to focus their nation on forgiveness, reconciliation, and healing, practices that will be explored at length in later chapters (especially part II of the book).

In his book *No Future Without Forgiveness*, Desmond Tutu, retired archbishop of Cape Town and 1984 recipient of the Nobel Peace Prize, describes how the world came to a standstill as Nelson Mandela was inaugurated as the first democratically elected president of South Africa. Following Mandela's twenty-seven-year imprisonment under apartheid, he refused to continue the legacy of violence. Despite all that had been done to break his spirit and fill him with hatred, Mandela emerged as an embodiment of the power of restorative justice, winning the respect of the global community.

Mandela appointed Desmond Tutu to chair the "Truth and Reconciliation Commission." The commission was given the task of responding to the evils perpetrated under apartheid. Archbishop Tutu recalls that the members of the commission were silenced in awesome respect as persons who suffered or saw their loved ones suffer massacres, sadistic torture, abductions, or brutal killings refused to sink to the same level of dehumanizing violence against their assailants. These persons sought healing for their fellow South Africans and nation rather than revenge. They wanted justice and rightful punishment, but not revenge.

Many of them drew strength and inspiration from their Christian faith and the witness of Christian churches. Archbishop Tutu himself emphasized the religious convictions that shaped their responses, such as the powerful influence of gospel parables (e.g., the Good Shepherd) and Christ's own response to sinners.[1] This faith was the inspiration for those who suffered to distinguish the sinful deed and the perpetrator, to refuse to reduce people to one-dimensional monsters, to hope in the possibility of moral transformation, and to believe that we inhabit a fundamentally moral universe. Nelson Mandela envisioned the people of South Africa as providing a beacon of hope and new paradigm for dealing with human evil within the global community. On this issue, his nation lived up to his vision, providing the exceptional moral leadership so needed in the contemporary world.

Likewise, the United States provides leadership for freedom and human rights in the world. But the question of leadership is difficult for us to raise in relationship to the death penalty. The use of the death penalty continues in the United States, but for most of us the death penalty has little to do with our lives. Periodically a news story might mention a particular execution or latest nuance in the legal debate. Sometimes in a conversation, someone mentions a point or a fact that gets under our skin. For example, in chapter 1, Kim Hansen asked us to look more deeply into the reality of executions. In this chapter, Amanda Beal, a professor of political science, offers a look at our American practices of capital punishment from the perspective of the global community. How do others view us—with respect and admiration? Whose company do we share through this practice—countries whose principles and policies we revere and praise?

Amanda's chapter offers a broad overview of the current international response to the death penalty and its historical background. Americans are well aware of our European cultural and historical legacy. However, many are unaware of a widespread critique of our retention of the death penalty. For example, in June 2011, US secretary of commerce Gary Locke turned to Germany for assistance in acquiring needed execution drugs. Without hesitation German economic minister Phillip Rösler refused, and he went even further. He prohibited the sale by German pharmaceutical companies of any drugs used in executions. In developing his justifica-

---

[1] Desmond Tutu, *No Future Without Forgiveness* (New York: Image Books, 2000), 83–87.

tions for his refusal, he cited his own Catholic faith.[2] Rösler was hailed as a hero for his moral stand. In other words, the issues explored in this chapter continue to generate international tensions on moral grounds. Many are shocked when they learn the facts that this chapter discloses. In relationship to the death penalty, we in the United States are, paradoxically, on the side of countries that we often oppose for their human rights violations, such as China and Iran. On the issue of capital punishment, our country seems to be inconsistent with its broader role in the world.

An International Perspective on the Death Penalty

Amanda Beal

As Kim Hansen noted in chapter 1, drug manufacturers and European governments are making increasing efforts to stall executions in the United States.[3] These efforts began in 2010, successfully delaying the execution of Jeffrey David Matthews in Oklahoma and pushing Governor Steven Beshear to delay the signing of two death warrants in Kentucky. In August, Oklahoma had two prisoners scheduled for execution but only one supply of thiopental (pentothal), a barbiturate used to sedate people before they receive the drugs that paralyze them and stop their hearts. There was no longer a domestic manufacturer of the drug. Hospira, an Illinois-based pharmaceutical company, was previously the sole supplier of thiopental in the United States; it announced a shortage due to problems with its

---

[2] "German Minister Denies U.S. Request for Execution Drugs," *Spiegel Online* (June 9, 2011), www.spiegel.de/international/world/european-opposition-to-death-penalty-german-minister-denies-us-request-for-execution-drugs-a-767613.html.

[3] Kim Hansen also noted in chapter 1 that the scramble to find lethal injection drugs intensified as European suppliers have found ways of preventing their products from making their way into American execution chambers. In response to these developments, some states in the US explored the possibility of using propofol, an anesthetic, to execute inmates. But as new solutions are proposed, new forms of resistance emerge. It turns out that the major supplier of propofol is Fresenius Kabi, a German pharmaceutical company. Maya Foa, head of the Lethal Injection Project of Reprieve (a legal action organization), expressed deep concern over the involvement of Fresenius Kabi: the company's involvement in executions would make a mockery of its noble commitment expressed in its corporate motto of "Caring for Life." The mounting resistance of domestic and international pharmaceutical companies to playing a role in death sentences will continue to be a problem for the continuing use of lethal injection.

raw material producers. There were also no FDA-approved international manufacturers of the drug, so Oklahoma was left without a supplier.[4]

The Oklahoma Department of Corrections wanted to use a substitute drug for Matthews's execution, but switching to another drug requires a lengthy approval process that takes time and potentially invites lawsuits. In Matthews's case, Oklahoma tried to switch to pentobarbital, a drug used to euthanize animals, but Matthews's attorneys argued that the substitution was a form of human experimentation and, therefore, inhumane. A federal judge delayed the execution until there was enough time to evaluate the new drug.[5]

While Oklahoma may have been the first state forced to delay an execution due to shortages in the drug supply, many states soon began scrambling for international manufacturers or looking for substitutes. Despite objections from the US Food and Drug Administration (FDA), some states illegally imported the drug from European manufacturers; the FDA seized much of the international supply, but they also passed it on to the states even though the drugs had not gone through FDA testing. In response, the European Union (EU) issued a ban on the exportation of the drug to the United States, and Hospira officially announced that it would no longer manufacture thiopental, upholding claims that the company was purposely stopping production because they no longer want to make a drug that was used in executions and that, over the previous years, was being used less and less by the medical community.[6]

Drug manufacturers are responding to pleas from the medical community and foreign governments to stop supplying drugs used in executions. While the motives of drug manufacturing companies are not entirely clear, it is obvious that business concerns about public relations are a driving force for the drug supply problems in the United States. These efforts to stall executions in the United States should not come as a surprise. Since the seventeenth century, public opinion around the world shifted toward a concern for human rights. Corresponding to the shift, governments began to acknowledge the death penalty as a denial of the right to life and freedom from inhumane

---

[4] See Jessie Halladay, "Sodium Thiopental Shortage Delays Executions in Several States," *The Law Med Blog* (August 28, 2010); Nick Allen, "Shortage of Lethal Drug Halts U.S. Executions," *The Telegraph* (September 28, 2010).

[5] Bruce Japsen, "Hospira Ceases Production of Anesthetic used in Executions," *Chicago Tribune* (January 21, 2011).

[6] Sidley Austin LLP, "Filed Lawsuit Against FDA to Prohibit the Importation and Use of Unapproved Sodium Thiopental in Lethal Injections," press release (February 2, 2011), http://m.deathpenaltyinfo.org/documents/FDALawsuit.pdf.

treatment—regardless of the crime committed or the manner of the execution. This transition is most clearly manifest in the global abolition movement that began in the 1800s and now includes 105 countries.

A Global Abolition Movement

Early reformers often eliminated the death penalty in practice (*"de facto abolition"*) before abolishing the death penalty legally (*"de jure abolition"*). In addition, most countries abolished the death penalty for ordinary crimes (not including war crimes) before moving on to eliminate the death penalty for all crimes. Soon after the end of World War II, however, many of these pioneers had taken another step; they began forming organizations to build an international consensus on human rights issues and establish norms of behavior, one of which was the limitation or abolishment of the death penalty throughout the world. In doing so, they helped to foster a global movement toward abolition.

San Marino was the first country to abolish the death penalty for ordinary crimes in 1848, followed by Venezuela, the first country to abolish the death penalty for all crimes in 1863. San Marino and Portugal soon followed with the abolishment of the death penalty in 1865 and 1867.[7] From the 1870s until the 1920s, the Netherlands, Costa Rica, Norway, Ecuador, Uruguay, Colombia, Sweden, Panama, and Iceland abolished the death penalty. By the end of World War II, fourteen countries were *de jure* abolitionist countries and have maintained that status until the present day.[8]

European countries were among the first to abolish the death penalty, and after World War II, many of these countries wanted to establish international human rights instruments to address the atrocities of the war and future actions of states.[9] The first international instrument to address

---

[7] The state of Michigan was the first territorial entity to abolish the death penalty for ordinary crimes in 1846. Argentina, Austria, Brazil, Italy, Romania, and Switzerland abolished the death penalty in this time period as well, but they reversed this decision later.

[8] "Abolitionist and Retentionist Countries," *Amnesty International 2011*, http://www.amnesty.org/en/death-penalty/abolitionist-and-retentionist-countries; *Death Penalty Worldwide Database*, The Center for International Human Rights at Northwestern University School of Law, http://www.deathpenaltyworldwide.org/; Roger Hood, *The Death Penalty: A Worldwide Perspective* (Oxford: Oxford University Press, 2003).

[9] By "instruments," I am referring to international treaties or other documents that address human rights, whether they are legally binding or not. International instruments are either declarations (not legally binding) or conventions (legally binding).

the death penalty was the *Universal Declaration of Human Rights* (UDHR), adopted in 1948 by the General Assembly of the United Nations. It specifically addressed the right to life and protection from torture in articles 3 and 5. It became the foundational instrument for human rights laws at the international level.[10]

Subsequently, five major international instruments were constructed to address issues of torturous or cruel, inhumane or degrading, treatment, as stated in article 5 of the UDHR.[11] Then, in the 1980s, three instruments explicitly called for the elimination of the death penalty, often citing UDHR, articles 3 and 5, as well as a later instrument, the *International Covenant on Civil and Political Rights* (ICCPR, article 6). In 1983, the Council of Europe was the first to call for the abrogation of the death penalty for any ordinary crime in *Protocol No. 6 to the Convention for the Protection of Human Rights and Fundamental Freedoms concerning the Abolition of the Death Penalty*. Each of these instruments of the 1980s left room for the lawful execution of war criminals, only abolishing the death penalty for ordinary crimes.[12] Finally, in May of 2011, the Council of Europe drafted *Protocol No. 13 to the Convention for the Protection of Human Rights and Fundamental Freedoms concerning the Abolition of the Death Penalty*, which called for the complete elimination of the death penalty. As of this writing, it has been signed

[10] Though the committee deliberated about whether the death penalty was a right to life issue when constructing article 3, as a compromise, the final wording of the article makes no mention of the abolition or retention of the death penalty. UN General Assembly, *Universal Declaration of Human Rights*, 217 A (III) (December 10, 1948).

[11] International Committee of the Red Cross, *Geneva Convention Relative to the Protection of Civilian Persons in Time of War (Fourth Geneva Convention)*, 75 UNTS 287 (August 12, 1949); UN General Assembly, *International Covenant on Civil and Political Rights*, UNTS 999 (December 16, 1966), 171; Organization of American States, *American Declaration of the Rights and Duties of Man* (May 2, 1948); Council of Europe, *European Convention on Human Rights* (November 4, 1950); Organization of African Unity, *African Charter on Human Rights and People's Rights ["Banjul Charter"]*, CAB/LEG/67/3 rev. 5, 21 I.L.M. 58 (June 27, 1981).

[12] Council of Europe, *Protocol No. 6 to the Convention for the Protection of Human Rights and Fundamental Freedoms concerning the Abolition of the Death Penalty*, ETS no. 114 (April 18, 1983); UN General Assembly, *Elaboration of a 2nd Optional Protocol to the International Covenant on Civil and Political Rights, aiming at the abolition of the death penalty: resolution/adopted by the General Assembly*, A/RES/44/128 (December 15, 1989); Organization of American States, *Additional Protocol to the American Convention on Human Rights to Abolish the Death Penalty*, OASTS No. 73 (June 8, 1990).

and ratified by forty-one countries—all but four of the forty-five member countries.[13]

These instruments put international pressure on those countries that had not yet eliminated the use of the death penalty and created a platform for people within those countries to speak out against the death penalty as a violation of human rights. In this way, pioneering abolitionist countries and the international instruments they constructed have laid the foundation for abolishment in numerous countries throughout the world. The impact of these international instruments is most evident through direct citations of these documents when countries take steps toward eliminating capital punishment. It is also shown by the growth of abolition after the ratification of these documents.

Since the evolution of these instruments, especially those in the 1980s, the number of abolitionist countries has steadily increased. From 1988 to 2010, the number of *de facto* abolitionist countries increased from 27 to 48. Countries with *de jure* abolition, whether it is for all crimes or for ordinary crimes, increased from 52 to 105 in that same time period. The trend toward abolition is most clearly indicated in the total percentage of countries in the world that have abolished or retained the death penalty since 1988: the percentage of abolitionist countries has increased from 44 percent to 78 percent, and, inversely stated, the percentage of retentionist countries in the world (those that retain the death penalty) has declined from 56 percent to 22 percent (see table 1).[14] In most societies today, the majority of the population opposes the death penalty, and, consistent with public opinion, over three-fourths of the countries in the world have abolished the death penalty.

This progress continued in 2011: Latvia abolished the death penalty for all crimes; Amnesty International reported decreases in the use of the death penalty in Tunisia, Lebanon, China, and the Palestinian Authority; and many countries acknowledged additional international instruments; for example, Honduras joined the *Protocol to the American Convention on Human Rights to Abolish the Death Penalty*.[15]

---

[13] Council of Europe, *Protocol 13 to the European Convention on Human Rights and Fundamental Freedoms on the Abolition of the Death Penalty in All Circumstances*, ETS No. 187 (May 3, 2002).

[14] *Death Penalty Worldwide Database*.

[15] "Death Sentences and Executions: 2011" (London: Amnesty International Publications, 2012); Organization of American States, *Protocol to the American Convention on Human Rights to Abolish the Death Penalty*, A-53 (June 8, 1990).

Table 1. The Declining Use of the Death Penalty Worldwide					
Years	*De Jure Abolitionist*	*De Facto Abolitionist*	*Percentage of Abolitionist Countries*	*Retentionist*	*Percentage of Retentionist Countries*
By 1988	52	27	44%	101	56%
By 1995	73	29	53%	90	47%
By 2001	89	34	63%	71	37%
By 2010	105	48	78%	44	22%

Data Sources: Roger Hood, *The Death Penalty; Death Penalty Worldwide Database;* "Death Sentences and Executions: 2011" (London, UK: Amnesty International Publications, 2012).

The international community considers the abolition of the death penalty, one of the last vestiges of authoritarian and repressive regimes, a goal for stable and highly civilized societies. This belief, for the most part, is upheld. The vast majority of countries that retain the death penalty are authoritarian governments in Asia, the Middle East, and Africa. Official executions reported are most likely underestimated in many of these countries. In fact, in China, the number of executions is considered a state secret, and any published numbers are estimated by human rights organizations. For 2011, Amnesty International has yet to publish estimates of the number of executions in China, but the 2011 report suggests that the number of executions was well over 1,000. In addition, the Iranian government reported 360 executions in 2011, but some estimates for Iran are two times as many as those reported by the state. In total, twenty-one countries are known to have carried out executions in 2011.[16]

According to the *Death Penalty Worldwide Database,* many of these retentionist countries still employ the death penalty for a broad range of offenses. China and Iran are two well-known examples. Iran applies the death penalty for economic and secular crimes (robbery, recidivist theft, drug trafficking, drug possession, smuggling, counterfeiting, recidivist criminal offenses for alcohol consumption, murder, kidnapping, rape), political crimes (treason, espionage, spying, political dissidence, terrorism), religious crimes (apostasy, blasphemy, witchcraft), moral crimes (adultery, same-sex relations, incestuous relations, fornication), and military offenses. Prior to 2012, China applied the death penalty for political crimes (treason, espionage, and civil disorder or rioting), secular crimes (murder and other offenses

---

[16] "Death Sentences and Executions: 2011."

resulting in death, terrorism, rape, arson, kidnapping, and drug trafficking), economic crimes (robbery, graft and bribery), and military offenses,[17] but the country recently made some progress when they announced that they would no longer use the death penalty for thirteen of these crimes.[18]

Still, China and Iran far exceed their peers in number of executions, killing hundreds to thousands of people each year. China executes more people each year than all other countries combined—estimated at over 6,000 in 2010. Iran ranks second in the world for number of executions with 650 in 2010. Since 2007, China is known to have executed over 13,000 people, and Iran has executed over 1,700 (fig. 1).[19]

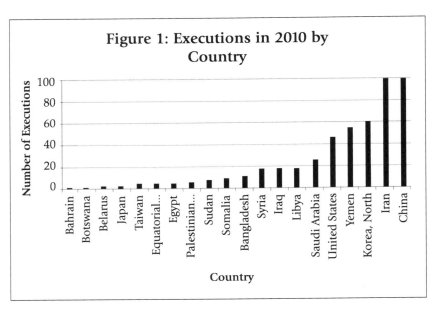

Figure 1 shows the twenty countries that held the most executions in 2010. Following China and Iran, North Korea reportedly executed 60 people, Yemen reported 53 executions, the United States held 46 executions, and Saudi Arabia executed 27 people (see fig. 1). As should be obvious from this figure, the United States is the only Western democracy in this list, ranking among a number of authoritarian governments in East

[17] *Death Penalty Worldwide Database.*
[18] "Death Sentences and Executions: 2011."
[19] Figure 1 and the corresponding statistics were created using data from the *Death Penalty Worldwide Database.*

Asia, the Middle East, and North Africa.[20] Only four countries executed more people than the United States in 2010: China, Iran, North Korea, and Yemen. This trend persists regardless of the year in question. Notably, over the four-year period from 2007 to 2010, Saudi Arabia executed 341 people, Iraq reportedly held 210 executions, the United States reported a surprising 177 executions, and Pakistan reported 171 executions.[21]

Today, only 9 percent of democracies in the world retain the death penalty, while 71 percent of the authoritarian or semiauthoritarian governments are retentionist countries. In addition, if we evaluate these countries based on the predominant religion in each of them, only 8 percent of Christian countries retain the use of the death penalty. In comparison, 51 percent of Muslim countries and 50 percent of Buddhist countries retain the use of the death penalty.[22] There is only one developed, predominately Christian democracy in the world that still retains the death penalty—the United States. It was also the only G8 country to carry out executions in 2011.[23]

US Exceptionalism

The phrase "US exceptionalism" is used in many different contexts. Often claims to exceptionalism are patriotic, suggesting that the United States serves as a model for freedom and democracy in the world. However, the record in terms of human rights demonstrates a paradox in US exceptionalism. In this respect, the United States stands out as an exception in the Western world. In fact, this US exceptionalism has sparked numerous debates regarding why some countries retain the death penalty while others do not. There are no easy answers to this question, but, generally speaking, American culture and political institutions tend to impede the abolitionist movement. The cultural difference is most evident in public opinion data. While less than 35 percent of the population in most predominately

---

[20] Japan and Botswana are also democratic governments that held executions in 2010.

[21] *Death Penalty Worldwide Database.*

[22] This data was calculated using the following four sources: (1) *Freedom in the World 2010*, Freedom House Organization, http://www.freedomhouse.org/; (2) *Human Development Indicators 2010*, Human Development Report Office, a partner in the United Nations Development Programme, http://hdr.undp.org/en/reports/global/hdr2010/; (3) *Death Penalty Worldwide Database*; (4) *The World Factbook 2009*, Central Intelligence Agency, https://www.cia.gov/library/publications/the-world-factbook/.

[23] Botswana and Saint Kitts-Nevis are also predominately Christian democracies that retain the death penalty, though they are both only moderately developed countries.

Christian countries support the use of the death penalty, almost 68 percent of Americans support the death penalty (as of 2000). It is important to note that support declines when respondents are given the alternative option of life in prison without parole; the wording and emphasis in the question have an impact on the way that people respond. Yet, it is still unclear why more Americans support the death penalty, though arguments regarding retribution and the protection of society and its members seem to be the most common survey responses.[24]

What is perhaps most interesting is the effect of religion in the United States. Protestants (65 percent) in the United States are more likely than Catholics (60 percent) and nonreligious people (61 percent) to support the death penalty, and white Evangelical Protestants are the most likely to support the death penalty (74 percent).[25] These results suggest that American Christians in general and Evangelical Protestants in particular may focus more on a popular interpretation of Old Testament passages of "an eye for an eye" rather than the atonement of sins through Christ's sacrifice in the New Testament.[26]

However, it is clear that religion is not the main influence on public opinion. Those who are religious and those who are not religious both support the use of the death penalty in the United States. Race and political affiliation seem to have a larger impact than religious beliefs. Whites and Republicans are overwhelmingly more likely to support the death penalty than other constituencies, while blacks and liberal Democrats are much less likely to support the death penalty.[27]

This cultural effect is complicated by the fact that the United States is a very large and diverse country with a federal system of government. At this point, seventeen states have abolished the death penalty. The abolition of the death penalty is left up to each state and, until a majority of states abolish the death penalty, it is unlikely that nationwide abolition will occur. The United States's progress in the last few years has been mixed at

---

[24] James Unnever, "Global Support for the Death Penalty," *Punishment and Society* 12:4 (2010): 463–84.

[25] "Public Opinion on the Death Penalty," The Pew Forum on Religion and Public Life 2010, http://www.pewforum.org/Death-Penalty/Public-Opinion-on-the-Death-Penalty.aspx.

[26] The proper interpretation of "an eye for an eye" will be discussed in chapter 7.

[27] "An Enduring Majority: Americans Continue to Support the Death Penalty," The Pew Forum on Religion and Public Life 2007, http://www.pewforum.org/Death-Penalty/An-Enduring-Majority-Americans-Continue-to-Support-the-Death-Penalty.aspx; "Public Opinion on the Death Penalty."

best, but some advances have been made. In 2009, New Mexico repealed the death penalty, followed by Illinois in 2011, and, recently, Connecticut became the seventeenth state to abolish the death penalty in 2012. The international community, especially the European Union, welcomed this progress, expressing hope that other states would soon follow suit.

In contrast, however, many states have been resistant, if not overtly defiant, in their attempts to carry out executions in the face of the recent drug shortage. In early 2011, thirteen states turned to the US Department of Justice, asking them to "[identify] an appropriate source for sodium thiopental or [make] supplies held by the Federal Government available to the States."[28] In addition, some of the drugs were shipped in illegally from overseas manufacturers and sent through the US Food and Drug Administration to the states without the required testing. Several death row inmates filed a lawsuit, contending that the imported drug was un-approved and could cause problems during execution.[29] Richard Leon, a federal district court judge, agreed, ruling that these supplies of thiopental were inappropriately approved by the FDA and must not be used in ex-ecutions, and all corrections departments in possession of the drug must return their supply to the FDA.

To avoid such thiopental supply problems, most states have switched to pentobarbital as a substitute. In Jeffrey David Matthews's case, his exe-cution was successfully stalled by the drug shortage of 2010, but he was executed five months later in January of 2011 using this substitute. By Au-gust of 2011, twenty-three people had been executed using pentobarbital. Lundbeck, the Danish manufacturer of pentobarbital, strongly objects to its use in capital punishment. After they found out about the execution of Jerry Jackson in Virginia in August of 2011, they placed restrictions on the exportation of pentobarbital, refusing to sell the drug to prisons in the United States and requiring all buyers to sign a form guaranteeing that they will not use the drug in capital punishment or sell the drug without Lundbeck's approval. However, as of July 2012, all executions in the United States were carried out using pentobarbital.[30]

---

[28] "Thirteen States Seek Help from Justice Department for Lethal Injection Drug," Death Penalty Information Center (January 25, 2011), http://www.deathpenaltyinfo .org/thirteen-states-seek-help-justice-department-lethal-injection-drug.

[29] Sidley Austin LLP, "Filed Lawsuit Against FDA."

[30] "Execution Database," Death Penalty Information Center, http://www.deathpenalty info.org/views-executions; David Nicholl, "Lundbeck and pentobarbital: pharma takes a stand," *The Guardian* (July 1, 2011), http://www.guardian.co.uk/commentisfree

Drug manufacturers and the European Union have been somewhat successful in stalling executions, and it is likely that they will continue such attempts. These attempts to delay or dissuade executions in the United States are directly related to the global abolition movement, reflecting the growing international consensus that capital punishment is a human rights violation. European and Latin American countries were the first to abolish the death penalty and support the formation of international instruments calling for abolishment of the death penalty around the world. These countries continue to be a driving force for abolishment today. The United States, however, remains the sole member of the G8 (and only Western democracy) to retain and regularly use the death penalty. Therefore, the European Union, in combination with drug manufacturers, is working diligently to pressure the United States to finally abolish this inhumane punishment.

While some progress was made in the last few years, it seems that many states are highly resistant to changing their death penalty policy and will continue to find ways around domestic and international attempts to stall or deter executions. Thirty-three states still use the death penalty, and many of these states have persistently sought alternative paths for obtaining drugs needed to carry out executions by lethal injection, even if this requires the use of untested, illegally shipped drugs. Attempts to both proceed with and stop executions will continue so long as the United States retains the practice of the death penalty.

Review and Looking Forward

Editors

Amanda Beal traces a trajectory of global movement toward abolition. Nations have joined this movement, international organizations have articulated the fundamental principles directing this movement, and individuals and societies have worked hard to advance and speed up this movement. All of this has been done based on the conviction that important matters of human concern are at stake. In considering this trajectory, abolitionists often draw on the hopeful words quoted by

---

/cifamerica/2011/jul/01/pentobarbital-lundbeck-execution-drug; "United Kingdom Acts to Ban Export of Lethal Injection Drug," Death Penalty Information Center (July 2012), http://www.deathpenaltyinfo.org/united-kingdom-acts-ban-export-lethal-injection-drug.

Martin Luther King: "The moral arc of the universe is long, but it bends toward justice." Such hope sustains both the international and national movements toward abolition.

Amanda writes of the difference between *de jure* and *de facto* abolition. Often before legally eliminating the death penalty, countries cease applying death sentences. The current US situation involves these distinctions. A number of retention states have gone decades without executing any inmates; other states have massive death row populations, while executions become increasingly uncommon. The last five years have shown a steady increase in the number of states repealing the death penalty *de jure*. The momentum of the trajectory toward abolition is also shown in the *de facto* repeal. The dynamic of this trajectory in the United States will be explored in the next chapter.

Amanda's chapter also gives an overview of the growing consensus on human rights, the global abolition movement, and the role international instruments play in building that consensus. Early in the process, individual states in the United States eliminated the death penalty on the basis of particular principles. Other states show a history of conflicted debate eventually leading to abolition, and a number of states stand poised to play a role in building the sufficient consensus needed for national repeal. Such a global and national trajectory is made possible because of (1) the commitment of individuals to learn and educate other citizens about the realities of executions, (2) the principles at stake in this practice, and (3) the consistency with which we apply the truths and principles we judge worth preserving over time.

From this chapter, we learn of the important role of pioneering countries in creating a platform for people in other countries to begin to speak out against the death penalty. These efforts began through the hard work of individuals who cared deeply about human dignity and human rights. The postapartheid government of South Africa recognized all that hinged on the issue of the death penalty. Their constitutional rejection of the death penalty made crystal clear to the world their choice of restorative justice over retributive justice, an issue also explored in the next chapter. The framers of their new constitution paid due regard to the fact that one of the country's greatest assets was the passion for human rights and respect, even veneration, for human life shown by the generation who fought the hardest against the grave injustices of apartheid.

The 1995 judgment in South Africa, *State v. Makwanyane and Mchunu*, interpreted the new constitution and ruled, "Everyone, including the most abominable of human beings has a right to life, and capital punishment is therefore unconstitutional" (no. 388).[31] The Constitutional Court concluded that the framers of the South African constitution recognized that the death penalty had "brutalized us as a people and diminished our respect for life" (no. 391). The framers of the constitution articulated the new South Africa's deeply cherished principles on human rights and bound themselves to applying them with a consistency that continues to exemplify true leadership in today's global community.

Questions for Discussion

1. Americans are often proud of the leadership role they envision our nation playing in the world, especially in the area of human rights. What was your reaction to learning where the United States stands on the death penalty in relationship to other nations?

2. This chapter states that race and political affiliation have a greater impact than religion on persons' support of or opposition to the death penalty in the United States. Discuss whether and why this is the case.

3. Given the Catholic Church's opposition to the practice of the death penalty, how do we explain the high percentage of Catholics (60 percent) supporting the death penalty cited in the 2010 Pew Forum? The church's position on the death penalty will be outlined in part III of the book.

---

[31] The Constitutional Court of the Republic of South Africa, Case No. CCT/3/94, The State v. T. Makwanyane and M. Mchunu (Heard on: 15 February to 17 February 1995, Delivered on: 6 June 1995), http://law.gsu.edu/ccunningham/fall03/DeathPenalty -SouthAfrica-Makwanyane.htm.

Chapter 3

Trying to Get It Right

Editors

In her book *Don't Kill in Our Names: Families of Murder Victims Speak Out Against the Death Penalty*, Rachel King tells the story of the healing of the soul of Azim Khamisa.[1] On January 21, 1995, Tariq Khamisa, a nineteen-year-old art student at San Diego State University, looked forward to ending his pizza delivery shift. After knocking on doors in a housing project, he recognized he had been set up for a pizza-jacking. When a boy demanded the pizzas at gunpoint, Tariq threw them in the car and attempted to drive off. At that moment a single bullet shattered the window, taking Tariq's life. His father, Azim, woke early the next morning to learn of his son's death, describing the announcement as a nuclear bomb detonated within him, shattering him into a million broken pieces. He then had to break it to his wife, his daughter, and Tariq's girlfriend, Jennifer—the tragic news of the loss of this beautiful young man of such good character and promise.

The police quickly located the suspect, Tony Hicks, a teenager already identified for stealing a shotgun from Ples Felix, the grandfather who raised him. Shortly before the murder, California had passed a severe law allowing children under the age of sixteen to be prosecuted as adults. If Tariq's murder had occurred in December, Tony would have been processed through the juvenile system with a maximum sentence of youth detention until the age of twenty-five. The new ruling changed everything. Tony's life had already taken a dramatic change with his decision to run away from Ples, his strict grandfather, to smoke weed and drink with friends before selling the shotgun to head out on his own. Hungry and without money, the pizza-jacking sounded easy. Egged on to hold a pistol,

---

[1] Rachel King, *Don't Kill in Our Names: Families of Murder Victims Speak Out Against the Death Penalty* (New Brunswick, NJ: Rutgers University Press, 2003), 250–74.

angered by Tariq's refusal to give up the pizzas, and hearing the shouts encouraging him to shoot, Tony fired the fatal shot.

Mourning the loss of Tariq through the rituals and strong support of his Muslim community, Azim found it incredible that three fourteen-year-olds and one eighteen-year-old had been arrested in connection with the killing. How could teenagers too young to drive cars be carrying guns? As pressure mounted to prosecute Tony as an adult, Azim found himself troubled by the repeated retributive demand of "an eye for an eye." Seeing the depth of his grief, a religious teacher in his community counseled him to break the paralysis of his grief and free his son for his eternal peace by doing something good in Tariq's name. From his sorrow came his inspiration—he would become a foe, not of Tariq's killer, but of the forces that contributed to this shocking, senseless act of juvenile violence. Rather than demand retaliatory justice, he threw his energy into building a foundation committed to ending youth violence.

Little did Azim then know that the Tariq Khamisa Foundation would grow and eventually thrive, and with the support of Tony's grandfather, Ples, and finally Tony himself. Ples never expected Azim to reach out to him in shared grief over the tragedies in *both* their lives. Their desire to know and support each other, their prayers for each other, and their shared commitment to the foundation transformed their lives, helping them to heal and Tony to accept responsibility. Tony pleaded guilty to first-degree murder to avoid the pain a trial would cause these two families. Expressing deep regret for his senseless act of violence, he hoped for Azim's forgiveness, which in turn filled Azim with hope for this young man's moral transformation.

After hearing Tony's sentence of twenty-five years to life, Azim's response focused on restorative rather than retributive justice.[2] He sought to relieve his anger through forgiveness, to heal and restore all persons affected by Tariq's murder, and to work to address conditions contributing to youth violence and prison recidivism. Azim and Ples worked to develop a school-based program teaching youth that violence is a bad choice with terrible, irrevocable consequences. Tony began to participate

---

[2] The US continues to struggle with the issue of juvenile punishment. On June 25, 2012, in a 5–4 decision the Supreme Court struck down as unconstitutional mandatory punishments of life without parole for juveniles (18 and younger) convicted of homicide. The dissenting opinion supported harsh retributive justice in response to deliberate killing even by youthful offenders. Two thousand convicted juveniles serving such sentences were given hope in the possibility of release during their lifetime with this ruling. The 2005 ruling *Roper v. Simmons* struck down the death penalty for juvenile offenders.

through letters explaining his regrettable choices and their consequences. The program's success led to national recognition and funding, but, more importantly, to Azim visiting Tony, forgiving him and hearing Tony commit himself to living a better life. Seeing his transformation, Azim asked him to complete his GED and walk a straight path in prison, possibly leading toward parole after twenty-five years, and work for the foundation upon his release. Azim draws on his Islamic faith to continue the work of his foundation, and Tony draws on Azim's faith in him to work on attaining this goal. Azim also gains strength and fellowship through his work with Murder Victim Families for Reconciliation to end the death penalty and shift our society's focus from retributive to restorative justice.

In the introduction to chapter 1, Vicki Schieber (an editor of the book) made brief mention of her own experiences of having a child murdered. Shannon Schieber was full of the same beauty, goodness, and promise as Tariq. Vicki understands deeply the journey Azim Khamisa has traveled and is still on. Similar to Azim, she has been sustained by the depth of her faith—for her, the Catholic faith that teaches the transformative power of forgiveness and reconciliation. Like Azim, she continues to speak across the country, especially to students, of the need to end the death penalty and promote restorative justice. Both parents know that the pain of the loss of their children will never end, but both know the joy that comes from honoring their lives through work promoting restorative justice.

The lives of Azim and Vicki and their responses to the loss of their children to murder offer a means to rethink the death penalty. The two previous chapters revealed how unsettled and unsettling the death penalty is. Americans keep rethinking the *way* we execute, trying to get it right so it won't be inhumane, cruel, or unusual punishment. We try incorporating new resources—electricity, gas, and now pharmaceutical drugs. At the same time, we keep rethinking *why* we execute, confident we can strengthen the justifications, refute the objections, and marshal the supportive data. As we keep at it, persons within our society and across the global community find deeply unsettling these endless attempts. They follow a different path, confident that we will reach the point that was foreseen by former US Supreme Court Justice William Brennan when he stated, "One day the Court will outlaw the death penalty. Permanently."[3] Many stand convinced the only way to get the death penalty right is to abolish it.

In this chapter, Trudy Conway, a professor of philosophy, offers a broad overview of this history, focusing on rethinking the death penalty

---

[3] Justice William Brennan, "What the Constitution Requires," *New York Times* (April 28, 1996).

in the United States. The abstract debate and the concrete changes in how, where, and before whom we execute have a long and complex history. Her chapter highlights the wave of landmark Supreme Court rulings since 1972. Following these rulings, we didn't expect the very honest revelation by some former justices that, had they known then what they know now, they would have ruled against the death penalty. If they could have foreseen how practices would unfold, our country's rethinking of the death penalty might have ended in the 1970s.

As Azim and Vicki's lives show, rethinking the death penalty has come from an unexpected group of people. Who would expect family members of murder victims to stand firmly against, and even actively resist, often under criticism, the execution of the murderer of their loved one? Over the course of this book, readers will learn of these persons, so numerous they formed support and advocacy organizations. This chapter argues that the only remaining defense of the death penalty rests on the human desire for just retribution. We expect families of murder victims to demand retaliation, even revenge, through the death penalty. We even can imagine ourselves voicing this demand if we suffered such deep loss and sorrow.

Rethinking the Death Penalty

Trudy D. Conway

The death penalty has been part of American society since its founding, but responses to it have been conflicted throughout its history. Dramatic changes have occurred over time, from persons being quickly executed following even minor offenses (such as petty theft, killing chickens, or trading with Native Americans) in public settings witnessed by local communities to current executions that are hidden, secretive, precisely mechanized, bureaucratically administered, highly impersonal, and preceded often by decades of death row incarceration. Most advocates of the death penalty want such ultimate punishment to be used on the basis of strong justification, in a fair manner without bias or inhumane cruelty, and only against the truly deserving. Opponents question its justification, the fairness of its application, and the effects it has on our society, those administering it, and a broad range of persons deeply affected by it. Since the passionate opposition of Benjamin Rush, a cosigner of the Declaration of Independence, the American death penalty has been riddled with ambivalence and frustration that continue to unsettle persons in our current age.

Deepening reservations about the death penalty finally resulted in a national moratorium enacted by the 1972 Supreme Court ruling of *Furman v. Georgia.* This ruling set the standard that punishment would be deemed cruel and unusual, thereby violating the Eighth Amendment, if it was too severe for the crime, was arbitrarily imposed, offended society's sense of justice, or was not more effective than a lesser penalty. Although concerns had been repeatedly raised about racial disparity in the application of the death penalty, this ruling focused solely on challenges that capital punishment was being administered in a capricious and arbitrary manner. The court ruled that the current Georgia death penalty statute (which gave the jury full discretion in setting sentences) would result in arbitrary sentencing and was thereby cruel and unusual. The ruling voided existing death penalty statutes across the country, in effect suspending the death penalty. Such suspension consistently followed the steady decline in the use of the death penalty in Western societies. With good reason, expectations arose that executions might no longer be part of American society.

But in response to the ruling, states seeking reinstatement introduced revised sentencing guidelines. Under the 1976 landmark ruling collectively referred to as *Gregg v. Georgia,* the Supreme Court reinstated capital punishment, ruling that the newly proposed sentencing statutes in Georgia, Florida, and Texas, which would guide and restrict prosecutors, judges, and juries, were in theory nonarbitrary and therefore constitutional. The court approved a list of aggravating and mitigating factors to be considered in death sentence cases in a new, bifurcated format entailing separate determinations of guilt and then sentencing. It also introduced automatic appellate court review of capital convictions and sentences.

Supporters of the death penalty assumed challenges had been sufficiently addressed, while in fact the data supporting the challenges increased over time. Since 1997, the American Bar Association has called for a national moratorium on executions, arguing, "Two decades after *Gregg,* it is apparent that efforts to forge a fair capital punishment jurisprudence have failed. Today, the administration of the death penalty, far from being fair and consistent, is instead a haphazard maze of unfair practices with no internal consistency" (ABA House of Delegates 1997 Resolution). A study was released in 2011 on the thirty-fifth anniversary of the *Gregg* ruling. It cataloged the factors of race, geographical location, money (economic status of the accused and county budgets), and other arbitrary dimensions to the use of the death penalty. The study concluded that capital punishment continues to be applied in arbitrary, inconsistent, and unfair ways.[4]

---

[4] See "Struck by Lightning: The Continuing Arbitrariness of the Death Penalty Thirty-Five Years After Its Re-instatement in 1976," Death Penalty Information Center (July 2011), www.deathpenaltyinfo.org/documents/StruckByLightning.pdf.

It is not surprising that a majority of the nine justices serving at the time of reinstatement eventually concluded that the attempt to apply capital punishment fairly had failed. Three of the justices in the *Gregg* majority (Justices Blackmun, Powell, and Stevens) changed their views over time, stating that they now would have joined Justices Brennan and Marshall in supporting the complete banning of the death penalty as unconstitutional. Had these justices reached these insights at the time of this important ruling, a 5–4 rather than a 7–2 ruling regarding the constitutionality of the death penalty would have ended the death penalty in America in 1976.

Following the landmark *Furman* and *Gregg* decisions, subsequent Supreme Court rulings still continued to tinker with particular dimensions of the practice, in hopes of righting the wrongs of the application of capital punishment. The court has continued to focus on refining and limiting the practice with the hope of bolstering its legitimate retention. Most significant among these rulings were the 1977 *Coker v. Georgia* ruling excluding the death penalty for nonlethal child rape convictions and 2002 *Atkins v. Virginia* along with 2005 *Roper v. Simmons* banning the execution of persons with intellectual disabilities and juvenile offenders respectively. While retaining capital punishment, the court would continue to limit the persons condemned to it and refine its procedures of application. Expressing the frustration of some justices with such endless whittling away at capital sentencing, Justice Harry A. Blackmun dramatically announced in 1994:

> From this day forward, I no longer shall tinker with the machinery of death. For more than twenty years I have endeavored—indeed, I have struggled—along with a majority of this Court, to develop procedural and substantive rules that would lend more than the mere appearance of fairness to the death penalty endeavor. Rather than continue to coddle the Court's delusion that the desired level of fairness has been achieved and the need for regulation eviscerated, I feel morally and intellectually obligated to concede that the death penalty experiment has failed. (*Callins v. Collins*, 510 US 1141, 1144)

The Supreme Court's stream of rulings on the death penalty gives evidence for ongoing unease and conflicted response to its practice.

Aside from passing exposure to brief media coverage of these rulings, few Americans are aware of the endless attempts to limit and repair this practice with the hope of making it morally and legally more palatable. Sister Helen Prejean emphasizes that support for the death penalty in this country may be a mile wide but is only an inch deep. As persons become more educated regarding the morality, human costs, ramifications, and unequal and seriously flawed application of this punishment, their reservations and opposition tend to increase significantly. Most troubling to both death penalty supporters and opponents is the ever rising number of exonerated death row inmates. Despite preoccupations with legal safeguards and refinements, it is anticipated that the number of exonerations will continue to increase beyond the current figure of 141 death row inmates freed after wrongful convictions.

Nothing troubles citizens more deeply than the ever present risk of inflicting on innocent persons a punishment that is irreversibly and permanently unjust. Execution stands forth uniquely as the only wrongly applied sentence that can never be corrected. Increasingly informed persons echo the succinct conclusion reached by Cardinal McCarrick, archbishop emeritus of Washington: "The use of the death penalty cannot really be mended. It must be ended."[5] Given these troubling reservations and loss of belief in the effective reform of capital punishment, the steady march of state repeal is far from surprising (currently seventeen states plus the District of Columbia have no death penalty).

Historically support for the death penalty has hinged on its deterrent and retributive value. For many persons, it was taken for granted that capital punishment has a clear and enduring deterrent value. They reasoned that the death penalty prevents executed persons from committing further crimes and deters other persons from committing capital crimes. In this sense its deterrent value is prospective, in the sense of being future oriented. Early in our American history, Benjamin Rush challenged this assumption, arguing that rather than serving as a crime deterrent, the death penalty, as a social practice that responds to violent and tragic crimes with violent and tragic punishment, has a brutalizing effect on society. Extensive and varied studies have failed to build strong empirical support for the deterrent value of this most extreme punishment, leading scholars to conclude, "As to whether executions raise or lower the homicide rate, we remain profoundly uncertain."[6] Such punishment might deter only in

---

[5] "Catholic Bishops Launch Major Catholic Campaign to End the Use of the Death Penalty" (March 25, 2005), http://old.usccb.org/comm/archives/2005/05-064.shtml/.

[6] John J. Donohue and Justin Wolfers, "Uses and Abuses of Empirical Evidence in the Death Penalty Debate," *Stanford Law Review*, vol. 58, no. 3 (December, 2005): 791. If the death penalty were an effective deterrent, homicide rates should be lower in states and countries that execute. This is clearly not the case. This study revealed that it is impossible to isolate the impact of executions from other factors influencing homicide rates.

the very unlikely case that criminals rationally assessed the likelihood of their being caught and sentenced, and executions occurred very certainly, frequently, and swiftly. Criminals' reasoning and concerns with just legal proceedings undermine such likelihood.

The steady decline in death sentences and executions over the past decade, the lingering of inmates on death row for decades, and the total suspension of executions in some retention states further erode confidence in capital punishment having a deterrent value. Since 2007 five states (New York, New Jersey, New Mexico, Illinois, and Connecticut) have repealed the death penalty. Of the thirty-four states retaining the death penalty, executions occur increasingly more rarely and are limited to a very small number of states, with Texas having the most executions since 1976 (482 in Texas, and Virginia following with 109). The number of new death sentences imposed in 2011 declined by 75 percent since 1996 (from 315 to 78).[7] Even in states that frequently sentence people to death (Texas, Virginia, Alabama, California, Florida, and Oklahoma), sentencing occurs very selectively in a limited number of counties. New Jersey legislators supported repeal for a range of reasons, but emphasized that the state had spent a quarter of a billion dollars to maintain capital punishment for twenty-five years even though New Jersey had not executed a person in over four decades. They concluded that such funding could be better used to support crime prevention and crime victim support. Since reinstatement in 1978, Pennsylvania has executed only three people and only after they no longer tried to appeal their cases. Yet over two hundred persons linger on its death row. Not surprisingly, Pennsylvania has recently established a state commission to review the death penalty. Support for the death penalty on the assumption of its deterrent value has been eroded through lack of compelling supportive evidence.[8] Despite politicians' references to the deterrent defense, the evidence supports Supreme Court Justice John Paul Stevens's conclusion that "despite thirty years of empirical research in the area, there remains no reliable statistical evidence that capital punishment in fact deters potential offenders" (*Baze v. Rees*, 2008).

---

[7] "The Death Penalty in 2011: Year End Report," Death Penalty Information Center (December 2011).

[8] A Gallup Poll Briefing (March 16, 2004) revealed most Americans do not believe the death penalty deters criminals from committing murder (http://www.deathpenalty info.org/node/711).

The most resilient argument in support of the death penalty today continues to be the retributive justice argument.[9] This approach is retrospective: it focuses on righting the wrongs of the past. In this approach laws are seen as binding persons across generations and within communities, rendering civil society possible. Violations of laws evoke what is seen as righteous anger, followed by a desire to retaliate and make wrongdoers pay for their crimes. Punishment is thus seen as a matter of just retribution or "payback" for victims and members of society. Violations of societal laws are seen as demanding commensurate retaliation. Some retributivists argue that in feeling anger and expecting just retribution, society shows a level of respect for persons committing crimes in holding them to be free and responsible agents. Just retribution is thus seen as a matter of rectificatory justice, wherein we right the wrongs done by making the convicted suffer as the victim suffered. On the basis of such reasoning, the most heinous crimes evoke the greatest anger and demand the greatest punishment—execution.

According to the famous Enlightenment philosopher Immanuel Kant, a strong retributivist, we punish wrongdoers simply because it is the right thing to do, because justice demands that we render to each what each deserves.[10] The offender has unbalanced the scales of justice by violating laws; society is obliged to right this wrong. The standard guiding the determination of justice must be *jus* or *lex talionis*, the right or law of retaliation, governed by the principle of equality. The courts must use reason to determine a punishment that fits and thereby equalizes the crime. Strong retributivists argue that capital crimes require capital punishments. But, interestingly, Kant adds the very important requirement that the convicted person's death be kept from all maltreatment or inhumane suffering and be done in accordance with a system of law insuring that only the deserving are punished following fair procedures of judicial deliberation.

Consistent with such a retributive approach, the American judicial system, in theory, reserves capital punishment for the "worst of the worst" offenders who commit the most heinous aggravated acts of murder. The Supreme Court stressed in its 2008 ruling that capital punishment "must be limited to the category of offenders who commit 'a narrow category of the most serious crimes' and whose extreme culpability makes them

---

[9] A 2006 Gallup poll revealed that most Americans who support the death penalty do so primarily because they are convinced it promotes just retribution (http://www.gallup.com/poll/23548/Support-Death-Penalty-Years-After-Supreme-Court-Ruling.aspx).

[10] *Metaphysical Elements of Justice*, 2nd ed. (Indianapolis: Hackett, 1999).

'the most deserving of execution'" (*Kennedy v. Louisiana*, no. 07-343). Supporters of the death penalty continue to believe the courts can fairly apply such retributive punishment. However, study after study undermines such belief. Numerous studies reveal that who is sentenced to death depends on a wide range of factors, such as an individual prosecutor's discretion in deciding to pursue a death sentence; the competence, workload, and available resources of the defense; the makeup of the jury and appellate court that reviews the verdict; and the race of the victim and the defendant. The economic situation of the accused plays a major role, leading to the troubling reality that people with capital do not face capital punishment. Justice William O. Douglas noted in *Furman*, "One searches our chronicles in vain for the execution of any member of the affluent strata in this society" (408 U.S. 238).

As will be shown in chapters 13–15, the death penalty is selectively reserved for the poor, marginalized, and powerless. It is simply not the case that the worst offenders get sentenced to death. Whether persons are sentenced to death is effected by contingent factors such as geographical location (state and county) rather than degrees of crime and culpability. Death sentences are applied so unevenly and sporadically that they fail to uphold retributive reasoning. Surprising and unsettling to people who defend the death penalty on retributive grounds is the escalating opposition of murder victim family members to executions. Numerous murder victim family members have become outspoken death penalty abolitionists. Supporters of retributive justice in the abstract face difficulties in attempting to reconcile such principled support with the disturbing realities of the death penalty—its inconsistent and arbitrary application, its exorbitant costs compared with alternative punishments, its failure to grant murder victim family members the healing they seek, and its risk of transforming righteous anger into retaliatory revenge.

Interestingly some persons who do support retributive conceptions of punishment argue that retributive justice itself no longer justifies the death penalty.[11] Our American history regarding executions clearly manifests evolving standards of decency. We look with horror on historical executions by disemboweling, quartering, gassing, and electrocuting. A retributive approach does not require doing the same kind of retaliatory act. Retributive justice requires proportionate but not identical punishment. It assumes there is a range of just punishment. A punishment *beyond* what is

---

[11] Jeffrey Reiman offers an excellent example of this reasoning in "Justice, Civilization, and the Death Penalty," *Philosophy and Public Affairs*, no. 2 (Spring 1985): 130.

deserved is unjust to the convicted. A degree of punishment *below* what is deserved is unjust to the victim. But the upper limit of punishment, strictly equaling the crime, is unacceptable if such punishment violates morally acceptable forms of punishment. Just as we refuse to torture torturers and rape rapists because these acts degrade both ourselves and the punished, so too should we refrain from the most extreme retaliatory act of execution. The severity of punishment is not without limits—respect for life and dignity set such limits. In our act of executing, we allow offenders, even those who commit the most heinous acts, to dictate our punitive response, even when it crosses a moral boundary. Numerous murder victim family members recognize that justice is not served through retaliatory, legalized homicide. We do not rectify killing by killing.

Along other lines, retired Supreme Court Justice John Paul Stevens argues that John Robert's opinion in *Baze* evidences that the court has rejected the premise that executions serve a retributive purpose. Stevens assumes the account of lethal injections that Kim Hansen challenges in chapter 1. Justice Stevens reasons that

> the Eighth Amendment has been construed to prohibit needless suffering and significant risks of harm to the defendant. As a matter of constitutional law, what was once a gruesome event has been transformed into a procedure comparable to the administration of anesthesia in a hospital operating room. By requiring that an execution be relatively painless, we protect the inmate from enduring any punishment that is comparable to the suffering inflicted on his victim. We have thus undermined the premises on which public approval of the retribution rationale is based.[12]

Echoing an earlier opinion of Justice White, Justice Stevens, drawing on his thirty-four years of experience after the *Gregg* ruling, concluded that the death penalty should be deemed unconstitutional since its imposition represents "the pointless and needless extinction of life with only marginal contributions to any discernible social or public purposes. A penalty with such negligible returns to the state [is] patently excessive and cruel and unusual punishment violative of the Eighth Amendment" (*Baze v. Rees*, 2008; quoting *Furman v. Georgia*).

Increasingly jurors and citizens express support for alternate forms of maximum punishment short of execution, such as long prison sentences or sentences of life imprisonment without parole, based on the reasoning that

---

[12] John Paul Stevens, *Five Chiefs: A Supreme Court Memoir* (New York: Little, Brown, 2011).

execution is not necessary to ensure the safety and security of communities. Many citizens argue that the exorbitant costs of funding capital trials can be better directed to crime prevention, victim support, and enhanced prison security. Like Benjamin Rush, many fear that killing in response to killing is both incoherent and carries a brutalizing effect by emphasizing violent solutions to societal problems.

As will be seen in subsequent chapters, the Catholic position on the death penalty is rooted in a fundamentally and substantively different approach to issues of crime and punishment. Rather than focusing narrowly on retributive justice, the Catholic response to crime substantively and holistically addresses the contributing factors of crime, the harms done to persons through crime, and the need for addressing such harms in ways that promote respect for all persons and the common good. With great clarity the US bishops' statement on crime, Responsibility, Rehabilitation, and Restoration, emphasizes that restorative justice, not retaliatory vengeance, is to be sought and that punishment must have a clear purpose: to protect society, restore the common good, and rehabilitate those who violate the law and harm persons. As will be seen in the following chapters, central to this understanding is the affirmation of human dignity and concern for all persons. Catholics are called both to stand with crime victims in their suffering and search for justice and healing and to recognize that no person is reducible to his or her worst act, unworthy of hope for transformation. Christians are called to recognize the face of Jesus in all persons, be they victims or offenders, and to seek responses to crime that heal and restore persons. The Christian response to such a radical call is shown most powerfully in showing respect, even love, to those who have done grave harm to others.

Subsequent chapters lay out in detail the depth and richness of the moral vision central to the Catholic approach to the death penalty. Catholics have played and continue to play a major role in state repeals of the death penalty. They have brought persons to understand that "we cannot overcome crime by simply executing criminals, nor can we restore the lives of the innocent by ending the lives of those convicted of their murders. The death penalty offers the tragic illusion that we can defend life by taking life."[13] It is hoped that as more Catholics come to understand the Catholic position on why the death penalty is wrong, Catholics will come to play

---

[13] United States Conference of Catholic Bishops, *A Good Friday Appeal to End the Death Penalty* (Washington, DC: USCCB, 1999).

an increasingly significant role in finally ending the practice of the death penalty in the United States.

Review and Looking Forward

Editors

This chapter provides an overview of ongoing debate about and tinkering with the practice of the death penalty in the United States. The sheer number of Supreme Court rulings on the death penalty reveals how this peculiar punishment is still unsettled and unsettling. More and more rulings are likely if we retain the practice of executions. The chapter also points toward the Catholic position on restorative justice, developed in subsequent chapters.

Azim Khamisa drew on his faith in responding to the violent murder of his child. The most frequent description of God in the Qur'an, the holy book of Muslims, is All-Compassionate and All-Merciful. Islam acknowledges the right of persons to seek retributive justice, the righting of wrongs in a fair and commensurate way. But it emphasizes that restorative justice is always the better response. Rather than narrowly focusing on punitively righting wrongs, restorative justice seeks to address the sources of wrongdoing, respond to the needs of the persons wronged, and restore relations. Attention is focused on what can be done to make our shared, communal life better.

Rachel King's book *Don't Kill in Our Names* explores the transformative insight of Bill Pelke, an insight shared by Azim Khamisa and Vicki Schieber. Bill's grandmother was murdered by teenagers feigning interest in her Bible classes. They intended to rob her and in the process stabbed her to death—by countless blows as she lay helpless on her living room floor. The Pelke family's immediate response was to demand the severest punishment possible in the state of Indiana. For them, anything less than capital punishment would be a travesty of justice. But when fifteen-year-old Paula Cooper was sentenced as the youngest death row prisoner in the country, the family was shocked. Some relatives expressed appreciation that the judge "had the guts" to give Paula exactly what she deserved.

Bill soon found himself haunted by the faith in Christ his grandmother had lived by. He found himself praying that God would help him have love and compassion for Paula and her family on behalf of his grandmother. He wrote to Paula, explaining he forgave her and his work to help her would be done for the glory of God. Azim, Vicki, and Bill recognized that their Muslim, Catholic, and Baptist faiths called them to forgive. But Bill's insight focused on the realization that forgiveness is a self-directed act, in the sense of an act that begins the journey of one's personal healing. Azim, Vicki, and Bill focused on forgiveness as a matter of faith, personal healing, and honoring their loved ones. Forgiveness freed them from the suffering of anger and hate triggered by bereavement.

With strong support from European activists, Bill worked to overturn Paula Cooper's death sentence. Under international pressure, the Indiana legislature changed its juvenile death penalty statute, raising the minimum age for death sentences from age ten to sixteen. But this new ruling would not apply retroactively to Paula Cooper. In disagreement with this finding, the Indiana Supreme Court in 1989 commuted Paula's sentence from death to sixty years. Like Azim and Vicki, Bill devoted all of his energy and passion to ending the death penalty. His organization, Journey of Hope . . . From Violence to Healing, gathers murder victim family members and family members of death row inmates to speak about the power of forgiveness and restorative justice.[14] Bill, like Azim and Vicki, speaks to people across the country and sits on the boards of major abolition organizations. But Bill says, "I don't like going to meetings. I'd rather be on the road telling my story and sharing my message of love and compassion for all humanity." Just like Azim and Vicki, Bill adds, "When I speak, I don't give a talk on the death penalty, I tell a story. People listen to stories. They open their minds, and then you can touch their hearts."[15] All three know well the arguments and facts about the death penalty but prefer telling their stories. Bill, Azim, and Vicki know the power of stories to change hearts and minds, a topic to which we turn in our next chapter.

Questions for Discussion

Editors

1. Retributive justice focuses on righting wrongs through punishment. It emphasizes that wrongs can be righted. Discuss whether restorative justice abandons this focus or reconceives what "righting wrongs" entails.

2. Azim, Vicki, and Bill speak of their journeys as if they have a new perspective that frees them. All focus on a future that honors their loved ones rather than a past that tragically harmed them. Discuss the role death penalty trials and decades of appeals play in murder victim family members' focusing on the past or the future.

---

[14] See http://journeyofhope.org/.
[15] King, *Don't Kill in Our Names*, 114.

3. Supreme Court rulings keep adding procedures, modifying protections, and narrowing the number of people who can be sentenced to death. Discuss whether any of the specific court rulings discussed in the chapter appear to be addressing the issue of restorative justice. Is our death penalty system of punishment exclusively focused on retributive justice? Discuss whether or not an exclusive focus on retributive justice is too narrow.

Chapter 4

The Power of Stories

Editors

Jean Vanier is the founder of L'Arche, an international movement with homes throughout the world. In these homes, "ordinary" people (not disabled) live together as a family and share the joys and struggles of daily life with persons with severe physical and intellectual disabilities. In his work *Becoming Human*, Jean Vanier recounts the story of how, "the night before he died, Jesus knelt down humbly before his disciples, washed their feet and called them to do the same." Vanier then asks, "Was it not because he knew how power can be used to crush and enslave, rather than to empower and free? In order to empower and free others, we need to discover this new force of love and communion, which comes from God."[1] We learn of this new force through stories about the life of Christ.

Vanier goes on to tell the powerful story of the Trappist abbot Christian de Chergé, murdered with six fellow French monks in Algeria in 1996. John Kiser's *The Monks of Tibhirine* and the 2010 film *Of Gods and Men* tell the story of how these men lived and died. They lived and died serving the spiritual and physical needs of their local Muslim neighbors amidst the protracted, brutal Algerian civil war of the 1990s. In this terror-filled context fraught with the deep-seated postcolonial hatred and resentment, these monks sought to continue their loving service to others, even extended to those who threatened and finally killed them. The film takes us on the slow, deliberate steps of their daily lives that witnessed their love of God and humanity. Abbot Christian de Chergé wrote a "testament" as he anticipated his death. He asked his family, religious community, and church to accept that Christ was no stranger to such a violent departure. He encouraged them to link their impending deaths to all the other violent

---

[1] Jean Vanier, *Becoming Human* (New York: Paulist, 1998), 160.

46

deaths that remain forgotten in anonymity. He cast his thanks broadly, including his killers, in a powerful gesture of forgiveness and reconciliation. Vanier repeats his words of thanks:

> In this "thank you," which is said for everything in my life, I certainly include you, friends of yesterday and today . . . and you also, friend of my final moment, who would not be aware of what you are doing. Yes, for you too, I want to say this "thank you" and *à Dieu* [to God], whom I have seen through you. May we meet again in Paradise as two blessed and good thieves, if that is what God, the Father of us both, wants. Amen! Inch'Allah [God willing]![2]

The words of the monks' chants, sung throughout the film, speak of their fidelity that brought them to "turn to the Man of Sorrow who beckons us from the Cross." The monks died devoutly, believing they are brothers to all, even those who do evil, and that love, their eternal hope, is what endures. The story captured so beautifully in this film is haunting, stirring reflection long after its viewing. The power of the film takes us right to the heart of the story, bringing us to ask pointedly—how would I respond if I were Christian?

In the same way, the story of Sr. Helen Prejean's journey on death row, told in *Dead Man Walking* and powerfully presented in the film of the same name, brings us to face a wide range of questions raised by the death penalty and faced by Abbot Christian. This film provided Americans an opportunity to grapple with the reality and morality of the death penalty. Now the Dead Man Walking School Theatre Project brings the story to life in school productions across the nation. Over 220 schools have participated in the theatre project since it began in 2004.[3]

Numerous teachers and students have written about the power of these student performances.[4] Maureen Ryan of Ohio State University explains how "*Dead Man Walking* puts the act of retribution in our view. It forces us to confront it, to question it, to personalize it. That's the point." One actor who performed in nearly seventy other shows said that no other performance had the personal intensity and affective power of his role as Matthew Poncelet, the death row inmate awaiting execution. Other actors

---

[2] Ibid., 161.

[3] See a script based on Sr. Helen Prejean's novel: Tim Robbins, *Dead Man Walking* (San Francisco: Dead Man Walking School Theatre Project, 2003).

[4] The comments by students and teachers in this section are found at Dead Man Walking School Theatre Project, "Testimonials," www.dmwplay.org/make_theatre/testimonials.html.

explained that they had never thought about the death penalty until the play powerfully drew them into the issue. One teacher at Justin-Siena High School in Napa, California, described how the play project generated numerous other projects:

> To be honest, I don't know why every catholic high school in the country isn't working on the show. Producing *Dead Man Walking* had an incredible impact, not only on the theatre department, but within the entire school community. Our English Department had every Junior and Senior in the school read "A Lesson Before Dying" as well as [work on] projects on different areas of capital punishment. Our Religious Studies department was inspired to expand their capital punishment and social justice segment. Our Campus Ministry students presented an entire Mass around the subject. Our Visual & Performing Arts Department was able to use the movie AND the play to discuss the ways that theatre and film are similar/different [and] to provoke discussion around the subject. And our Student Leadership filmed a documentary around the experience which they are going to show at a school wide forum . . . [The play and its performance] took on a life of its own and was unlike anything I have ever experienced.

Noting how the performance brought their entire community to care about and reflect on important social issues, this teacher concluded, "And, if you ask me, that's what theatre is all about!"

Other educators wrote of the power of the play's characters to create "teaching moments" about a range of issues concerning the place of drama in education and the death penalty. Father Douglas K. Clark of Benedictine Military School described the power of the play to generate reflection and dialogue. He found that the "audience will make up its own mind as to the issues presented. The actor and production team members came to this project with a range of views on the death penalty. The experience of mounting this production [made] us think." Dr. John H. Taylor of Adams State College recounted how his school's production redefined the role of theatre within their community. He found the greatest achievement of their production was the play's power to "engage the hearts and minds of a significant portion of our community in a dialogue about the death penalty."

In this chapter, Kurt Blaugher turns to this issue, exploring how drama "stirs minds and hearts" and why doing so is vital to our common, personal, and social life. Students and teachers often draw on stories, especially those portrayed in films. They turn to them repeatedly in class discussions to explain, expand, and illustrate points. We are drawn into stories; we remember and recount them to others. Our thinking often takes off from and is interwoven with them. Kurt is a theatre director and professor of visual and performing arts. In the chapter, he explores how stories, especially those enacted on stage, break down barriers between people, trigger reflection, motivate action, and, in some cases, bring about social change.

By bringing stories to life, drama and theatre expand our world and broaden our imagination. We find ourselves imagining other persons' lives—especially seemingly distant ones—and gaining new insights and envisioning new possibilities. Often we are not the same after the story. With theatre, we are immediately pulled into the story. We find ourselves caught up in the journey of another character while at the same time being able to reflect critically on that journey. Kurt captures well how these works evoke our reflection and concern, how they engage both our hearts and our minds. His chapter brings us to understand what we already experience—the power of stories, the power of empathy and living through someone else's point of view. The stories of our lives are the groundwork of the moral life.

Stirring Hearts and Minds

Kurt Blaugher

Scholarly writings and Supreme Court rulings are for the most part unknown by most citizens. Occasionally they receive passing attention in the national media. But for the most part the arguments, rulings, and empirical studies summarized in chapters 2 and 3 engage and sustain the interest of activists and academics already engaged in reflection on the death penalty. Yet in recent years the practice of the death penalty *has* increasingly engaged the interest of many citizens. Americans *are* thinking about the death penalty. Stories of exonerated death row inmates deeply trouble us. Across the nation we were riveted to hourly developments leading up to the execution of Troy Davis. Stories of real, living persons put a human face on the abstract issue of the death penalty. It can be argued that Sr. Helen Prejean's story of her journey on death row with Patrick Sonnier, told in *Dead Man Walking* and even more powerfully presented in film and theatre performances, is what brought Americans to reflect on and care about the death penalty.[5] For many persons it was the film, subsequently reworked

[5] See Sr. Helen Prejean, *Dead Man Walking* (New York: Vintage, 1994).

as an opera and straight play, that riveted their attention and began their own journey to understanding the death penalty. For many Americans, film provides the closest experience of a theatrical performance of stories, and good films provoke concern about and reflection on important social and moral issues. The death penalty became present through Sr. Helen's powerful storytelling—present to us in all its human reality bearing on the lives of the convicted and victimized, both their family members, local communities, legal and prison personnel, and spiritual advisors.

Peter Brook describes the moral power of story as a sharing of life that intervenes between two "silences": a dead silence and a silence that is a moment of deeply felt empathy. He is well situated to comment on story. He is one of the few theatre artists alive who rates the title of "genius." He is a playwright, director, filmmaker, and founder of the International Centre for Theatre Research.

> You see, this is exactly how it starts. With a silence. There are two silences. Perhaps there are many, but there are two ends of the pole of silence. There is dead silence, the silence of the dead, which doesn't help any of us, and then there is the other silence, which is the supreme moment of communication—the moment when people normally divided from one another by every sort of natural human barrier suddenly find themselves truly together, and that supreme moment expresses itself in something which is undeniably shared, as one can feel at this very moment . . . Here is a human being, other human beings watching. Now, can we tell the whole story we want to tell, and bring to life the theme we want to bring to life, doing no more than that?[6]

From his landmark productions of *King Lear*, *Marat/Sade*, and *A Midsummer Night's Dream* in the 1960s to his more recent adaptations of the Indian epic *The Mahabharata* and *L'Homme Qui* (from Oliver Sacks's *The Man Who Mistook His Wife for a Hat*) in the 1990s, Brook has consistently proven himself to be a visionary, capable of creating theatre that invigorates and reinvents the essential nature of the genre. In the cited quotation from Moffitt's book, Brook speaks of the most essential aspect of theatre, storytelling at its most basic—the shared communion between performers and audience.

No one knows exactly when, in some prehistoric moment, a storyteller began to characterize, to *perform*, the persons in a story, rather than just tell

---

[6] Dale Moffitt, ed., *Between Two Silences: Talking with Peter Brook* (Dallas: Southern Methodist University Press, 1999), 5.

the story. For most theatre historians, that "moment" is considered something akin to the birth of theatre, the moment when the human impulse to imitate and to tell stories coincides with the equally strong human impulse simply to report. Most theorists suggest that this impulse to perform is hardwired into our humanity; humans have from our very beginning performed for one another. Whether through communal ritual experiences or more personal storytelling, humans have always seemed driven to perform for each other. It is also generally accepted that as imitation developed, deepened, and became more consciously performative, various other trappings of theatre—costumes, settings, props, et cetera—were added to these performance events, until these nascent performances became events unto themselves, separate from other ritualized or storytelling activities.

As Brook explains, theatre—the act of performing a story for an audience—breaks down barriers between actors and audience, allowing those "supreme moment[s] of communication" and communion to occur. Performances powerfully draw audiences into a sharing of human conditions. Performances also have the power to persuade, motivate, and even bring about change in local communities and societies. In this sense, as an agent of change, theatre can take on political significance, bringing about critical reflection and transformation within social communities. "Theatre of the Oppressed," developed by the Brazilian theatre practitioner Augusto Boal, is used by theatrical and nontheatrical groups to engender grassroots political action in communities of all sizes.[7] Theatrical performances are seen as evoking reflection on and response to important social and political realities. But many critics argue intellectual engagement presupposes an emotional connection with and through performances. If we are to reflect on, care about, and take action against oppression as Boal calls us to do, we must somehow be "moved" to do so. Storytelling dramatized in theatre must somehow on a fundamental level engage our sense of human empathy.

Tim Robbins offers his reflections on the power of performance. His reflections are part of his introductory remarks to Sr. Helen Prejean's keynote address, in 2007, to the Association for Theatre in Higher Education. Robbins comments, "I've found that there is no more effective way to truly stir the hearts and minds of people than a live event. . . . Hundreds if not thousands of people sit in a dark room and share an experience with a

[7] See Augusto Boal, *Theatre of the Oppressed* (New York: Theatre Communications Group, 1985).

group of actors."[8] In her book *Dead Man Walking*, Sr. Helen stresses that an understanding of her experiences of Louisiana's death row requires "work of the eye"—an intellectual seeing and understanding. But she quickly adds that if we are to reach fuller and deeper understanding, such seeing is not enough. Her narrative, subsequently transformed into theatrical, operatic, and filmed embodiments, brings readers and audiences to realize the life experiences of Elmo Patrick Sonnier, Robert Lee Willie, Matthew Poncelet, and others they deeply affect.[9] Such realization requires "heart-work"—our being drawn into the human dimensions of executions. This "heart-work" is the spark that makes the issue of the death penalty come alive within us, allowing it to be fanned and grow to flame. Her narrative, embodied in varying forms, is what draws us into the hard and compelling work of the eye *and* the heart.

Why and how is this so? Why did the arts provide the spark that ignited both personal and national discourse on the death penalty? Why do the arts make human things matter so much to us as persons and citizens? Clearly answers to these questions lie in the realm of aesthetics, the province of philosophers who have asked the "why art works" questions since the musings of the ancient Greeks. For the theatre practitioner, however, the asking of *why* art works is perhaps nowhere as important as the visceral assurance that *art does work*, and on both the hearts and minds of an audience. Indeed, if it does not work—if it fails to engage the audience—then it can be easily argued that art hasn't happened. This heart/mind engagement can best be understood as entailing a type of empathy. David Krasner writes,

> The lived body has significance for the theater. The actor onstage is not an abstraction, but a living organism expressing emotions, actions, gestures, movements and sounds. . . . I exist in the audience as observer. . . . We are in communication, actor and audience are living forms that adapt and adjust to the environment, the circumstances of the play, and the spaces we inhabit. I *empathize* with actors not in order to lose myself in them, or allow myself to be manipulated by them, but to absorb their experiences that in turn assist me in comprehending and enlarging the full meaning

---

[8] Tim Robbins, Introductory Remarks (Association for Theatre in Higher Education, 2007), www.press.jhu.edu/timeline/athe/2007_robbins.html.

[9] Sonnier and Willie are portrayed as a composite character, Matthew Poncelet, in the film.

of the play, and in turn, the meaning of my life as well (emphasis added).[10]

Drawing on the philosophical works of ancient (e.g., Aristotle) and modern (e.g., Martha Nussbaum) thinkers, Krasner argues that theatrical performance by its very nature draws audiences toward empathy, toward the stirring of "heart and mind" alluded to by Robbins. Why does such engagement of performers and audience occur? Why does theatre work the way it does? Scholars argue that compared to other art forms, theatre audiences engage with performers and performance "in the moment," as the performers are actually creating the narrative event in the same space with them, bringing them to think and feel along with them. This powerful immediacy of response is what separates performance from other art forms. Performance literally embodies the story for the audience, placing human actors with human responses into the situations being performed for the audience. Such embodiment makes human concerns, motivations, reflections, and actions present, stirring the minds and hearts of actors and audience.

Theater has been—and always will be—a way for humanity to reexperience, reevaluate and reinvent itself. Theater pushes us to recognize and evaluate our deepest desires, fundamental beliefs, and highest goals. In the telling of the story in the gripping moment of performance, actors and audiences link themselves with a long line of other actors and audiences—in Greek amphitheaters, Elizabethan playhouses, Spanish *corrales*, Japanese *Noh* theatres—anywhere people gather for the performance of stories. Catholic theologian Bill Portier calls this never-ending link between performers and audiences "the communion of saints." For Portier, the communion of saints is the endless stream of humanity from our earliest beginnings through the present into the future, each with its own particular story. In these moments of communion with this stream, whether stepping into the stories of murderers, victims, beloved family members, seekers of justice, forgiveness, or reconciliation, we draw closer to human aspirations, concerns, and truths—and to each other.

Krasner, in his "Empathy and Theater," stresses that empathy *"allows us to transcend the limits of our own world,"* bringing us into contact with a "vastly different living circumstance" (265). In embodying a character

---

[10] David Krasner, "Empathy and Theater," in D. Krasner and D. Saltz, eds., *Staging Philosophy: Intersections of Theater, Performance, and Philosophy* (Ann Arbor: University of Michigan Press, 2006), 270–71.

and conveying a story, the actor makes present "an attention-grabbing and dynamic human being" who commands our interest. Theatre heightens our awareness of how life is experienced and lived by others. Krasner is convinced that empathy is based on "a need for exercising the capacity for human communication, fruitful cooperation, and reciprocal interchange of values and ideas" (ibid., 258). Sister Helen's narratives vividly bring to life the range of human harms and sufferings tied to death sentences. In doing so, she brings us deep into the American practice of the death penalty in all its human dimensions. Krasner stresses that empathy entails four elements: (1) our identifying with others, envisioning ourselves in their circumstances, (2) our feeling compassion for others wrongly treated, as bound up with our sense of justice and related judgments of value, (3) our sympathy evoking the desire to aid or assist others in their pain, and (4) our critical understanding that brings us to comprehend and judge others' beliefs, responses, and actions (ibid., 258–59).

In short, empathy clearly engages both mind and heart. Empathy enhances our capacity to comprehend persons and their social conditions. On this point, Krasner cites the work of Norwegian philosopher Arna Johan Vetlesen: empathy facilitates a "reaching out process, enabling us to walk in someone else's shoes without sacrificing critical reflection" (ibid., 263). Narrative performances can evoke both reflection and concern, a cognitive and emotive response to the lives of others, which in turn can motivate us to become involved in social action. Krasner stresses that performance of stories strengthens an audience's capacity to care about characters, events, circumstances, and conditions. Such caring can be a powerful inspiration for societal change. Krasner concludes that "care and empathy are inextricably bound up with social action and heightened cognition, which are essential components to critical awareness and objective assessment" (ibid., 272).

Sister Helen's journey into the death penalty began when she first encountered a man on death row. This encounter initiated her inquiry about the death penalty and shaped her own subsequent life story. She ends her second book, *The Death of Innocents*, with what she calls "the last cry of the heart," which is her own. She invites readers to join her in the struggle to end the death penalty in the United States and the rest of the world, for "its practice demeans us all" as persons.[11] She reaches out to those who are ambivalent about the death penalty, seeking to begin a dialogue. Her

---

[11] Sr. Helen Prejean, *The Death of Innocents: An Eyewitness Account of Wrongful Executions* (New York: Vintage, 2006), 270.

hope is that her stories, expressed in narrative, film, opera, and play, set us on fire regarding the death penalty, as the literary and performative arts have the gripping and transformative power to do so.

Review and Looking Forward

Editors

Music plays a significant role in the film *Of Gods and Men*. The quiet peace of the monks' daily lives flows naturally into their beautifully sung chants expressing their beliefs and aspirations. As the film builds to its expected conclusion, the monks share a deeply thoughtful and powerfully emotional meal together. Their faces disclose the depth of their joy in the world—their enjoyment of their communal friendship, the wonderful wine, and the beautiful music of *Swan Lake*—and their sadness in recognizing these will be their last days together in this community. Clearly God is present to them in and through this world. Given this distinctly Catholic sensibility, it is not surprising that Catholics value the sensible aspects of experience and produce literary, visual, and performing art works.[12]

Given this appreciation, it is not surprising that Sr. Helen Prejean's story of her journey has been transformed into a film, an opera, and finally a theatre production. Through *Dead Man Walking* she brings us to hear all the voices from her journey coming from their differing experiences and places—the voices of the families of the victims, the condemned and their families, the legal and correctional personnel, and persons fighting to abolish or retain the death penalty. She lets each character speak to us in a way that draws us into this story, which is part of a larger story about our nation, our communities, and ourselves. Sister Helen's story is unquestionably rooted in the faith that shaped her journey on death row.

To this Catholic understanding of the death penalty we now turn in chapter 5 on the Eucharist and chapter 6 on Christ's sacrifice. We should remember that what God gives us in Jesus Christ is God's own being. God is communicated to us in the life and death of Jesus, which is passed from generation to generation by story—by the gospels, by the performance of the Mass, by stories of discipleship, and by the story of the church's ongoing service to the world. These stories are the topics of part II of the book. They are the sources of the Christian life.

---

[12] See sociologist (and Catholic priest) Andrew Greeley's *The Catholic Imagination* (Berkeley: University of California Press, 2000).

Questions for Discussion

1. In light of this chapter's analysis, discuss the role and power of the parables in the gospels.

2. Discuss how you understand and what you think of Bill Portier's analogy of performers and audiences as being part of "the communion of saints."

3. Jean Vanier states, "Reality is the first principle of truth. . . . Each of us needs to work at searching for truth, not be afraid of it. We need to strive to live in truth. . . . And the truth sets us free only if we let it penetrate our hearts and rend the veil that separates the head and the heart, our attitudes and our way of living" (*Becoming Human*, 15–16). Sister Helen Prejean's two books (*Dead Man Walking* and *The Death of Innocents*) are full of revelations about the reality of the death penalty. She weaves these into stories of her journey with four men to their executions. Discuss how Vanier's words speak to her way of writing and how they speak to the challenge of your own striving to live in truth.

Part II

A Christian Rethinking
of the Death Penalty

Editors

The first part of the book attends to views and practices of capital punishment across the world and in the United States. The use of the death penalty persists. However, it is becoming less and less defensible as people are trying to think about what is really going on. At first, capital punishment seems right, but as we look closer we find that we need to rethink the issue. This process of "rethinking" continues in the second part of the book. We will look at the death penalty through the lens of faith. We investigate the foundations of Christianity: Jesus' death and resurrection, worship, and the Bible as they relate to the issue of the death penalty. As the apostle Paul frequently proclaims in his New Testament letters, we are called to live "in" Christ (Rom 6:3; Gal 2:19; Col 2:12). The story of God in Jesus Christ is the story of our lives.

Chapter 5

Forgiveness and Healing

Editors

In her book *Choosing Mercy*, Antoinette Bosco describes her reaction to the news that her son and daughter-in-law, John and Nancy Bosco, were murdered on August 12, 1993: "There is a collapse in the heart and the soul that cannot be described. . . . For murder is the entrance of the worst evil into your home . . . forever shattering any illusion you might have had that good can protect you from evil."[1] Later she would ask herself if she had enough of God's love in her to pray for the killer. Antoinette remembers,

> My beloved son and his beautiful wife were dead at the hand of someone I could only believe to be, at that moment, an agent of Satan. I found myself screaming, sometimes aloud, sometimes with silent cries tearing at my insides. I tormented myself, wanting to know who was the faceless monster that had brought such permanent unrelenting pain into my family. I wanted to kill him with my own hands. I wanted him dead. (13)

About four months later, Antoinette received word that the killer had been arrested. He was a first-year college student, who gave no motive for the murders of John and Nancy. Sadistic whim? Experiment? Fantasy? The only connection he had to John and Nancy was their house; they lived in a home recently purchased from their killer's parents. Antoinette wanted answers, hoping they would relieve the pain. She was given no answers.

Antoinette remembered the question of the death penalty being raised in an ethics class, while working on her master's degree a few decades

---

[1] Antoinette Bosco, *Choosing Mercy: A Mother of Murder Victims Pleads to End the Death Penalty* (Maryknoll, NY: Orbis Books, 2001), 13. Subsequent references will be noted within the text.

before. Amid the spirit of Vietnam War protests and the civil rights movement, she asserted—to the class—that she was against the death penalty. The professor turned confrontational: "Suppose someone raped and murdered one of your daughters. What would you say then?" Antoinette did have a daughter. She recalled, "I was stunned. I had not expected such a crime to be a personal matter. Without thinking, I blurted out, 'I'd say kill the bastard'" (40).

Most people think that victims' families will want the death of a murderer, and, therefore, we all should support the death penalty. But after much soul-searching, Antoinette found a better way:

> I know the claim that vengeance can make on your soul when you are devastated by the injustice of losing a love at the hand of a murderer. It fills every part of you, with rage tearing the very molecules of your existence. Yes, you feel like destroying the person who has so permanently clawed away a vital part of your life. This rage puts you on the point of a defining moment that will determine who you will become and what will happen to your relationship with God. (17)

Along the journey of pain and confusion, Antoinette learned a "new slant on forgiveness." She realized that she would be destroyed by hatred and revenge. She began to understand that the desire for revenge was just another way that the murderer was in control of her life—she was "emotionally handcuffed to him." Forgiveness became that pathway to her own healing. "I saw clearly that what forgiveness is really about is putting the spotlight on ourselves to reveal who we really are when we become the victim of brutal evil." Forgiveness "doesn't mean to give in; it means to let go, and letting go is a precondition to becoming free" (50).

Antoinette shares an unexpected experience with others whose family members have been murdered. She realizes that she cannot forgive the killer; yet, she does forgive and knows this experience of healing, freedom, and peace to be a work of grace (106). This experience of wholeness is real and concrete for Antoinette in receiving Holy Communion—in the unity of the Eucharist (104–8). In the following chapter on the Eucharist, Rodica Stoicoiu, a liturgist and scholar of the liturgy, reflects on forgiveness in the context of the Mass. She notes that "to forgive is to face the full reality of what we are called to forgive." This statement is strikingly similar to an insight that Antoinette learns along her spiritual path: that forgiving is not forgetting because what is forgotten cannot be healed (113). The Eucharist is given to us by Jesus Christ—the gift of God's own self—to bring our brokenness before God who will transform it. This chapter focuses on forgiveness and conversion. This focus is not "academic." It represents the experiences of many family members of murder victims.

The Eucharist: Forgiveness and Personhood

Rodica Stoicoiu

Sometimes the inability to forgive comes from the misunderstanding of what forgiveness is and is not. Forgiveness is not pardon. That is the function of the president or governor in the United States. Forgiveness is not forgetting; some actions are too terrible to forget, and some should never be forgotten. "Forgive and forget" is not always applicable to real life. Forgiveness is not the same as reconciliation; it may be possible to forgive persons but not possible to reconcile with them and be present to them or form a relationship with them. Antoinette Bosco, for example, does not attempt to befriend the murderer of her son and daughter-in-law.[2]

Forgiveness means none of these things. Rather, to forgive is to face the full reality of what we are called to forgive—to face it, to experience that reality to its fullest depth—and only then through forgiving will we find healing. When we forgive, we give up certain rights we may feel we have. We give up the right to hate, to retribution, to revenge. Instead we are asked to embrace understanding and even compassion for the person who has done us such wrong. Antoinette seeks understanding and compassion, especially for the killer's parents, who have also lost a child to his own brutality. By seeking to let go of our hate, we are open to embrace forgiveness as a grace, a gift that we may reject or accept. The gift of forgiveness reveals both the deepest level of human frailty and our capacity to share in the strength of God's love.

As Christians our model for forgiveness is that of God, especially as this is embodied in the ministry of Jesus. In his ministry, Jesus forgave and demonstrated the love of God to those who were dead to his society, the disenfranchised, the outcast, and all those who most needed to experience the love of God. He loved and forgave those who were least lovable and most in need of the compassion of God. We could draw a parallel in the

---

[2] Some relatives of murder victims have done so, as discussed in Rachel King's account of Ron Carlson. See chapter 3 of Rachel King's *Don't Kill in Our Names: Families of Murder Victims Speak Out Against the Death Penalty* (New Brunswick, NJ: Rutgers University Press, 2003).

modern world and speak in terms of those most in need of compassion today: the homeless, IV drug users, teenage prostitutes, and so forth. The breadth of his forgiveness encompassed even those who were killing him as he hung upon a cross.

How are we to find the strength to carry out such an understanding of forgiveness? It would seem, under some circumstances, to require superhuman strength. Nevertheless, each of us is asked to forgive with hope and love and to do it over and over again, "not seven times but seventy-seven times" (Matt 18:22). We are asked to embody the love of God, to imitate Christ. How is this possible since we are frail? We are only human. But that is where the answer lies, in our humanity as created and graced by God.

We are most fully human when we are in relationship. Humans are not meant to be isolated and alone. We know this to be true because we are created in the image of a relational God, Father, Son, and Holy Spirit, who mutually indwell each other in the unity of the divine communion of persons. To be most fully who we are, authentic persons, we will live in open, honest relationships, able to give ourselves away to others, to share ourselves. This is possible because forgiveness brings healing, and healing turns us toward wholeness. In other words, true humanity is experienced in community, in a web of relationships that allow us to image our God, in justice, forgiveness, healing, and love. As creations in the image of this God we carry the potential to authentic personhood within our relationships. This potential for authenticity is actualized in the waters of baptism, the foundational sacrament of forgiveness, through which we enter a web of relationships, and hence allows us to express the fullness of our humanity as part of the Body of Christ—the church.

In the waters of our baptism, we die to our old selves and are reborn in the image of the triune God. Through our baptisms, in a very real sense, we die to who we were, and emerge from the font a new creation committed to the actions of Christ. We emerge, no longer as isolated individuals condemned to death but rather we rise from the water as new persons, part of the community of the church, now actualizing what it means to be fully human. As part of this new authenticity we are called to reach out in radical forgiveness and a love so encompassing we may be called to stretch wide our arms and offer our very selves.

Since this new identity is fundamentally ecclesial (embodied in the community of the church), it finds expression when we gather together as the Body of Christ. It is most fully expressed when we gather to celebrate the Eucharist, the most radically social act of our lives. In the celebration of the Eucharist we model as one Body what every moment of our lives should be. Here we experience what it is to forgive because we are forgiven and are called, in turn, to forgive others. Together we experience what it is to be loved and, in turn, are called to love all. The eucharistic liturgy confronts us with truth. It challenges us to embody the fullness of our humanity. It reminds us who we are called to be through Jesus. To truly celebrate the Eucharist is to become a member of a community where fundamental acts of forgiveness, love, and compassion lead to healing and conversion.

The word for "conversion" in the New Testament is *metanoia*, which literally means "to turn around" in Greek. We are called to turn around so that we will live out the fullness of who we are destined to be. To truly celebrate the liturgy leads us to be human as Jesus taught us to be human, to give ourselves away utterly and completely. This is such a transformative experience that we are never the same people at the end of the liturgy as we were at its beginning. We are forever changed; our hearts have been turned; we are forever being converted, over and over again, as often as we come together to celebrate this most central mystery of our faith. To celebrate the liturgy is to walk out the doors of the church and embody the experience of celebration in such a way that we live this out in the world. We love and forgive and call others into this relationship of authentic personhood. We bring peace, we heal, and we call the world to *metanoia*.

There is nothing private about the public/communal rituals of the church. The eucharistic liturgy is the most public, social act we perform. In it, we are powerfully made the Body of Christ and enact our membership as part of the Body. The liturgy both forms us and transforms us. It challenges us to be like Christ and in so doing transform others. As the baptized we are never alone; we are part of the community. That community prays with and for us, models what it means to be a member of the Body of Christ, comforts us, and challenges us. It is in our midst that the living Word is proclaimed, preached, and inculcated into our being. It is as one voice that we sing our prayer, voice our intercessions, and proclaim our faith. It is as one ecclesial community we ask forgiveness, give thanks for the One who is the focus of our actions, and together at the high point of the eucharistic celebration eat and drink the Body and Blood, given into our hands by the Body to convert the Body.

The eucharistic liturgy begins with the gathering rites and, in most communities, with a gathering hymn. Keeping in mind that hymns are sung prayer, the singing that begins our worship seeks to draw us together, reminding us of our ecclesial identity. We are gathered together through song, reminded that we are one body, one community. It is as members of the community of the baptized that we ask forgiveness of God and one another. There are numerous options provided for this in the opening rites of the eucharistic liturgy. None of these are meant to treat sin and forgiveness as private issues between individuals and God. Rather, all the opening rites recognize that sin never hurts just one person. Sin sunders relationships and hence always affects others, as recognized in the *Confiteor*:

> I confess to almighty God and to you, my brothers and sisters . . . .[3]

Just as sin is never a private matter, just as it is always a wound to or rupture of a relationship, so too our need for forgiveness requires the recognition of community.

> [T]herefore I ask blessed Mary ever-Virgin,
> all the Angels and Saints,
> and you, my brothers and sisters,
> to pray for me to the Lord our God.

We are not alone, and whether it is the *Confiteor* mentioned above or the "Lord have mercy," the opening prayers of the liturgy acknowledge that we are a community that hurts one another but also a community that forgives one another. It is through the experience of being forgiven that we can also begin to heal and grow in our humanity.

The entire liturgy follows this communal dynamic. When the opening rites conclude, we then hear the Scriptures proclaimed. The three Scripture readings speak a word that calls us to live out our commitment to authenticity, that reminds us how Christ calls us to live: to forgive (as described above), to care for those who have no one else to care for them, to feed the hungry, to visit those in prison, in essence to give ourselves away as Christ gives himself away. We are reminded of the identity we embraced in our baptism. Strengthened by the connections that the homily makes for us between the readings and our lives, we dare to intercede for one another, to pray for those in need, to ask forgiveness, healing, and mercy for ourselves and for those who have died.

The word Eucharist comes from the Greek *Eucharistia*, which means "thanksgiving." When we gather for the eucharistic liturgy, we are giving thanks for the gift of Christ. In the thanks we give over the gifts of bread

---

[3] The prayer is named for the first word of the Latin, *Confiteor*, or "I confess." The prayer is said during the penitential rite at the beginning of the Mass.

and wine, the ramifications of the gift are clearly communicated. The second eucharistic prayer of reconciliation states,

> For though the human race
> is divided by dissension and discord,
> yet we know that by testing us
> you change our hearts
> to prepare them for reconciliation.

> Even more, by your Spirit you move human hearts
> that enemies may speak to each other again,
> adversaries join hands,
> and peoples seek to meet together.

> By the working of your power
> it comes about, O Lord,
> that hatred is overcome by love,
> revenge gives way to forgiveness,
> and discord is changed to mutual respect.

Here we can clearly see what we are called to be and to do. The transformation of bread and wine brings forth a transformation of human reality. As a community, living like Christ, through the power of the Spirit we experience conversion. We experience a fundamental transformation of persons. We forgive others, are healed, are made whole, and become authentic expressions of the God in whose image we are created.

What is expressed in the eucharistic prayer becomes reality in communion. It is why communion is the high point of the entire eucharistic liturgy. Having been forgiven, having been reminded of our communal identity, having passed Christ's peace to one another, having gathered around the table and given thanks to the Father for the gift of the Son, we then eat and drink the Body and Blood as the body and blood. In the words of St. Augustine, "So if it's you that are the body of Christ and his members, it's the mystery meaning you that is placed on the Lord's table; what you receive is the mystery that means you. . . . Be what you see and receive what you are."[4] We receive the bread and the cup as the Body of Christ, as members of the Body, in the midst of members of the Body. What we do is a radically collective act; we do not eat and drink alone. This

---

[4] *Works of Saint Augustine*, pt. 3, vol. 7: *Sermons on the liturgical seasons 230-272*, trans. Edmund Hill, OP (Hyde Park: New City Press, 1993), 297–98.

truly relational experience of eating and drinking together in the midst of the Spirit embodies the reality of following Christ.

The fullest expression of this communion reality is to both eat and drink. In the Scriptures when Christ speaks of the cup, it is always as a symbol of the cost he will pay for his actions. "Will you drink the cup I drink?" By sharing in this cup we accept the price of participating in the life of Christ. By both eating and drinking we publicly acknowledge the cost of following Jesus. As one community we eat and drink the Body and Blood of Christ, accepting the challenge of our baptism to end violence, to bring peace, to show mercy, to forgive, to accept the cost of such actions.

One prayer we all know and that we all pray together during the eucharistic liturgy, before we make the sign of peace (in and of itself a reconciling gesture), is the Lord's Prayer. It is a prayer that is far more extreme than people realize, with its clear reminder of the cost we are called to pay:

> Our Father, who art in heaven,
> hallowed be thy name;
> thy kingdom come,
> thy will be done,
> on earth as it is in heaven.
> Give us this day our daily bread,
> *and forgive us our trespasses,*
> *as we forgive those who trespass against us;*
> and lead us not into temptation,
> but deliver us from evil.
>   (*The Roman Missal*, quoting Matt 6:9-13, italics added)

We pray this by rote and rarely give thought to what we are really saying. We are praying to God the Father that we will be forgiven with the pledge we are willing to forgive others. Here, set out clearly is the challenge of forgiveness. It is a prayer that calls for our own transformation. Given our baptismal call to authentic personhood, are we willing to offer our fullest expression of forgiveness? If we can reach out in forgiveness and compassion, we can truly be open to God's forgiveness and healing. Antoinette Bosco attests to this experience of freedom from the "claim of vengeance" and for wholeness and healing. Authentic personhood requires forgiveness to be a mutual, communal, relational reality.

Having experienced the transforming power of the Eucharist, we are sent out into the world to embody this reality. This is not ever easy, and hence we pay the cost of letting go of our anger and desire for revenge. According to victims' family members, we have to give up the hatred that seems to be holding our lives together. We give up control. But we do not do so alone; we are never alone. We are persons born of the waters of baptism, fed by the Body of the church, embraced by the relationship of the community. Forgiveness, Antoinette explains, is not giving in or forgetting, but "letting go." Our openness to wholeness and new life comes in the measure of our willingness for God's mercy and forgiveness to come through us. As grace comes through us to others, we are healed. We experience the support of the community that shows us what it means to forgive and be forgiven; we celebrate this reality in the Eucharist and out of this transformative experience we can offer the gift of forgiveness. With forgiveness comes life; with compassion and mercy comes hope. With life and hope comes the kingdom of God.

Review and Looking Forward

Editors

"It was a contradictory path for his [Jesus'] times, and it remains a contradictory path in our time."[5] The "it" is forgiveness, and the author is Antoinette Bosco. In a book on *Radical Forgiveness*, she reflects, for a moment, on how difficult it was to forgive the man who murdered her son and daughter-in-law, John and Nancy Bosco. She explains that, however contradictory, the alternative to Jesus' way of forgiveness was, for her, being "emotionally handcuffed" and "bound" to the killer in a destructive way. Antoinette experienced the pathway of forgiveness as a way of freedom and new life. The same holds for Rodica's chapter on the Eucharist. In the Mass, new life—authentic human life in relationship to God and one another—is the promise of gathering together, confessing our sins before God, and accepting God's reconciliation in sharing the Body and Blood of Christ.

Rodica presents us with two principles of operation in the celebration of the Eucharist. First, we are reconciled and transformed by sharing God's life—by God's self-giving in the Eucharist. As we become part of God's good company, we become extensions of sharing God's reconciliation with the world. Antoinette recounts this experience of communion during Masses celebrated at prisons,[6] and she becomes an extension of "the

---

[5] Antoinette Bosco, *Radical Forgiveness* (Maryknoll, NY: Orbis Books, 2009), 75.
[6] Bosco, *Choosing Mercy*, 105–8.

way of reconciliation" through her work to abolish the death penalty and her spiritual writings.[7]

The second principle offered in this chapter on the Eucharist is this: the measure of our openness to God's forgiveness is the measure we are open to showing forgiveness, mercy, and reconciliation toward others— and vice versa. This relationship between being forgiven and forgiving others is not payment or tallying points (e.g., ten points of forgiveness of others gives you ten points of forgiveness from God). It is not that God withholds forgiveness until we pay up. Being forgiven and forgiving others are intimately connected through *metanoia*—"conversion" and "turning around." Being forgiven requires that we "let go," that we admit we are not the masters of our own lives. We admit that our wholeness and peace are founded on God's mercy. When we are filled with God's mercy, we become an embodiment of God's peace in the world. God's mercy works through us to others. Therefore, the measure of our openness to transformation by God is the measure of our capacity to forgive others. Because of this connection, Antoinette—in letting go of her hate and anger—experienced freedom and grace.

Forgiveness is facing up to the reality of a situation. The ultimate reality is that God's love is the source of all life. Practically speaking, facing up to reality means that forgiveness is remembering rather than forgetting, and it requires taking responsibility rather than overlooking evil and sin. Twelve years after he murdered John and Nancy, their killer wrote a letter of apology to Antoinette and her family. He asked for forgiveness.[8] In response, Antoinette told him that she and her family have forgiven him, and she emphasized that they still do not understand, nor will they ever be able to conceive, why he committed the murders. She did not relieve him of responsibility; she did not forget. Elsewhere, she has noted that he ought to be punished and imprisoned for the rest of his life. In forgiveness, she recommended to him that he face up to the reality of his acts.

Facing up to reality is the framework through which Rodica describes the Eucharist. It is the reality of God's gift to the world. It is the reality of authentic human relationships. It is the reality that we are invited to be God's embodiment of self-giving and reconciliation in the world. The chapters that follow will develop the themes of the Eucharist through discussion of the Mass as sacrifice (chap. 6) and Jesus' teachings (chap.

---

[7] See, for example, Antoinette Bosco, *The Pummeled Heart: Finding Peace through Pain* (Mystic: Twenty-Third Publications, 1994); and *One Day He Beckoned: One Woman's Story of the Difference Jesus Made* (Notre Dame: Ave Maria Press, 2004).

[8] Bosco, *Radical Forgiveness*, 102–3.

8). In the chapter on sacrifice, David Cloutier will indicate that God's self-giving in Christ provides an answer and end to the common human desire for a scapegoat. God's reconciliation calls an end to our desire to "solve" problems of sin through violence. In chapter 8, Sr. Mary Kate Birge will present to us Jesus' teachings on radical forgiveness—on the way of "choosing mercy" that freed and gave new life to Antoinette Bosco.

Questions for Discussion

1. In the chapter, Rodica highlights the communal (not private) nature of penance and forgiveness. They are acts that bind human community in God. Discuss this point in relationship to how hard it is to be open with our need for forgiveness. Why do we want to keep forgiveness private?

2. Following Rodica's suggestions in the chapter, discuss the communal elements of the *Confiteor*:

   > I confess to almighty God
   > and to you, my brothers and sisters,
   > that I have greatly sinned,
   > in my thoughts and in my words,
   > in what I have done and in what I have failed to do,
   > through my fault, through my fault,
   > through my most grievous fault;
   > therefore I ask blessed Mary ever-Virgin,
   > all the Angels and Saints,
   > and you, my brothers and sisters,
   > to pray for me to the Lord our God.

3. It is hard, perhaps impossible, to imagine Antoinette's pain and despair after John and Nancy were murdered. It is equally difficult and also almost impossible to imagine that she started to meet with murderers in prisons and share the Eucharist. We are not likely to be able to explain her experiences, but it might be helpful to discuss how the two hardly imaginable experiences might fit together *and* give us insight into the reality of the Eucharist.

Chapter 6

Jesus Christ and Sacrifice

Editors

Kirk Bloodsworth was not a saint. But from 1984 to 1993, he was called a monster. He grew up among watermen (fishing oysters and crabs) in a small town on the Chesapeake Bay. He was never a great student. He left Cambridge High School and attended a nonaccredited Open Bible Academy.[1] Afterward, he served as a marine and distinguished himself on the Marine Corps track and field team. He threw the discus. Three years later, in August 1984, Kirk was arrested for the brutal rape and murder of a nine-year-old girl in Baltimore. He was no longer a clean-cut marine. When the detectives saw him, they might have thought he looked "seedy"—long hair, thick mustache, muttonchop sideburns, burly, barrel-chested, just under six feet tall and over two hundred pounds (66). At the time of the rape and murder, he was in Essex, Maryland (just north of Baltimore). He was in the process of leaving a short, tumultuous marriage, a life of hard drinking and drug use, and a low-paying job loading and unloading furniture for an outlet store. By the time of his arrest, he was trying to start over. He was back at home in Cambridge. No job, no car, no clear way forward, he was no saint. But after his arrest, he was labeled a monster.

Understandably, the city was in shock. A nine-year-old girl was sexually assaulted and murdered on July 25, 1984, in the woods near the Fontaine Village neighborhood in Baltimore. "The community was afraid. The community needed an arrest" (44). Witnesses had seen a strange man in the neighborhood. Their descriptions varied, but a composite sketch was made. Within three days, over 500 calls came in to identify men who matched the sketch of the killer. Kirk's name was offered by an anonymous

---

[1] Tim Junkin, *Bloodsworth: The True Story of the First Death Row Inmate Exonerated by DNA* (Chapel Hill: Algonquin Books, 2004), 61. Subsequent references will be noted within the text.

caller, number 286 (75). Understandably, the victim's family and the community sought justice and closure. At the trial, the state's prosecutors asked the jury to look at two things—at the brutality of the rape and murder and at Kirk. In the courtroom, he was wearing dress shoes, dress pants, and a sweater, and he no longer looked the part (neither seedy nor dangerous). The lead prosecutor asked the jury to look beneath the surface to see the "monster inside the mind" of Kirk Bloodsworth (154).

Kirk had alibis. But persons supporting the truth (that he was not anywhere near the murder) were not considered "upstanding" citizens (and some were not). The witnesses for the defense had no credibility with the jurors. The prosecutors argued that Kirk's alibi was "too perfect" and "too consistent" to be true. Ironically, the jury believed the prosecutors' case (in a trial and retrial) despite its imperfections and inconsistencies. They rejected Kirk's story because it was "consistent" and they believed the "inconsistent" of the prosecution. The case against Kirk provided no physical evidence. Some physical evidence, like a shoe print, suggested that Kirk was not the killer. Witnesses said that his hair was too red and that, unlike Kirk, the suspect did not have sideburns. Nevertheless, Kirk was identified in a lineup, but only after a weekend of local coverage when his face appeared frequently on the television news. There really is no reason why Kirk was on trial, except for a few unfortunate coincidences, a troubled and "disordered" life that could be loosely fit into a psychological profile, no money to pay for an adequate defense, an overextended public defender, and, of course, the need for resolution for the public good.

In 1984, Kirk was arrested, and once the wheels of justice started turning, they could not be easily stopped. In 1985, he was sentenced to death. In 1986, he was retried and received two life sentences. Kirk, however, never gave up on proving his innocence. Due to unrelenting perseverance, he became the first convicted murderer to be exonerated by DNA evidence in 1993. In 2003, the DNA evidence was finally entered into Maryland's DNA database of convicted felons (274). The database identified the real killer, who was in prison for an attempted rape and stabbing. This man was also identified, in 1984, in one of the five hundred responses to the composite sketch. After almost twenty years, the killer of nine-year-old Dawn Hamilton confessed and now serves life in prison. In 1984, there was a rush to put the case in order and to seek closure, but real justice turned out to be a long time in coming.

The police detectives, prosecutors, witnesses, and jurors were all people of goodwill. They wanted the best for Dawn's family and the community. They wanted justice. They believed Kirk was a monstrous killer. We—also people of goodwill—are foolish if we think that we are better than these detectives, attorneys, witnesses, and jurors. Each played a role in trying to do what was right. How did it go so wrong? David Cloutier's chapter, "Jesus Christ as Scapegoat," attempts to explain how our good intentions can go so terribly wrong. In the chapter, David identifies a common human desire for a scapegoat. He notes that we are able to identify this desire because Jesus' life, death, and resurrection free us to confess our sins and to live a new way of God's love in the world. Like the chapters in part III of the book, David cites the *Catechism of the Catholic Church* and Christian doctrine. Catholics believe that the incarnation of God in Jesus Christ has radical implications for human solidarity and the inalienable dignity of human life. Much like the chapter on the Eucharist, this chapter emphasizes that a faithful approach to the death penalty, like the Christian life as a whole, requires conversion, a reversal of perspective, and a pledge to turn our lives around.

David brings together Rodica Stoicoiu's chapter on the Eucharist (chap. 5) and Kim Hansen's analysis of execution by lethal injection (chap. 1). The Eucharist remembers and reenacts a public execution. In contrast, Kim notes that lethal injection is performed in a way that attempts to remove the violence. It is made to look like a medical procedure rather than an execution. Even so, the reality of the "procedure" seeps through. The clean room, professional atmosphere, and medical instruments do not, in the end, hide the fact that a person is being killed.

Unexpectedly, the Eucharist goes in the opposite direction. It is a sacrament that makes present and visible what we usually do not want to admit full on: that God has died for our sakes, and we have done the killing. On this last point, David notes that on Palm/Passion Sunday, the narrative of Holy Week is read, and the congregation is directed to cry out, "Crucify him! Crucify him!" We are called to identify with Jesus as innocent victim, certainly. We also are called to admit that we are persecutors. Kim's chapter is about the "masking" of violence in the methods of lethal injection. David's chapter is about "unmasking" of human violence through God's self-giving in Jesus Christ.

Jesus Christ as Scapegoat:
Christology, Sacrifice, and the Death Penalty

David Cloutier

Jesus, the Son of God, was executed by the state. This fact, which lies at the heart of Christian faith, is the reason why Christians should view capital punishment as such an important moral issue. Catholics see the crucifix, with the executed body still on it, as the central symbol of their faith. We know that Jesus' death is not merely a passing moment on the way to some heavenly paradise. Rather, the death itself reveals something supremely important. Other essays in this collection very ably demonstrate a whole array of practical arguments against the death penalty. But in this chapter, I want to explain the deeper, theological significance of opposing the use of mortal violence by explaining and utilizing the work of theorist René Girard.[2]

For Girard, the cross is meant to reveal the very mystery of human violence and sin "hidden since the foundations of the world." The cross reveals the perverse nature of our attempts to deal with that violence by designating "scapegoats." Violence against the scapegoat is supposed to bring an end to violence, but it does not. The cross, however, breaks apart the human tendency to believe that through violence, we can somehow maintain human social order. Girard's theory, therefore, has enormous implications. Most specifically, it calls into question the pro–death penalty argument that capital punishment is a necessary act of retributive justice. Instead, I will suggest that by singling out particular crimes that are supposedly "worthy of death," the death penalty perpetuates the cycle of scapegoating violence that the cross is meant to end.

René Girard's work in history and literary criticism has led him to a conversion to Christianity. After his conversion, he gradually developed an extraordinarily important theory of the underlying mechanisms of religious violence, and, by extension, the role of forms of "sacred violence" in the (false) maintenance of social order. Most importantly, Girard develops the idea of a scapegoat: the scapegoat is a victim that channels the collective violence generated by social conflict onto a common and shared victim, who is "magically" identified as the source of the violence and disorder. We might consider the way Adolf Hitler used the Jewish people as "scapegoats" for Germany's social problems in the aftermath of World War I and the Great Depression. Hitler's anti-Semitism is a classic instance of how this scapegoat mechanism works. Jews were not in fact responsible for various social problems facing Germany. But they were a useful "solution" to the problem by taking the hostility generated by the social problems and naming a source that all could then turn on and attempt

---

[2] René Girard is a French scholar, whose teaching career has been spent at American institutions, including the State University of New York at Buffalo, Johns Hopkins University, and Stanford University.

to destroy. Girard's work shows how "myths" of this sort occur constantly throughout the history of culture.

Key to understanding Girard's views are two other ideas: (1) mimetic desire, that is, to copy or to mimic and to want what others have, and (2) the inability of our laws to limit conflicts caused by mimetic desire. Why is there social conflict in the first place? Girard argues that conflict happens when two (or more) people or groups desire the same thing, and therefore must fight over it. This conflict is inevitable. Why? Because, according to Girard, our desires themselves are produced through mimesis—that is, through imitating models. We come to desire this or that thing because we "learn" to see it as desirable through imitating models, first and foremost our parents. Mimetic desire drives all societies. It may be particularly potent in our consumer- and media-driven society. Our economy depends upon comparison: wanting something better or something more. But in any situation, humans have many possible desires. The many options intensify both our search for appropriate models and our anxiety about our identification of the "right" model. Mimesis is simply a fact of our human condition—that is, this is how we learn to desire this or that food or person or job or lifestyle, through imitating models. Because of this imitation, conflict ensues when (as might be expected) we end up desiring the same object as our model. Our models then become our rivals.

Laws are the way in which societies ordinarily deal with these kinds of conflict. Rules against stealing or killing or incest or adultery exist to diminish the disorder produced by this rivalry. Yet the conflict is consistently spilling over these rules. One can think about how the intensity of romantic desire is used by some as a "justification" for breaking the rule against adultery. Then think about how tempting it is to react to adultery by resorting to violence. How much theft is caused by envy of what others have? Again, think about how tempting it is to respond to a home invasion (an act of violence) by further violence. How much political corruption is caused by viewing politics as a competition for power? Think about how tempting it is to respond to cheating by cheating. We cheat because we say it is only fair to level the playing field. Put simply, social disorder appears to exceed the capacity of laws to maintain order.

Thus, competing self-interest, envy, and social rivalries cannot be fully resolved by laws. Ironically, the solution appears to be more intense rivalry to the point of violence. Again, Girard means to explain basically how societies work. But how do societies deal with this problem? The violence can be "peaceful" when it is ritualized, say, through professional football, hockey, or mixed martial arts. Competition is intensified but made relatively harmless by sports at all levels. Yet, even in sports, it is striking how passionate and irrational, often "fanatical," fans can be. If we live in a time or space of relative social peace, we mean that our ways of ritualizing violence and competition are basically effective. Yet, even in those times, we are conscious of the possibility of social chaos or disorder that might happen if the laws fail, and so we continue to seek new, more powerful ways to institutionalize violence in order to maintain order. Of course, earlier, less developed societies might confront this breakdown more routinely, not least because the basic needs of life—say, food—were considerably more scarce and hence more subject to mimetic rivalry.

Girard claims that it was at these times that societies developed "sacred" or "religious" violence as a way of defusing conflict that couldn't be handled by law; it is here where his famous theory of the "scapegoat" comes in. The society is breaking down into violent conflict because of its rivalries. What is to be done? The authorities come to rely on the scapegoat mechanism. We still see this: when there is a major crisis, people want "answers." People want someone to blame. We see examples of this all the time. For example, in a globalized economy that outsources jobs, immigrants are targeted as "causing" the problem. We resent their desires to have what we have, especially when we are "losing" it. We need to identify a rival against whom we can institutionalize violence. We need a scapegoat.

The scapegoat mechanism prevents an analysis of the complexity of the given problem, especially the extent to which "we" share in the blame for the problem. In the above example of job loss and scapegoating immigrants, we ignore aspects of the problem: the extent to which our economy relies on low-wage labor in order to provide us with cheap vegetables and cheap restaurants, or the extent to which the globalized economy does not serve the common good, but rather the good of those at the top of our economy. Instead of criticizing multiple aspects of a national economy that includes outsourcing jobs to poorer countries, we oversimplify and deflect criticism, blaming immigrants from poorer countries for our problems. We are unable to see that our conflict is the result of our rival (economic) desires and willingness to do whatever it takes to defeat our rivals in order to pursue these desires. Instead, some individual or group of individuals is identified by authorities as "the source of the problems," and all the violence that is seething is whipped up into an even greater frenzy and heaped on these scapegoats. For Girard, religious rites offer a ritualization of this sacrifice. For example, in the Old Testament, the sins of the people are heaped upon a goat, which is then sent out into the wilderness to die (Lev 16:20-28).

Thus, the scapegoat mechanism defuses social violence by identifying a common victim against which the society can come together. It is, Girard writes, "a collective action of the entire community, which purifies itself of its own disorder through the unanimous immolation of a victim."[3] This mechanism is ingenious, in the sense that it does settle competition and violence . . . for a time. But it is problematic for two reasons. (1) It doesn't actually name the social conflict accurately, but merely evades it, so that it constantly recurs—hence, the need to ritualize the violence in some institutional manner. (2) It creates an innocent victim or set of victims. It is one thing to ritualize this mechanism through the use of an animal, but of course such rituals may more ordinarily (and effectively!) include actual human individuals or groups who must be killed or driven out. A related problem is that, ironically, such rituals ordinarily encourage the "sacred" breaking of the exact laws used in the first place. Someone has killed, so we must now kill. Or consider this: a deep problem with immigration today in the United States is the willingness to violate people's civil liberties in order to catch "illegal" immigrants. The very violence that the laws are meant to prohibit is now encouraged, but in a "sanctioned," even sacred, form.[4]

Jesus as Scapegoat

Such is Girard's theory. Now we have to identify how it works in the case of Jesus, and then return to our actual topic of capital punishment. For Girard, Jesus' innocent death is precisely the *unmasking* of this mechanism, for "once understood, the mechanisms can no longer operate."[5] Space prohibits a full exposition here, but some details from the gospel stories should suffice. He points out that Jesus' death is described as the result of collaboration among the Jewish religious leaders, the Roman political authorities, and "the crowds." These groups themselves were often at odds, most notably the Jewish people and the Roman occupation forces. But they are able to come together to kill this man (ibid., 105). Girard points out how the chief priests seek to kill Jesus in order that, as Caiaphas says, "one man should die instead of the people" (John 11:50).

---

[3] René Girard, "Mimesis and Violence," *The Girard Reader*, ed. James G. Williams (New York: Crossroad, 1996), 11.

[4] Ibid., 13.

[5] Girard, *The Scapegoat*, trans. Yvonne Frecerro (Baltimore: Johns Hopkins University Press, 1986), 101.

Instead of dealing with the actual rebellion against Roman authority, let's have them kill one man.

Girard notes that Pilate's supposed "reluctance" to condemn Jesus is, in fact, indicative of his own position of rivalry against others for the favors of the empire. Thus, the crowd, which has no real power over Pilate, "convinces" him that it is better to kill someone he deems innocent than endanger his position. Meanwhile, for Girard, "the crowd" remains the most important actor, because even "sovereign authority is forced to yield [to the mechanism] despite its impulse to resist." Setting aside (unending) historical conflicts about whether the crowd was incited by the priests, the gospels clearly mean to show Jesus' death as ultimately the "solution" for the threat of social violence and disorder produced by these rival social powers. By creating a victim, Pilate and the priests can be allied, with the priests saying, "We have no king but Caesar" (John 19:15), and the crowd can be quieted down.[6]

Jesus' execution saves us as it exposes the scapegoat mechanism in boldest form. The cross reveals human violence and sin and offers God's peace. When the basic mechanism of human sin is exposed, the disciples are able to call people to repentance because they now see, at the time, the people "acted out of ignorance" (Acts 3:17). That is, they were acting under the false consciousness of sin and the scapegoat mechanism, which God means to expose, once and for all, through the innocent suffering servant.

All stand under condemnation. The crowd cries for Jesus' crucifixion, Peter denies him, and the disciples abandon him. Could anyone be more innocent than Jesus? The self-giving of God is the true sacrifice, which unmasks the sinfulness of all institutionalized violent sacrifices. As Girard points out, the "most important" difference between God's offering and the scapegoat mechanism is this: scapegoating "comes from a cultural mechanism and is not approved by God."[7] That the Son of God himself is *subjected to* this mechanism is the strongest possible sign that it is not approved by God.

Scapegoating and the Death Penalty

What does this understanding of Christ's sacrifice say about the death penalty? One might object to my use of Girard's theory. One might object

---

[6] Girard, *The Scapegoat*, 106.
[7] Girard, "Epilogue: A Conversation with René Girard," *The Girard Reader*, 262–88, at 266.

that modern capital punishment involves not the innocent scapegoat, but rather the *guilty* criminal, one being punished justly for crimes of which he or she was convicted. Let's set aside the problem of executing innocent people. It is an injustice that certainly haunts the use of the death penalty. Let us instead consider how capital punishment is identified as a supposedly fair and righteous penalty *for the guilty*.

Among the arguments in favor of the death penalty, the strongest is based on its appropriateness for those guilty of terrible crimes, the moral claim that some criminals and some crimes simply "deserve" the death penalty. According to this view, life in prison is simply not "retributive" enough. We must kill the criminals because of how bad their actions were. Capital punishment is moral because it is retributive justice. The punishment matches the crime. Notice here that the *guilt* of the perpetrator is not what is being debated, nor even the fact that the guilty "deserve" punishment. The debate is how to determine what punishment is actually fitting and just. On this view, there are certain crimes so heinous that they "deserve" death.

This defense necessarily raises another question: What crimes deserve death? Most commonly, these would be acts of mass murder—genocides, terrorist attacks, and the like—as well as serial killers, especially those who also commit sexual violence against their victims. Additionally, those who kill public authorities—typically, police—are also singled out. Now this list of crimes is notoriously variable from culture to culture. We see in the Bible itself that acts of adultery and of sorcery (a kind of idolatry or blasphemy) are subject to the death penalty (Deut 22:22-27; Exod 22:17). In these ancient cases, the retributive character of the penalty is clear: adultery is a direct attack on the sanctity of the social institution of marriage, and various forms of religious blasphemy are an attack on the social institution of the right worship of God.

These lists should push us to recognize that the death penalty's value lies in its *symbolic significance*, rather than in "eye for an eye" justice or even the protection of society from further violence. Adulterers have not killed anyone, nor does the Bible give any evidence that the adulterer must be a danger to all. In fact, biblical stories of adultery usually do *not* involve multiple affairs, but a focus on one particular person! Why, then, the death penalty? It is not for "practical" reasons, but for symbolic ones. The death penalty is institutionalized violence—Girard would say "ritualized violence"—to be displayed in certain key cases.

Which ones? Crimes that involve the violation of *whatever is particularly sacred* in the society merit death. We no longer punish adultery or blasphemy through the court system. These "wrongs" are not believed by many people to be wrong at all. Rather, we have based our social order around *other* sacred symbols. For example, we value sexuality more as a sacred *personal* right dependent on free *consent* between adults; therefore, we severely punish those who commit serial acts of sexual violence, or who are pedophiles (e.g., sex offenders being forced to register and be publicly identified). We value law and order; therefore, we feel particularly violated when a police officer or a member of the military is killed. In the case of Jesus (who, after all, was not accused of killing anyone!), characters in the gospel narrative make clear that his death is "deserved" precisely because of his violations of sacred institutions, both religious and secular.

Thus, the death penalty, even when it is reserved to a small number of cases, appears vitally important to its defenders. Why? It is a symbol and ritual of order. It allows for the "sacred violence" of scapegoating when particularly sacred aspects of the social order are violated. Even if very few people are executed, those who support the death penalty find its very existence to be morally necessary, for its symbolic value (precisely as Girard explains it). As noted above, laws serve to contain social conflict, but when they prove inadequate, we turn to collective violence as a desperate measure for expressing our righteous anger and restoring order. It is this symbolic sense that, according to Girard, is a matter of identifying certain scapegoats, certain figures, on whom we can heap particular responsibility for social disorder. Capital punishment is exactly this kind of collective violence, reserved for when law is radically disregarded and socially sacred symbols are violated. Girard's theory thereby allows us to recognize the logic behind using institutionalized violence, but also the problem of identifying *certain* crimes as "worthy" of death.

The symbolic importance of capital punishment, as scapegoating, has a prominent place in American history. Robert Johnson, in writing about public executions in colonial America, explains how clearly they exemplify the scapegoat mechanism. Often, these spectacles involved "marginal members" of the community. The offenders executed in this way were "typically . . . *in* but not *of* the community." As members of the community, they can serve as "suitable substitutes for the whole group" in casting out the group's "impurities." The crowds who gathered for these events served as "the assertion of a common social order drawn together against the threat posed by the offender," even presided over by sermons featuring common themes of repentance.[8] While slowly but surely public

---

[8] Robert Johnson, *Death Work: A Study of the Modern Execution Process* (Belmont, CA: Wadsworth, 1998), 28–29.

executions receded in the North, they continued to feature heavily in the South, focused most notoriously on African Americans after the Civil War. The status of African Americans as "impure" elements of the community was so strong that Johnson notes, "once the mob was on the move, *any* black person could serve as a suitable candidate for a lynching," with friends or relatives "explicitly chosen by mobs as stand-ins when the alleged offenders could not be found."[9]

The rage that accompanies certain crimes even today mimics this kind of ritualized casting-out of impurity. In coming to recognize the scapegoat mechanism at work, we can also come to see as mistaken the argument that some crimes "deserve death." Properly speaking, we can say, according to current Catholic teaching, no crime "merits" death.[10] No one "deserves" death, because, as the *Catechism* teaches, all life is sacred. Such recognition requires that we love others, all neighbors, in God, seeing the human family as a unity, one in radical solidarity with another. This radical solidarity means, according to Girard, that there really is no "scapegoating" possible. As God's creations, we recognize the fundamental dignity of all life as loved by God.[11] As Pope Benedict XVI reiterated recently, Catholic efforts to "eliminate the death penalty" are to be praised, specifically as a part of efforts to conform penal law to "the human dignity of prisoners."[12] It is this dignity of all that is a gift from God; it is not something that we "earn," nor something that can be taken away. God's gift to us is the reason why the death penalty cannot be justified.

Yet the crucifixion of Jesus reveals *even more* than our common dignity. It ultimately shows us how we are all complicit in sin, and thus in radical

---

[9] Ibid., 34, emphasis in original.

[10] In the 1997 revision of the *Catechism of the Catholic Church*, the paragraphs on capital punishment make this clear, as we will see in chapters 10 and 11. In the earlier version, reference is made to certain circumstances in which the death penalty is the appropriate retribution, but all this language is dropped in the 1997 revision. The earlier version states "the right and duty of legitimate public authority to punish malefactors by means of penalties commensurate with the gravity of the crime, not excluding, in cases of extreme gravity, the death penalty." But the 1997 revision, after Pope John Paul II's encyclical *Evangelium Vitae*, drops this entire phrase and any mention of the death penalty as "commensurate" with a crime. See *Catechism of the Catholic Church*, 2266–67.

[11] It is worth noting here how often death row prisoners are "reduced" to the status of their worst acts, and defined as "monsters" or in other subhuman terms. Would we all want to be defined by our worst acts? And deprived of all basic dignity?

[12] Pope Benedict XVI, Address to Members of the Sant'Egidio Community (November 30, 2011), http://catholicmoraltheology.com/pope-benedict-xvis-most -recent-statement-on-the-death-penalty/.

solidarity even with the guilty and sinners. We cannot simply drive them out, for we are also the guilty. During the reading of the passion on Good Friday, Catholics are charged as a congregation to shout out, "Crucify him! Crucify him!" This is an odd, unsettling moment. It exemplifies how we are to see Jesus' death as overcoming what Bruce Ward calls the "persecution-victimage mechanism that pervades the world." For in this moment, even as we are in solidarity with Jesus as the innocent victim, we also show forth our solidarity with Jesus' *persecutors*. We are all crucified with him, and yet we are also all crucifiers of Christ. In this scene, we then can imagine "the possibility of a human solidarity that transcends the 'us or them' mentality of persecutor *versus* victim."[13] It is where we recognize there are no scapegoats.

When we look at the crucified Jesus, then, we should remember that he was "a marginal Jew," as Catholic biblical scholar John Meier titled his massive study of Jesus' life. He was put to death by defenders of the law and the dominant social institutions because he represented a (supposed) threat to these institutions. In his rising, however, we recognize God's self-giving and nonviolent victory over our acts of collective violence, in the hopes that we will come to see that "I desire mercy, not sacrifice" (Matt 9:13; cf. Hos 6:6).

Review and Looking Forward

Editors

We opened the chapter with the story of Kirk Bloodsworth's arrest and conviction. Kirk's case hinged more on the brutality of the crime, the need for an arrest, and a supposed psychological profile than on the evidence against Kirk. He serves as a clear example of the scapegoat mechanism because he is innocent. David Cloutier, however, challenges us to see the injustice of scapegoating even in relation to the guilty, especially when we are inclined to believe that they have forfeited their dignity and deserve death. Such a challenge is found in the faith and forgiveness lived out by SueZann Bosler.

In December 1986, SueZann and her father, Reverend Billy Bosler, were attacked at their home. The attacker stabbed Billy to death and left SueZann for dead. A week after the deadly assault, police had the attacker

---

[13] Bruce K. Ward, *Redeeming the Enlightenment: Christianity and the Liberal Virtues* (Grand Rapids, MI: Eerdmans, 2010), 149.

in custody. They had fingerprint evidence and a confession. SueZann made a positive identification. There was no doubt that the suspect was the man who murdered her father and nearly took her life.[14] There was also no doubt in SueZann's mind that the killer should be held accountable but not be put to death. Her father Billy had been clear, years earlier, when the subject came up in conversation. He was against capital punishment and would not want even his own murderer put to death.

The killer was sentenced to death twice. However, due in large part to SueZann's persistence, James Bernard Campbell is now serving four consecutive life sentences. During the first sentencing hearing (in 1988), SueZann stated her father's stance against the death penalty and her own wishes: life in prison without parole. A jury voted nine to three for death. Later, the Supreme Court of Florida reversed the decision because the judge had not adequately taken into account the offender's intellectual capacity (IQ of 68) and the years of abuse and abandonment that he suffered as a child. The judge held that the determining factor in his decision to affirm the death penalty was James's "evil mind."[15] During the second sentencing hearing, SueZann stated her father's convictions and her own again. Again, the jury disagreed and voted in favor of death. This time the vote was ten to two.

A second time, the Supreme Court of Florida reversed the decision, citing "improper conduct by the prosecutor." The transcript of the Supreme Court decision states that "[the prosecutor's] 'cop-killer' rhetoric and 'message to the community' statements played to the jurors' most elemental fears, dragging into the trial the specter of police murders and a lawless community that could imperil the jurors and their families."[16] In other words, James was made into a scapegoat by the prosecutor, and the judge and jury were convinced by what David Cloutier has referred to as the scapegoat mechanism.

In 1997, during the third sentencing hearing, SueZann was not allowed to state her views to the jury. The judge would not allow her to speak of her father's stance against the death penalty and threatened SueZann with six months in jail and a fine. After this order, the judge asked her what she might say to the jury. SueZann answered, "I forgive James Campbell for what he has done." In addition to her view on the death penalty, the judge did not allow her to state her feelings and opinions in relation to

---

[14] Rachel King, *Don't Kill in Our Names: Families of Murder Victims Speak Out Against the Death Penalty* (New Brunswick, NJ: Rutgers University Press, 2003), 144.

[15] Ibid., 147.

[16] *Campbell v. Florida*, 679 So.2d 724-5; cited in King, *Don't Kill in Our Names*, 153.

Jesus Christ and Sacrifice 83

the defendant.[17] Expressions of forgiveness were considered contempt of court. As a result, SueZann did not take the stand. Instead, she sat in court where the family of the defendant (the murderer) usually sits. She did not speak with him, and still has not met him. Rather, she made a stand in solidarity with him as a human being. Her solidarity (along with additional evidence of his life of suffering and abuse) finally made a difference. The jury voted: four in favor of the death penalty and eight for life.

Questions for Discussion

1. Usually, the views of the victim will carry a great deal of weight with a jury. In SueZann's case, however, her petition for a life sentence was overridden by the prosecutor's references to evil and its threat to community. Was the scapegoat mechanism at work?

2. A case like Kirk Bloodsworth's is often explained by blaming a vicious prosecutor or a hysterical community. This explanation, like the scapegoat mechanism, puts blame on "bad characters" so that we do not have to take responsibility or to look at ourselves. Let's go the other direction. Can we see that it could happen to us—that we could be convinced of a person's guilt regardless of the evidence?

3. Jesus' calls for reconciliation and radical solidarity make people anxious. It is comforting when we hear a call to be nice to the people we know and like. It is frightening when we are called to share life with sinners and outcasts. No wonder Jesus was a threat to law and order. Discuss how we would have to live differently in order to see Christ in the prisoner (Matt 25:31-46).

[17] King, *Don't Kill in Our Names*, 158.

Chapter 7

Hebrew Scriptures—
"an Eye for an Eye"

Editors

George White has much to say about the death penalty. In 1985, he
and his wife Char (short for Charlene) were robbed and attacked at a
building supply company where George was vice president. They were
confronted, when the store was closed for the day, by a man wearing a ski
mask and waving his gun. During the robbery, Char was shot twice in the
head and killed. George was shot three times (arm, thigh, and abdomen)
and survived, thanks to emergency surgery.[1] George and Char had two
children at home. During the following months, George thought favor-
ably about vengeance and the capital punishment. But in 1986, he was
arrested and charged with Char's murder. The state of Alabama sought the
death penalty for George. He was convicted and given a life sentence by
what the Alabama Court of Criminal Appeals later called "a mockery and
a sham" (ibid.). He spent over two years in prison before the conviction
was overturned. Evidence not presented at the trial came to light, and,
after another three years, the case was dismissed.

For seven years—from the murder of Char in 1985 to his exoneration
in 1992—George says that he was full of hate for the murderer, the courts,
and God. Amid the hate and hopelessness, his incredible experiences have

[1] Susan Olp, "Wrongly Convicted Man Speaks Against Death Penalty," *Billings Ga-
zette* (January 30, 2010), http://billingsgazette.com/lifestyles/faith-and-values/religion
/article_63b52f94-0d4e-11df-b423-001cc4c03286.html.

84

brought wisdom. "I came to understand that he [God] kept loving me. It wasn't hatred that sustained me, it was love. It was the love of family and friends and a country lawyer who wouldn't quit and who wouldn't walk away" (ibid.). Of vengeance and retribution he now says,

> I believe that society's laws must offer relief for a victim's anger and loss, and we must be afforded protection from those who would harm us; however, one cannot stop the shedding of blood by causing more blood to be shed. No amount of killing would restore Char to my family or take away the pain of losing her. What began with a horrible act of violence should not be memorialized with an act of vengeance.[2]

George's statement should be read carefully again and again. It is a nuanced set of claims that comes from the pain of being on all sides of the death penalty—victim, grieving husband, accused, imprisoned, and exonerated.

Too often, our approach to capital punishment is too simplistic. George, for example, has been accused of being a "bleeding heart liberal" by people who do not know his story.[3] We throw around catchphrases instead of seeking understanding. This is true of the phrase, "an eye for an eye." Not long ago, an article in *The Baltimore Sun* reported on various problems and moral questions in carrying out capital punishment in Maryland.[4] These problems and questions caused what the *Sun* reporter called an "unofficial moratorium" on the death penalty.[5] In response to the article, a reader of the *Sun* wrote a letter to the editor. This citizen appealed to a classic line from the Bible: an eye for an eye. The reader asked, "Why should they [the death row inmates] receive three meals a day when there are starving, homeless people who have nothing? I know as a humane nation we must treat the human race in a humane way, but how about how the murder victims were treated? What ever happened to an eye for an eye?"[6]

---

[2] George White, Journey of Hope . . . From Violence to Healing, http://journeyof hope.org/who-we-are/murder-victim-family/george-white/.

[3] George White, "Journey Speakers in Terre Haute," http://www.abolition.org/Bill AndGeorge.html#george.

[4] The snags and glitches pertained to legal procedures, a shortage of chemicals used for lethal injections, a lengthy review of protocols in the prison system, and moral doubts felt by legislators and the governor.

[5] Julie Bykowicz, "A Slow Death," *The Baltimore Sun* (Feb. 13, 2011), A1.

[6] "Md. death penalty: What happened to an eye for an eye?," *The Baltimore Sun* (Feb. 14, 2011)http://articles.baltimoresun.com/2011-02-14/news/bs-ed-death-penalty -letter-20110214_1_death-penalty-eye-murder-victims.

For the author of the letter and for most of us, the meaning of "an eye for an eye" is obvious, and too simplistic. Whether we accept it or reject it, we take the meaning casually with little reflection and depth of thought. For most Christians, it means that criminals ought to receive retribution in kind—"a burn for a burn, a wound for a wound." The author of this chapter, Richard Buck, will call this view "equality retribution," and he will show that this seemingly obvious meaning is not scriptural. Richard will give the phrase scriptural depth. He shows that we ought to take "an eye for an eye" very seriously. He does not say that the teaching no longer applies. Indeed, Richard shows that the common interpretation of "an eye for an eye" is mistaken. The common view of "equality retribution" does not attend to Scripture carefully enough. "An eye for an eye" is a line from Scripture that is used in a way that is not scriptural.

Many of us who like to quote "an eye for an eye" do not know where the statement actually is in the Bible and the context where it makes sense. To understand passages like "a wound for a wound," we need to understand the context of biblical commands and community life where these verses of the Bible have their proper meaning and use. Richard shows us that the so-called obvious, retributive meaning of "an eye for an eye" is not quite right. Out of context, the phrase takes on a meaning that is almost opposite from its biblical purpose. Richard outlines the plain sense of the passage by describing its context of Mosaic law and Jewish faith. He is a professor of philosophy and an Orthodox Jew. He offers us valuable understanding and insight. As Catholic Christians, we (the editors) find his chapter illuminating for how Jesus used the phrase "An eye for an eye" in Matthew 5:38. By rejecting retaliation and vengeance in Matthew 5:38-42, Jesus was not overturning the law (see Matt 5:17). He was, like the rabbis that Richard discusses, looking to restore the law to its original intention.

Biblical Principles: Mosaic Law

Richard Buck

Perhaps the most often quoted, and most often misquoted, passages in all of the Torah are the following from the books of Exodus and Leviticus:[7]

> When men have a fight and hurt a pregnant woman, so that she suffers a miscarriage, but no further injury, the guilty one shall be

---

[7] The Torah is the Hebrew word for the five books of Moses, known in English as Genesis, Exodus, Leviticus, Numbers, and Deuteronomy.

fined as much as the woman's husband demands of him, and he shall pay in the presence of the judges. But if injury ensues, you shall give life for life, eye for eye, tooth for tooth, hand for hand, foot for foot, burn for burn, wound for wound, stripe for stripe. (Exod 21:22-25)

Whoever takes the life of any human being shall be put to death . . . Anyone who inflicts a permanent injury on his or her neighbor shall receive the same in return: fracture for fracture, eye for eye, tooth for tooth. The same injury that one gives another shall be inflicted in return. (Lev 24:17, 19-20)

Many have appealed to these verses as direct proof for three independent claims: (1) the Bible not only permits but also *requires* capital punishment; (2) the Bible justifies capital punishment as *retribution*, the view that the aim of punishment is to *pay back* the offender for what he or she has done; and (3) the Bible employs a certain version of "payback" that we will call *equality retribution* ("an eye for an eye"). According to equality retribution, the only appropriate way to pay back offenders for what they have done is to do to them exactly what they have done to the offended parties. Taken together, these three claims are often used to justify the use of capital punishment. For example, in reaction to an article about a brutal and hateful murder, a respondent to a CBS news report holds that the murderer deserves death. "An eye for an eye, except unfortunately, his death will be much less painful than [his victim's]."[8] Such a claim seems persuasive because it appears to carry the authority of the Scriptures.

In this chapter, we will evaluate this argument by taking a closer look at its sources in the Hebrew Scriptures and in the Oral Law.[9] What we will learn about the biblical "an eye for an eye" is this: Causing injury to another person is a serious matter, in fact, so serious that the one who harms another deserves to suffer from the same type of injury. Causing

---

[8] "Miss. teen Deryl Dedmon could face death penalty in hit-and-run killing," CBSNews.com (August 22, 2011), comments section, www.cbsnews.com/8301504083 _162-20095429-504083.html.

[9] "Oral Law" is the phrase often used to refer to the Mishnah (compiled by Rabbi Judah HaNasi in the sixth century) and the Gemara, a series of discussions of the material in the Mishnah, redacted in the tenth century. For observant Jews, the principles of the Oral Law—contained in the Mishnah and the Gemara—were part of the revelation at Sinai. Without these texts, the Torah would be difficult, if not impossible, to understand. Indeed, as we will see, it is lack of attention to the discussions of capital punishment in the Mishnah and Gemara that leads to serious misunderstandings of its justification and practice.

injury is so serious that literally taking "an eye for an eye" is unthinkable. Few would consider cutting off hands and poking out eyes signs of faith. Although we do not implement such severe penalties literally, the language of the Scriptures is in place to ensure that we understand how grave a crime it is to cause injury to another person. The severe language points not to equality retribution, but to the need for recompense and the restoration of the victim.

The arguments of the chapter proceed in the following steps. While the Hebrew Scriptures do require capital punishment for certain crimes, they do not employ equality retributivism in order to *justify* the capital punishment or any other punishment. Recompense and restoration are more fundamental. In addition, even in situations where the death penalty would be required, the conditions for its use are so strict that it's nearly impossible to find a case in which it would be *permissible* to put a person to death. Finally, even if one could find a situation in which all the specific procedural conditions for the death penalty were satisfied (something that is very unlikely), it is not at all clear that the death penalty can be applied outside of a legal process that is governed by the legal principles outlined in the Torah and Oral Law. In other words, the specific punishment of death can only be applied when all the other components of the biblical legal system are in place.

Is Punishment in the Hebrew Scriptures Retributive?

The Hebrew Scriptures are often cited as evidence for the view that the aim of punishment is retribution, that is, to pay back the criminal for what he or she has done by doing to the criminal the very same thing that he or she did to the victim. But this is not the case. Rabbinic commentators provide many proofs—based on the actual text—to show that the plain sense of the text is that offenders must make monetary restitution to their victims.

Let's begin with Leviticus 24:17-20, which is the second passage cited in the introduction to this chapter. The Talmud provides numerous discussions that aim to show that this text actually calls for monetary compensation. For example, Rabbi Shimon Bar Yochai raises this question: If the Torah meant literally that a person who blinds another must be blinded in return (i.e., this is the only appropriate punishment), what happens to a blind person who injures another person's eyes? How is he to be punished?[10] One might cast aside Rabbi Yochai's questions as merely "academic." How likely is it that a blind person would blind another person in-

---

[10] Tractate Bava Kama, 83b–84a.

tentionally? But further discussions in the Talmud suggest other reasons for understanding these passages as requiring only monetary compensation.

Let's look at another passage from the Torah, which might be cited as further reason in support of the retributivist interpretation of Hebrew Scripture: "You will not accept compensation in place of the life of a murderer who deserves to die, but that person must be put to death" (Num 35:31). This verse clearly states that murder is punishable by death. But the specific mention of murder as a crime for which compensation (i.e., monetary payment) cannot substitute for the death of the murderer shows, according to the Talmud, that monetary payment can make restitution for nonfatal physical injuries.[11] In other words, the biblical teaching is not literally "an eye for an eye." But does this argument obscure the literal meaning of the text, since the text only mentions murder and not physical injury?

The medieval scholar Maimonides raises a similar question when he asks how we know that the statement "an eye for an eye" requires only monetary compensation. He answers this question by citing Exodus 21:18-19: "When men quarrel and one strikes the other with a stone or with his fist, not mortally, but enough to put him in bed, the one who struck the blow shall be acquitted, provided the other can get up and walk around with the help of his staff. Still, he must compensate him for his recovery time and make provision for his complete healing." The passage explicitly states that a person who strikes and injures another is only required to compensate the injured party for the recovery time (i.e., inability to work) and for the costs incurred in treating and healing from the injury.[12]

The texts of the Hebrew Scriptures do not support the retributivist philosophy of punishment. The physical injury is not the punishment for causing physical injury. Even though the death penalty is the required punishment for some crimes (given certain conditions), it is clear retribution is not the principle of justification. Hebrew Scriptures do not require that offenders be punished by doing to them what they have done to others. But this leaves us with an important question: If punishment is not to be retributive, why is the stark "eye for an eye" wording used? One would be wrong to conclude that the language of "wound for a wound" ought to be ignored. On the contrary, "burn for a burn" and "hand for a hand" make clear that causing injury is a serious matter, so serious, in fact, that

---

[11] Ibid., 83b.

[12] Rabbi Moshe ben Maimon (1135–1204) was one of the most prominent Jewish philosophers and sages of the Middle Ages. The discussion in our chapter is taken from his *Mishneh Torah* (*Hovel U'Mazik* [*Injuries and Damages*], chap. 1).

the measure of justice is as high as forfeiting one's own hand, foot, or eye. Although we do not implement such a severe penalty as equality retribution, the language of the Scriptures is in place to ensure that we understand how grave a crime it is to cause injury to another person.

This point bears further consideration. By using the language "an eye for an eye" the Hebrew Scriptures mean to make clear that injuring another person's body is a much more serious crime than damaging another person's property. We might think that such a distinction is obvious and, therefore that we need not be reminded of it with such extreme language. But without the severe "an eye for an eye," the severity of the harm and the need for compassion for the victim is lost. Imagine how the Scriptures might be read if they stated explicitly that one who injures another's body must make financial restitution. Since such restitution would also be required of the person who merely damages another person's property (willfully or accidentally), we might wonder why the restitution required for the more serious offense of personal injury is no greater than that required for property damage. Therefore, the instructions for handling such cases are written with language such as "an eye for an eye" in order to make it clear that the person who causes bodily harm cannot be compared to the person who merely damages property.

Also important is the manner in which this difference between property damage and personal injury is understood. Although making restitution to the victim is crucial, the offender must also *atone* for the sin of harming another's person or property. In the case of a person who damages another's property, atonement for the sin is achieved in making restitution for the damage. But this is not the case for the person who maims or blinds another. The person who causes physical injury has not made atonement until he or she has asked for forgiveness from the victim. The payment of compensation for the loss of sight or the loss of a limb can never make good the actual loss suffered by the injured party. Such a loss can never be made good. The severe language of "an eye for an eye" makes this point clear.

Conditions for Imposing the Death Penalty

Passages containing the famous phrase "an eye for an eye" are well known (and often cited) even by those with little experience studying the Hebrew Scriptures. But other passages equally important for understanding the nature of capital punishment in the Hebrew Scriptures are more often than not overlooked or ignored. Take, for example, the following passages from the book of Deuteronomy: "Only on the testimony of two or three witnesses shall a person be put to death; no one shall be put to death on the testimony of only one witness" (Deut 17:6). And again: "One witness alone shall not stand against someone in regard to any crime or any offense that may have been committed; a charge shall stand only on the testimony of two or three witnesses" (Deut 19:15). These passages point to the legal context for how teachings like "an eye for an eye" ought to be understood and used. The Hebrew Bible requires capital punishment for some crimes, but within the court system outlined by the Bible itself, significant safeguards and roadblocks are put in place to render the penalty of death practically nonexistent.

Deuteronomy 17:6 and 19:15 indicate clearly that the death penalty cannot be imposed without the testimony of two or three witnesses. Regardless of the amount or type of evidence indicating that a person has committed a capital crime, multiple witnesses are required to put the accused to death. In addition, a closer look at Deuteronomy 17:6 reveals something quite interesting. One might be puzzled by the apparent redundancy in the text: If two witnesses are sufficient for imposing the death penalty, it seems clear that three or more witnesses would also be sufficient. Why, then, does the text mention the greater number of witnesses? According to commentary on this passage, the redundancy brings to light crucial components of a capital case. First, wherever possible, multiple witnesses should be consulted; a court can never prevent additional witnesses from testifying. Every possible measure must be taken to find even one witness that will testify to the innocence of the accused. One might wonder why one witness's testimony should matter, if multiple other witnesses have already testified that the accused committed the crime in question. This brings us to the second point: The entire group of witnesses—regardless of its size—is treated as one unit (i.e., as if they were all one witness). If fifty witnesses are in agreement and one is discredited, the other forty-nine are disqualified as well.[13]

Deuteronomy 17:6 and 19:15, therefore, point to the legal context for understanding "an eye for an eye." These passages and rabbinic commentary on them show that even though the Torah clearly requires capital

---

[13] It is important to note that the Torah prescribes strict penalties for witnesses who knowingly and intentionally give false testimony. See Deuteronomy 19:18-19. The Talmud goes into extensive detail on what it means to discredit witnesses, the exact punishments prescribed for false witnesses, and the requirements for imposing these punishments. See tractate Makkot.

punishment for some crimes, much effort is made to show that the accused is, in fact, not eligible to receive the penalty of death. The biblical strictures concerning capital punishment explain why the legal context of the Bible makes it easy, by modern standards, to disqualify witnesses. But the Torah goes even further. A person cannot be sentenced to any physical punishment (e.g., death or lashes) unless he or she received a warning before the commission of the act that (a) the act was wrong and (b) capital punishment would be imposed on one who so acted.

The requirement of the warning is derived from the following biblical passages: "But when someone kills a neighbor after maliciously scheming to do so, you must take him even from my altar and put him to death" (Exod 21:14). "While the Israelites were in the wilderness, a man was discovered gathering wood on the sabbath day. Those who caught him at it brought him to Moses and Aaron and the whole community" (Num 15:32-33). Commentary on these passages focuses on the fact that in both verses the sinful actions are expressed in present (imperfect) tense. In Hebrew, the verb tense means that the offending actions (i.e., killing and violating the Sabbath) are still in process when they are discovered. From this, commentators conclude that in both cases the offender was given a warning to stop, which he ignored.[14] If this is true, it follows that if no warning was issued to the offender, physical punishment cannot be imposed. Like the requirement for multiple witnesses, this requirement of warning shows that the conditions for carrying out the death penalty made it virtually impossible to impose, even on those accused of the most heinous crimes.

One of the most oft-quoted passages in the Mishnah (the "Oral Law" attests to this fact, suggesting that executions should be extremely rare:

> A Sanhedrin that executes once in seven years is called a destroyer. Rabbi Eliezer ben Azariah says: Even once in seventy years. Rabbi Tarfon and Rabbi Akiva say: Had we been on a Sanhedrin [at the time when they still performed executions] no person would ever have been executed.[15]

---

[14] Tractate Sanhedrin, 41a.

[15] Mishnah Makkot, 7a. This statement is followed by a response from Rabbi Shimon ben Gamliel, who criticizes Rabbi Tarfon and Rabbi Akiva because their view would have increased the number of murderers (presumably because potential murderers would no longer have to fear execution). This response lends further support to the view that the Hebrew Scriptures do not endorse a retributive theory of punishment.

Following this statement, the Talmud explains that Rabbi Tarfon and Rabbi Akiva would have prevented executions by questioning witnesses in such a manner that it would have been impossible for the witnesses to have been sure that they in fact witnessed a murder. For example, in the case of a stabbing, they would have asked the witnesses if they were sure the victim was not a *treifah*, that is, a person who possesses a life-threatening bodily defect (e.g., a hole in a vital organ). Because of this defect, the murderer of a *treifah* would receive punishment but could not receive the death penalty. Since witnesses could not know of the victim's condition—and it would be possible for the defect to have been obscured by the fatal wound—the witnesses could never be sure that they witnessed a capital crime.

Two things should be clear from the discussion up to this point. First, the Hebrew Scriptures do require that the death penalty be imposed for certain crimes. Second, the prerequisites that must be met before the death penalty is imposed are so difficult to meet that it was nearly impossible for any offender to be executed. This second point is consistent with the first. Although executions will be very rare, we must recognize that for some crimes the offense is so severe that atonement for the offender is impossible in this world. Having the death penalty "on the books," so to speak, communicates the immense gravity of certain crimes. While the Hebrew Scriptures require that every effort be made to make an offender ineligible for execution, we must recognize that some offenses are so noxious that the soul of the offender is beyond the repair that worldly atonement can bring.[16]

Conclusion: Contemporary Jewish Approaches to Capital Punishment

For many contemporary Jews, the Hebrew Scriptures are a crucial source of moral and religious guidance. For Orthodox Jews in particular, the Torah and Talmud retain their standing as the chief guide for living an observant Jewish life. The development of new economic, social, and technological realities has given rise to literally thousands of complex questions concerning

---

[16] An alternative account of the strictures in place for the application of the death penalty is that the death penalty reflects G-d's original intention to create the world in accordance with strict justice, which would require that a murderer lose his or her life. But G-d quickly realized that very few (if any) human beings were capable of living according to such a strict standard. Therefore, G-d commanded that measures be taken to assure that human beings were not in practice made subject to the demands of this standard. *Editors' note: The author's use of "G-d" here is consistent with the Jewish tradition of refraining from writing or speaking the name of the divine.*

the application of Jewish law as revealed in the Torah and Talmud to contemporary life. One of these questions concerns the contemporary practice of capital punishment. In the United States, where the significant shortcomings of the capital punishment system have been carefully documented, the question arises as to how the members of the Jewish community should weigh in on the current debate over capital punishment.

This is particularly of concern for Orthodox Jews, since they hold the teachings of the Torah and Oral Law to be of universal and eternal authority. Several prominent authorities in Jewish law have weighed in on this issue. In a letter to the Orthodox Union—the largest Orthodox Jewish umbrella organization in the United States—Rabbi Aharon Soloveitchik argued that it would be "irresponsible and unfair" for Orthodox Jews to advocate for capital punishment and, furthermore, that from the perspective of Jewish law, "every Jew should be opposed to capital punishment." Rabbi Soloveitchik bases his view on the fact that the Torah does not permit carrying out the death penalty in the absence of the Sanhedrin (the Jewish court) and the holy temple in Jerusalem. Other noted authorities, such as Rabbi Moshe Feinstein—recognized as the supreme authority in Jewish law for North American Jews—contend that the restriction mentioned by Rabbi Soloveitchik only applies to a Jewish community operating a legal system in accord with Jewish law.[17]

One might infer from this debate that non-Jewish courts are not bound by any of the conditions for the application of capital punishment discussed in the previous section of this chapter. But another reading of this debate suggests an alternative conclusion: the discussions of capital punishment in the Hebrew Scriptures have no direct application to contemporary legal systems. Therefore, it would be misleading for one to claim justification for capital punishment by appealing to a system of punishment that both includes restrictions on meting out the death penalty that are not being followed and is not meant to apply at a time when neither the Sanhedrin nor the holy temple in Jerusalem exist.

---

[17] Rabbi Feinstein argues further that all of the requirements that must be met before a court can mete out the death penalty only apply where "the prohibition against murder has not been rendered null; but for someone who murders people because for him the prohibition against murder has become meaningless, and similarly when the number of murderers has become many, we apply [capital punishment] in order to deter murder for to do this is to save society" (*Igeerot Moshe*, Hoshen Mishpat II, pp. 293–94).

Review and Looking Forward

Editors

"An eye for an eye" is used frequently to defend capital punishment *as* retribution. Sometimes, the phrase is used to defend a right to revenge. Richard Buck shows that neither of these uses can be justified by appeal to Hebrew Scriptures. "An eye for an eye," as it is popularly used, is taken out of context, especially when some people use the phrase to claim divine sanction for their own desire for retribution. On the contrary, Richard notes that "an eye for an eye" does not translate to practices in modern secular court systems. He also shows, however, that biblical passages like "an eye for an eye" do point to the severity of crime and the need for just punishment and compensation. It is striking how this scriptural view parallels the perspective of victims' families who are against capital punishment. Recall the statement made by George White at the beginning of the chapter, as well as the stories of Antoinette Bosco at the beginning of chapter 5 and SueZann Bosler at the end of chapter 6. Antoinette and SueZann believed that the men who murdered their loved ones ought to be held responsible and kept in prison, but not killed.

Consider also the experiences of Ron Carlson, whose sister, Debbie Thornton, was murdered in 1983. Ron explains that just after Debbie was murdered, he thought that the killers deserved to die. "I was very angry. I didn't like the person that I was becoming. I felt that if I had the opportunity and it was possible, I would kill those who had killed my family."[18] Yet, over time, Ron's mind and heart change, and he begins to believe that the death penalty is wrong. More detail will be given about his experiences at the end of the next chapter. At this juncture, we will cite his reasons from his letter to George W. Bush, who was the governor of Texas at the time of the execution (1998):

> I write to you today concerning the fate of one Karla Faye Tucker Brown. . . . I realize that according to law Karla should be executed. However through all of this I see one thing that just does not go over well with myself. That is the fact that executing Karla will not bring back my sister . . . [T]he pain that I feel for the loss of my loved one will not be replaced with joy by the execution. . . . The fact of the matter is also that executing Karla will not bring me a sense of closure concerning this matter. . . . I feel that by executing those death row inmates, our society is not

---

[18] Rachel King, *Don't Kill in Our Names: Families of Murder Victims Speak Out Against the Death Penalty* (New Brunswick, NJ: Rutgers University Press, 2003), 65.

improved. If anything, it just makes the cycle continue and cause the pain to increase.[19]

Ron's thoughts and feelings encapsulate the wisdom of the Hebrew Bible and the Jewish legal tradition. "An eye for an eye" focuses on the severity of crimes that cause physical injury and death, but in the Jewish community, it also points, not toward retribution and vengeance, but toward restitution and the need for forgiveness.

Questions for Discussion

1. Richard Buck puts "an eye for an eye" (often called the *lex talionis*) in the context of Jewish law as a whole and its legal customs. He holds that phrases like "a wound for a wound" and "a hand for a hand" have an important meaning. What is the meaning of this severe language in the context of Jewish law?

2. Biblical scholars note that legal codes like Exodus 21 set out the purposes of divine justice, but "they do not necessarily record day-to-day legal customs."[20] Richard outlines the requirements of the "day-to-day" legal system. He states two main points. First, the death penalty can be imposed for certain crimes. But second, the legal and procedural requirements for the death penalty are so difficult to meet that it is "nearly impossible for any offender to be executed." Do you think that the first and second points are consistent? Do the two points consistently reflect divine justice and mercy?

3. Richard draws a contrast between a biblical system of justice and the current secular system. He suggests that severe crimes, like personal injury, require that the offender offer restoration to the victim and ask for forgiveness. Consider how the contemporary system of justice could be reformed in order to include both of these important practices.

---

[19] Ibid., 73.
[20] Richard Clifford, SJ, *Deuteronomy* (Wilmington, DE: Michael Glazier, 1982), 187.

Chapter 8

The Bible and the Church

Editors

"My tears were flowing like a river. I begged God, 'Please, please, please give me love and compassion for Paula Cooper and her family and do it for the sake of Nana.'"[1] This prayer was offered by Bill Pelke, about a year and a half after Nana was stabbed to death by teenage girls (in 1985). A group of four girls had skipped school and needed money to spend at an arcade. One of the girls "told the others that there was an old lady in the neighborhood who taught Bible lessons. . . . She suggested that they go to her house under the guise of seeking Bible lessons and, once inside, rob her." Ruth welcomed the girls into her home and "told them that she didn't teach the classes anymore but would get them the name and number of a woman who did."[2] They knocked her down, ransacked the house, and found ten dollars. Meanwhile, they stabbed Nana thirty-three times and left her to die. The robbery was not Paula Cooper's idea, but the murder seemed to be. Nana—Ruth Pelke—was seventy-eight years old.

You might recall the story of Bill and Ruth Pelke, as it was introduced at the end of chapter 3. Bill lived through and developed a "rethinking" of the death penalty that is the topic of chapters 3 and 4. We now return to his story, since his grandmother's faith is what began his journey to understand the gift of compassion. During the trial of the murderer, Bill agreed with the prosecution's pursuit of the death penalty. His grandmother's faith and Jesus' teachings changed his mind and heart. Central

---

[1] Bill Pelke, *Journey of Hope: From Violence to Healing* (Bloomington, IN: Xlibris, 2003), 79.

[2] Rachel King, *Don't Kill in Our Names: Families of Murder Victims Speak Out Against the Death Penalty* (New Brunswick, NJ: Rutgers University Press, 2003), 88, 89.

to the story of Ruth's life and death was her faith in Jesus Christ. Even after death, her faith and presence were alive in Bill's life.

Four months after Paula was sentenced to death, Bill's personal life was in disarray. He was becoming "unglued." He was at work, sitting in the cab of his overhead crane, waiting for coworkers to arrive. Bill found himself praying, "asking God why. Why? Why everything?" Images and memories passed through his mind of broken and lost relationships over the years and of his recent downward spiral. Then his thoughts shifted to his grandmother. "I asked God why He had allowed one of His most precious children to suffer such a horrendous death. Nana was such a good person and she had died trying to serve Jesus. Why? Why? Why?"[3]

Recalling Nana's faith started a shift in Bill's thinking. "I began to think about someone with many more problems than I had" (ibid., 76). He had an image of Paula in her death row cell, alone in the world, laying on her bed, staring upward, crying. He remembered her as she was on the day of sentencing, contrite, begging for forgiveness, full of tears and anguish. His thoughts turned to his grandmother and to Jesus:

> I pictured Nana with tears flowing out of her eyes and rolling down her cheeks. At first I thought they might be tears of pain, but I immediately realized that they were tears of love and compassion for Paula Cooper and her family. . . . And I didn't think Nana would want Paula killed for killing her—Nana had let Paula into her house to talk about Jesus.
>
> I began to think about Nana's faith in Jesus, and I immediately thought of three things that Jesus had said about forgiveness. I recalled the Sermon on the Mount when Jesus said if we wanted our Father in heaven to forgive us, we need to forgive others.
>
> I thought about Jesus talking to his disciples and Peter asking Him about the number of times that we should forgive someone. "Seventy times seven" . . . And as I sat in the crane, I pictured an image of Jesus crucified on the cross . . . I recalled what He said just before they killed Him. Jesus said, "Father, forgive them for they know not what they are doing." (ibid., 78)

Bill felt a transformation beginning. But he could not do it alone; he could not have compassion for his grandmother's killer. It was at this point when he prayed for love and compassion "for the sake of Nana." Bill experienced grace through what the apostle Paul calls living "in Christ" (2 Cor 5:17).

---

[3] Pelke, *Journey of Hope*, 73, 75.

Bill experienced *metanoia*: he turned his life around (see chap. 5). He began to work for a reversal of Paula's death sentence. He traveled across the United States and Europe talking about his grandmother's faith, and in 1989 the Indiana Supreme Court ruled that "'evolving standards of decency' made it intolerable for Paula Cooper to be the first and last person to be executed for a crime committed by a fifteen-year-old."[4] Bill "has traveled to over forty states and ten countries with the Journey of Hope and has told his story thousands of times."[5] At the heart of Bill's story is the central question of Sr. Mary Kate Birge's chapter on the Bible and church: Mary Kate asks, "What would Jesus do?" Her chapter brings together the themes of chapters 5, 6, and 7: accountability, repentance, and restoration.

WWJD? Jesus, the Death Penalty, and US Catholics

Sr. Mary Katherine Birge, SSJ

I have a panel from the now defunct comic strip *The Boondocks* taped to my office door. In it two African American boys are conversing with one another about the national political situation and the death penalty. In the final frame, the older and more worldly of the two delivers the punch line with a devastating directness and brevity worthy of Jesus' own teaching style. He asks, "I mean . . . Do you REALLY think Jesus would be pro-death penalty?"[6] His question is the lens through which I will consider how Jesus' words and deeds in the gospels offer a starting point from which Catholic Christians may examine the basis for their own attitudes and positions on the use of the death penalty in the United States.

To be clear, the death penalty, as practiced today in the United States by the federal government (and the various state governments that have not repealed it), is an exercise in retribution. Why else would officers of both state and federal governments want to end the life of someone who had been found guilty of murdering another human being? A sentence of life imprisonment without parole would effectively neutralize any future threat to society from such a perpetrator. So why kill a person who has been found guilty by the court of killing another person when there is an alternative for keeping society safe and holding the perpetrator accountable—unless it is

---

[4] King, *Don't Kill in Our Names*, 104.

[5] Journey of Hope, http://journeyofhope.org/who-we-are/murder-victim-family /bill-pelke/.

[6] Aaron McGruder, *The Boondocks*, *Washington Post* (November 16, 2004).

the desire to retaliate in kind (or retaliate in kind as closely as the criminal law code will allow)? "Retributive" justice, some reply. But what kind of justice did Jesus live and teach? Did he call for what Richard Buck calls "equality retribution" in the previous chapter—that every word or act of violence be answered with its equivalent? Did he teach that those who commit great evils are devoid of God's image and have forfeited their membership in the human community?

In Matthew's gospel, Jesus answers some of these very questions in the section called the Sermon on the Mount (chaps. 5–7).[7] In Matthew, Jesus does not intend this "sermon" to be a rejection of Torah teaching nor even a correction of it. Rather, Matthew has assembled a major collection of Jesus' pronouncements in which he recalls a particular Torah commandment. He states the commandment first; he then commands a practice that fulfills or completes the commandment's purpose.[8] Jesus states, "You have heard that it was said, 'An eye for an eye and a tooth for a tooth.' But I say to you, offer no resistance to one who is evil. When someone strikes you on (your) right cheek, turn the other one to him [or her] as well" (5:38-39). With his "[b]ut I say to you," he is completing the purpose behind a series of commandments exemplified in Exodus 21:23-25 (also Lev 24:20 and Deut 19:21).

Torah commands such as Exodus 21:23-25 ("an eye for an eye and a tooth for a tooth") are sometimes called the *lex talionis* or "law of the talon." The *lex talionis* limited violence and death to one person. It prevented the spread of deliberate injury and murder by the victim's family and tribe in retaliation for the initial injury or death. Even such limited "violence" was rare in practice (even if allowed in theory). As Richard Buck explains in the preceding chapter, the Jewish legal tradition interprets the *lex talionis* primarily in terms of restitution rather than retribution. The victim or victim's family should be compensated through payment of a

---

[7] Jesus also answers these questions in Luke 6:17-49 (which editors often call the "Sermon on the Plain") with almost the very same words as Matthew does. The majority of New Testament scholars believe that Matthew and Luke each had a copy of a collection of Jesus' sayings (no longer extant but called "Q" by scholars) when they were writing their gospels. Such an arrangement would explain the frequent agreement in the Greek wording of Jesus' speech in both gospels.

[8] Often, when translators of Matthew's gospel use the English word "perfect," both as a verb and an adjective for forms and derivatives of the Greek verb *teleioo*, they are indicating that some person or object has reached the "end" for which he or she was intended or created. In this sense Jesus is ordering his followers in Matthew 5–7 to complete the intention behind various Torah commandments. He orders them to follow the logical trajectory of a commandment's purpose and to act on it.

significant indemnity by the perpetrator, not unlike what contemporary insurance companies do in the case of a client's loss of life or limb. In addition, such commandments or laws applied to everyone in society, even the rich and the powerful. The law was applied to all, not an insignificant development in understanding God's desire for all people—that they recognize themselves as brothers and sisters to one another despite differences in their social, economic, and cultural milieus.

Jesus takes the *lex talionis* and builds on it. When he says, "But I say to you, offer no resistance to one who is evil" (Matt 5:39a), he articulates the purpose behind the Torah commandment and reveals its completion or perfection: "When someone strikes you on (your) right cheek, turn the other one to him [or her] as well" (v. 39b). Jesus is charging his followers to reject violence and to forego retaliation; Matthew requires this conduct of his own community members. He underscores its foundational nature for them as followers of Jesus in two ways: (1) by including this pronouncement in the first significant block of instruction to his community on how to live together while they await Jesus' return at the end of time, and (2) by following immediately upon it with another pronouncement (Matt 5:43-48) that repeats the essence of Matthew 5:38-42 in a positive formulation (cf. vv. 38-42).

> You have heard that it was said, "You shall love your neighbor and hate your enemy." But I say to you, love your enemies, and pray for those who persecute you, that you may be children of your heavenly Father, for he makes his sun rise on the bad and the good, and causes rain to fall on the just and the unjust. For if you love those who love you, what recompense will you have? Do not the tax collectors do the same? And if you greet your brothers [and sisters] only, what is unusual about that? Do not the pagans do the same? So be perfect, just as your heavenly Father is perfect. (vv. 43-48)

In effect, Jesus directs them to those actions they should pursue rather than not pursue. The message is not simply, "Do not retaliate," but also, "Follow the ways of God."

Jesus quotes from the Old Testament (Lev 19:18) when he states, "You have heard that it was said, 'You shall love your neighbor'" (Matt 5:43ab), but the final clause of his statement, "and hate your enemy," does not come from Scripture itself. It seems Jesus draws upon an interpretation of Leviticus 19:18 that had once understood the unwritten-but-implied corollary of the command to love one's neighbor as a command also to hate one's enemy.[9] The word "neighbor" of v. 43b (cf. Lev 19:18) had always been interpreted as another member of the Mosaic covenant and the word "enemy" as someone who stood outside the covenant. When Jesus commands his followers to "love your enemies, and pray for those who persecute you" (v. 44bc), he goes beyond simply widening the boundaries that delimit whom one must engage with loving action.[10] He removes such boundaries entirely and brings to completion, that is, to perfection, the purpose behind the commands in Leviticus 19:17-18: the radical transformation of the world through loving action. Every word and every action of Jesus in the gospels is directed toward this goal. He announces it, he preaches it, he reveals it in his miracles and his actions, and he invites—no, he commands—those who would follow him to do the same, to join him in initiating the "reign of God."[11]

Jesus reveals why the "enemies" of God's own people (and so also enemies of God) warrant such compassionate engagement in Matthew 5:45bc. He reminds his audience that God "makes his sun rise on the bad and the good, and causes rain to fall on the just and the unjust," recalling for them God's practice of compassion toward all whom God has made (cf. Ps 145:9; Wis 15:1). By bringing into the foreground the image of God as the author of humanity, Matthew draws attention to the likeness

---

[9] Later in this gospel, Jesus will indicate an additional interpretation of this same command in Matthew 22:34-40.

[10] Ulrich Luz, *Continental Commentary: Matthew 1–7*, trans. Wilhelm C. Linss (Minneapolis: Fortress, 1989), 342–45; W. D. Davies and Dale C. Allison, *International Critical Commentary: Matthew 1–7* (New York: T & T Clark, 1988), 548–49.

[11] This "reign," "rule," or "kingdom" (as it has been variously translated) was an unknown time in the future longed for by many Jews during Jesus' lifetime. For Jews, then, all of time was divided into two periods: now or the "present age" and the "age to come" or the "next age." This present age was filled with violence, hunger, disease, and injustice; the next age would be when God "ruled" or "reigned," when all violence, hunger, and disease would be turned upside down and God's justice would prevail, especially for the poor. All who had been broken or destroyed, lost or abandoned, would be restored. The prophets had preached about it (e.g., Isa 2:2-5; 9:1-6; 11:1-16; 30:19-26; 35:1-10; 49:8-13; 55:1-13; 61:1-2; Jer 31:7-14; Joel 4:11-16), as did Jesus. But he not only preached about the reign of God; he enacted it. Every time he healed someone's illness (Matt 4:23-25; 8:1-4, 5-13, 14-15, 16-17; 9:1-8, 20-22, 27-31, 32-34, 35-38; 12:9-14; 14:34-36; 15:21-28, 29-31; 20:29-34), restored someone's child to life (9:18, 23-26), and exorcised an evil spirit (8:28-34; 17:14-20), people encountered the reign of God; they smelled, heard, saw, tasted, touched, and were touched by it. Time and again, Jesus revealed that the reign of God was already active and present in people's lives through him.

of God that every person bears (Gen 1:26-27), yet leaves his audience to infer that even their enemies carry the divine image. In Matthew 5:46-47, Jesus appeals to his audience's sense of virtue and honor: If tax collectors, hated among ordinary citizens of the Roman Empire, love one another, what virtue is there for followers of Jesus who do not exceed the virtue of the despised tax collectors? Where is the honor for disciples of Jesus if they greet another only as the Gentiles do? Their own practice of justice ought to follow the pattern of God's justice.[12] They must go far beyond even what scribes and Pharisees do (cf. 5:20).[13] To be followers of Jesus they have to strive toward becoming whole, complete, and undivided the way God is.[14] They are to be like God rather than like tax collectors and Gentiles (cf. Lev 19:2; Deut 18:13).[15]

In the verses examined here (Matt 5:38-49), Jesus has instructed those who follow him to repudiate retaliation in word and deed, and to embrace the practice of nonviolence (vv. 38-42). He repeats this instruction in another way that is as unambiguous as the first and likely more demanding. He commands disciples to love their enemies, to go beyond the ordinary practices of their society and become like God because they are God's children (v. 48). At the beginning of the chapter, I introduced the reader to the "interpretive lens" through which I would explore various New Testament texts: Recall the *Boondocks* comic, "I mean . . . Do you REALLY think Jesus would be pro-death penalty?" The death penalty in the United States exists to retaliate against the perpetrator of a terrible crime. It is not needed to protect members of society from any future violence by that perpetrator. Life imprisonment without possibility of parole safeguards the public and provides very serious consequences to the perpetrator. No, it does not seem that Jesus would be pro-death penalty; rather, in light of Matthew's account of his teaching, it seems that Jesus would be adamantly and vociferously against the death penalty.

Yet, I have based my initial conclusion on one passage of Matthew's gospel. Although significant, it is only one passage. My claim for Jesus

---

[12] See Mary Katherine Birge, "Biblical Justice," *The Heart of Catholic Social Teaching: Its Origins and Contemporary Significance*, ed. David Matzko McCarthy (Grand Rapids, MI: Brazos, 2009).

[13] Scribes and Pharisees were the experts in the interpretation of Torah at the time Matthew and Luke were writing, ca. 80–90, and at the time John was writing, ca. 90–110.

[14] In the NABRE, the Greek word behind "whole," "complete," or "undivided" in 5:48 is translated "perfect."

[15] In the NABRE, the Hebrew word behind "whole," "complete," or "undivided" in Deuteronomy 18:13 is translated as "altogether sincere."

regarding the death penalty would be much stronger and more convincing if I could demonstrate that Jesus himself practiced such a difficult teaching or even rejected the death penalty's use. To this end, we will examine two other passages, one from Luke's gospel and the other from the Gospel of John.

In Luke 22:49-51, right after Jesus' anguish and prayer in the garden, when the chief priests, elders, and temple police come to arrest Jesus in secret at night (v. 52), the evangelist writes,

> His disciples realized what was about to happen, and they asked, "Lord, shall we strike with a sword?" And one of them struck the high priest's servant and cut off his right ear. But Jesus said in reply, "Stop, no more of this!" Then he touched the servant's ear and healed him.

In Luke, as in Matthew's gospel, Jesus has already commanded his followers to live in a new way. He has proclaimed to them,

> [L]ove your enemies, do good to those who hate you, bless those who curse you, pray for those who mistreat you. To the person who strikes you on one cheek, offer the other one as well. (Luke 6:27b-29a)

He continues in this vein for several more verses before he concludes the section with almost the same charge to his followers with which he begins the passage:

> [L]ove your enemies and do good to them, and lend expecting nothing back; then your reward will be great and you will be children of the Most High, for he himself is kind to the ungrateful and the wicked. Be merciful, just as [also] your Father is merciful. (Luke 6:35-36)

Like in Matthew's gospel, Jesus' command to love one's enemies figures early and prominently in Luke's gospel; it too draws attention to an essential attitude of mind and heart and prescribes a practice, both of which are constitutive for those who follow Jesus. He does so because he has taught those who would follow him to "[d]o to others as you would have them do to you" (6:31), and he has practiced it in word and deed throughout his ministry.[16]

---

[16] See examples of Jesus' restraint in word and deed with opponents from among the people and religious leaders, Luke 4:29-30; 5:17-26, 30-32; 6:1-11.

Consider Jesus' challenge to the practice of selling animals for sacrifice and changing money in the temple. This "market" was in the only place in the temple available for Gentiles to pray to the God of Israel (19:45-46). Luke portrays Jesus as he has portrayed him on numerous other occasions when Jesus exorcises evil spirits who desecrate their human host. He is firm, strong, commanding, and powerful.[17] Just as in these exorcisms, Jesus does not employ violent force, and neither does he in Luke 19:45-46. When driving out the money changers from the temple, Jesus shows great passion and even anger. But he does no violence. No one is harmed. His actions are a reminder that Jesus' nonviolence and his way to the cross do not come from "passiveness" but are essential to his embodiment of God's self-giving and reconciling passion.

Likewise, when they are still at the Passover meal, Jesus speaks to his disciples in metaphorical language about the strength and fortitude they will need to continue following him. They show enthusiasm in proclaiming that they have two swords to protect against the coming challenge. Jesus is vexed: "It is enough!" he thunders. The disciples fail to grasp the meaning of Jesus' warning about his own suffering (Luke 22:35-38) and his earlier commands to them to love their enemies and to do good to them (6:35).[18] A disciple tries to resist Jesus' arrest and cuts off the ear of a servant of the high priest (Luke 22:49-51). With one utterance—"Stop, no more of this!"—Jesus stops the violence that would have "protected" him and "saved" him from unjust arrest, brutal treatment, and inevitable death. Yet, even ending violence is insufficient for him. He must try to repair as best he can what an act of violence has ruined. He restores the servant's amputated ear, and follows his earlier teaching to "do good to those who hate you" (6:27c). He and those who would follow him are called to "[b]e merciful, just as [also] [their] Father is merciful" (6:36).[19]

---

[17] The verb "to drive out," in Greek *ekballō*, in Luke 19:44-45 is the same verb that Luke uses to describe Jesus' exorcisms in Luke 9:40, 49; 11:14, 15, 18, 19, 20; 13:32; cf. Luke Timothy Johnson, *The Gospel of Luke*, Sacra Pagina Series (Collegeville, MN: Liturgical Press, 1991), 299.

[18] Eugene LaVerdiere, *Luke* (Wilmington, DE: Michael Glazier, 1980), 262.

[19] In Matthew's gospel, Jesus urges his followers to become complete or whole as their Father is (5:48); in Luke's gospel, Jesus urges his followers to become merciful or compassionate as their Father is (6:36). Isn't this a contradiction? No, it is not a contradiction; to be complete or whole as God is to be merciful or compassionate as God, and to be merciful or compassionate as God is to be as complete as God. Each author has Jesus say essentially the same thing, but with words carefully chosen to address particular questions or circumstances dealing with discipleship that are specific to the two audiences.

In addition to studying the passage from Matthew's gospel, in which Jesus unequivocally forbids his followers to practice retaliation, we have considered a passage from Luke's gospel in which he himself "walks the talk" of Matthew 5:43-48 and Luke 6:27-36 and rejects the use of violence on his behalf to protect him from those who would do him harm. Jesus also does his best to render null the effect of violence against a servant in the company of those who have come to arrest him. In words and in action, Jesus rejects violence, rejects retaliation, and models the practice of nonviolent, inclusive love.

"I mean . . . Do you REALLY think Jesus would be pro-death penalty?" Assuredly not. Jesus was not then, nor is he now, "pro-death penalty." Would he be neutral toward its use by anyone or any institution? No. He commanded his followers to reject violence, to reject retaliation, and he himself barred a follower from protecting him with a sword. Today, then, it seems that Jesus would reject the use of the death penalty because it is both an act of violence and an act of retribution. The Gospel of John offers an example of Jesus outright rejecting the use of the death penalty in his own society.

John 8:2-11 presents Jesus as sitting early one morning in the temple area, surrounded by people who have sought him out. He is teaching these people. A group of scribes and Pharisees approach him with a woman who they say has been caught in adultery. They remind Jesus of the Torah prescription that calls for a woman who has been found committing adultery to be stoned publicly for her crime, and then they ask him to comment on the case. The Torah prescriptions to which the scribes and Pharisees allude are in Leviticus 20:10 and Deuteronomy 22:22-29. All of these commandments prescribe stoning as punishment for the commission of adultery for both the man and the woman involved, but the scribes and Pharisees present only the woman to Jesus for condemnation.[20] John makes clear that the motive behind the question of the scribes and Pharisees is to trap Jesus into contradicting the law (John 8:6). Jesus ignores them by doodling in the dust with his finger until he tires of them pestering him with the same questions. His response to their question, "Let the one among you who is without sin be the first to throw a stone at her" (v. 7), sends them silently away.

---

[20] There is one exception in the prescribed punishment. If the place where the adultery is supposed to have taken place happens to be a field or another remote area, the woman shall be considered innocent. For, if the man were to have attacked her there, any cry of hers for help would not have been heard, and so she is innocent of adultery (cf. Deut 22:25-27).

They cannot trap him with the law; rather, Jesus has trapped them with his interpretation of the law, and he has stymied their plan to execute the woman. When the scribes and Pharisees have slunk away in defeat, tasting some of the humiliation to which they had subjected the woman, Jesus, now alone with her, asks the woman two questions. He inquires where her accusers are, and if one of them has denounced her. "No one, sir," she answers, and then in one sentence, Jesus restores her to life: "Neither do I condemn you" (John 8:11). He refuses to apply the death penalty. He rejects the use of the death penalty in his own society.

"What would Jesus do?" (WWJD?). Another question, gleaned from the comic pages of the *Washington Post* and repeated throughout the essay, draws that initial question into a far more stark and probing search of the Catholic conscience: "I mean . . . Do you REALLY think Jesus would be pro-death penalty?" In words and in actions, we have watched Jesus reject the use of violence, reject the practice of retaliation, and reject the use of the death penalty. It cannot be clearer. Jesus would reject today's use of the death penalty in the United States just as he did during his life on earth. How will Catholic Christians today respond?

Review and Looking Forward

Editors

Before dawn on June 13, 1983, Debbie Thornton was murdered during a robbery at the home of Jerry Lynn Dean. Jerry and Debbie were killed with a pickax; the killers were possessed by drugs and a hatred for Jerry. Debbie, they did not know. The killers, Danny Garrett and Karla Faye Tucker, were turned in by Danny's brother and Karla's sister. Karla was the one responsible for Debbie's death. Ron Carlson, Debbie's brother, remembers that during and after the trial, "I wanted to take that same pickax and leave it in the heart of Karla Faye Tucker." He remembers the years after the murder as a blur of alcohol and drugs. On New Year's Eve 1989, he got down on his knees and "prayed the sinner's prayer." Then he asked Jesus, "Would you please take this hatred and fill it with love and compassion for those who destroyed my family?"[21]

A year later, Ron met with Karla at the Harris County Jail. She had to be present at an appeal hearing at the Harris County Courthouse. Karla was shocked by Ron's visit. She wept. Ron offered forgiveness. He remembers,

---

[21] King, *Don't Kill in Our Names*, 65, 66.

"I felt like a great weight had been lifted off of my shoulders; I felt like a burden I had been carrying was gone." From that point, he began to speak against the death penalty and to work for the reversal of Karla's sentence. At the close of chapter 7, we cited Ron's letter to then-governor of Texas, George W. Bush. Consider another portion of that letter:

> I leave you with this thought. Jesus of Nazareth walked upon the face of this earth for a very short period of time. It was through compassion for the people in this world that He gave his life on the cross. He himself was executed. He suffered a terrible death. However because of compassion he followed what his father in Heaven had to say. Through Him many changes were made, and are being made even today. Quite possibly by stopping the executions this will be another change that He wants. I am not saying that He said not to execute Karla. But He did say to love one another, and to forgive one another.[22]

Ron's words provide a fitting way to summarize this chapter on the Bible and to look ahead to part III on the Catholic tradition.

Questions for Discussion

1. Read Matthew 5:1-48 (the beginning of the Sermon on the Mount). We often assume that these teachings are difficult, if not impossible, to live by. Discuss why they are considered "hard" sayings. Discuss why and how the family members of murder victims, like Bill Pelke and Ron Carlson, have found that Jesus' teachings are liberating and healing. How can this be?

2. Bill Pelke likes to say, "I am a Christian, and Jesus said, 'Whosoever has no sin, cast the first stone.' Under that criterion, none of us can cast the stone of death."[23] Discuss Bill's statement and the story of Jesus and the woman caught in adultery (John 8:1-11). Is the woman simply "let off the hook"? What is the relationship between compassion and accountability?

3. Both Bill Pelke and Ron Carlson took faith-based positions on the death penalty that were at odds with family members who supported

---

[22] Ibid., 73.
[23] Journey of Hope, http://journeyofhope.org/who-we-are/murder-victim-family/bill-pelke/.

the death penalty. They both work to promote dialogue on the death penalty. Drawing on insights from this chapter, discuss how Christians who disagree about the death penalty might approach dialogue with each other on this issue.

Part III

Church Teachings on Capital Punishment

Editors

The third part of this book has four chapters that focus on the history of church teachings on capital punishment and the *Catechism of the Catholic Church*. The first chapter starts at the beginning of the story—the first few centuries of Christianity. The early church rejected the death penalty for use by Christians, but acknowledged that non-Christian rulers (that is, the magistrates of the Roman Empire) may use it when necessary. The contemporary end of the story, covered in chapter 12, is John Paul II's evangelical call against capital punishment for use by anyone, especially advanced nations like the United States.

Sometimes reading the history of the church conjures up worries about the truth of our faith. Can moral convictions change and still be true? The answer, in short, is yes. But the simple "yes" is too simplistic. Our moral convictions can change *and* still can be true, because amid the change there is a core of consistency, a continuous and unbroken foundation of the Christian life. That foundation was outlined in part II of the book. It is the church's continuing call and commitment to be faithful to the incarnation of God in Jesus Christ, to his life, teaching, death, and resurrection. It is the consistent acknowledgment that God is the Creator who orders human life. It is the continuing call from God to be transformed and to follow Jesus. These four chapters bring us to understand the changes and inner core of unchanging foundational beliefs found in the church teachings on the death penalty.

❖

Chapter 9

The Catholic Moral Tradition

Editors

Jesus suffered and died—was crucified—in accord with Roman law, under what had become the empire's harsh penal code along with its methods of inflicting slow and painful death. Pontius Pilate, governor of Judea, has an inscription placed on the cross: "Jesus the Nazorean, the King of the Jews" (John 19:19). This is the charge levied by Rome against Jesus. The message is clear: this is what happens when a Jewish liberator enters Jerusalem to make a claim to God's city. When Jesus turns his face toward Jerusalem (Luke 9:51), he does so as the Messiah and Redeemer of Israel. Nonetheless, rather than defeating and expelling the Romans by force, he is executed. Rather than taking our lives, God gives his life to us. He dies so that we might live. This reversal is the "miracle of the reign of God."[1] It is the defeat of the world's powers by God's own self-giving, and it sets in place a way of life for Christians—the imitation of Christ.

Today, Christians are among the most persecuted and martyred peoples worldwide.[2] This situation of hostility is not new. In his historical study of the death penalty, James Megivern emphasizes that following Jesus would

---

[1] Gerhard Lohfink, *Jesus and Community* (Philadelphia: Fortress Press, 1984), 180.

[2] Paul Marshall, "Persecution of Christians in the Contemporary World," *International Bulletin of Missionary Research* 22, no. 1 (Jan. 1998): 2–9. Marshall concludes, "In the last five years, the persecution of Christians has taken place in approximately forty countries, and legal repression and discrimination in an additional thirty countries. Reliable estimates of the number of religious believers in various countries are hard to achieve, and in any case they are subject to wide variation depending on definition. My best estimate of the overall situation is that, in total, some 200,000,000 Christians in the world are members of persecuted groups in countries where religious persecution includes imprisonment, beatings, torture, mob violence, and death. An additional 400,000,000 live in situations of nontrivial discrimination and legal repression. And

likely mean execution for the first-generation Christians. For three centuries after Christ's crucifixion, Christians were "members of an illegal religion . . . [and] were among the likeliest targets of capital punishment."[3] They were victims of Roman oppression, but Christians did not necessarily or automatically reject the authority of the empire. In following Christ, they did not seek or oppose oppression by force.

Although not revolutionaries, early Christians did seek to live in a new way, a way that reflected God's reconciliation and mercy. They did not reject capital punishment in particular; they were critical and wary of any kind of bloodshed, whether legal executions or the spectacle of gladiators.[4] When Christianity was given legal status in the fourth century, the role of the church and its view of coercive force were realigned and continued to shift through time, into the Middle Ages and the modern period. Throughout, however, bloodshed was never considered the norm and always required special justification. God's reconciliation and mercy do not allow us to be complacent with the ways of the world. The death penalty could never sit well with the church as a whole. In this chapter, Christian Brugger tells the story of this unsettled history.

Christian outlines periods of church history and their different attitudes toward capital punishment. He warns us a few times against oversimplification. In a brief chapter, it is difficult to achieve the nuance necessary to show both the continuity and the changes of the church through time. Christian's main task is to chart the changes, but he assumes the changeless continuity of our faith and the teachings of the church. An element of change is inevitable because the church professes faith in the incarnation. We profess faith that God in Christ is embodied and with us in various and changing times and places.

One role of the teaching office of the church is to identify the foundation of our faith and moral life amid differences in time and place. To this degree, the culmination of the story of the death penalty, developed in chapters 10 and 12, is John Paul II's teaching about the "gospel of life." In his life and through his papal teaching, John Paul II shows how the death penalty could have been rightly used in ages past (in narrowly defined circumstances) and why it ought not to be used today. Indeed, John Paul II gives us reason to be actively against it.

---

this persecution is increasing, notably in China, Vietnam, Uzbekistan, and parts of the Islamic world, especially Pakistan, Egypt, and Indonesia."

[3] James J. Megivern, *The Death Penalty: An Historical and Theological Survey* (Mahwah, NJ: Paulist, 1997), 19.

[4] Ibid., 20–26.

The Ancient, Medieval, and Early Modern Periods

E. Christian Brugger

Catholic moral thought on capital punishment is presently undergoing an epochal development in the direction of abolition. This is so obvious that it need hardly be said. However, what may not be so obvious is the theological pathway this development has traced over the centuries, a pathway with furrows going in both directions, at times supporting the death penalty, even enthusiastically, and at other times opposing it at the levels of both theory and practice.[5]

At the level of authoritative Catholic teaching, the church has consistently held the following concise proposition: *civil authority may (not must!) inflict a punishment of death on duly convicted criminals for the sake of maintaining the good order of the community.* The majority of Catholic writers, until recently, believed that Sacred Scripture affirmed this, especially St. Paul's words in Romans 13:1-4.[6] The proposition is admittedly thin and leaves unaddressed or unsettled a range of important questions related to crime and punishment, all of which bear to some degree on the practical support of Catholics for the death penalty over the centuries.[7]

---

[5] I use the term "theological" pathway and not "doctrinal" pathway because I think a distinction important to the faith of Catholics is rightly made between them. The pathway of Catholic doctrine on capital punishment has been relatively concise and consistent. The theological pathway has been more complex and circuitous. By "theological" I include the great ideas and treatises that have shaped Catholic teaching *and practice* over the centuries. Not all of these ideas and practices—rightly referred to as Catholic moral *tradition*—were set down as Catholic doctrine, that is, were authoritatively taught by the popes and bishops of the church and so became normative for Catholic belief and practice. But all constituted reflections on divine revelation and Catholic life aiming to clarify Jesus' will on the problems of criminal malefaction, just punishment, and the maintenance of social order.

[6] "Let every person be subordinate to the higher authorities, for there is no authority except from God, and those that exist have been established by God. Therefore, whoever resists authority opposes what God has appointed, and those who oppose it will bring judgment upon themselves. For rulers are not a cause of fear to good conduct, but to evil. Do you wish to have no fear of authority? Then do what is good and you will receive approval from it, for it is a servant of God for your good. But if you do evil, be afraid, for it does not bear the sword without purpose; it is the servant of God to inflict wrath on the evildoer" (Rom 13:1-4).

[7] Questions, for example, such as the nature of retribution and of due process, the implications of Christian discipleship for participating in bloodshed, the practical assignment of punishments, effective types of punishments for advancing the forward-looking aims of deterrence, criminal reformation, societal self-defense, and, finally, questions of

In the course of the church's history, there have been three dominant practical conclusions toward the use of capital punishment. Each is situated within a historical period:[8]

1. Prophetic rejection of the death penalty in the first three centuries of Christianity

2. Acceptance from the fourth to nineteenth centuries

3. Pastoral opposition to the death penalty in the twentieth and twenty-first centuries

Underlying the conclusions in these eras are questions, not only about the morality and theological justification of putting criminals to death (or not), but also about the church's role in the world, particularly in the modern era in an increasingly secularized world.

This chapter outlines the prophetic period in early Christianity (period 1) and the basic justification for acceptance of capital punishment from the fourth to the nineteenth centuries (period 2). The next chapter will begin with this period of acceptance and explain the shift to opposition in the twentieth century. Throughout, emphasis will be placed on the need for a theological approach to the death penalty consistent with the Christian vocation to discipleship and witness in the world.

Prophetic Christian Rejection (the First to the Third Centuries)

The fathers of the church prior to the conversion of Constantine (312 AD) held a bifurcated position (a two-sided view) on capital punishment.[9] On the one hand, civil authority, exclusively non-Christian during the period (and at times violently anti-Christian), could rightfully exercise lethal punishment, so long as it was exercised in accord with natural justice. This followed from

---

ethical principle stemming from the truth of the intrinsic dignity of the human person and the requisites of Christian mercy.

[8] Dividing Christian history into three subdivisions inevitably risks oversimplification. My threefold division, therefore, should not be understood monolithically. Each period admits a range of expressions of the prevailing view, together with differences in emphases and even bases of the theoretical justification for the position. In addition, more or less influential dissenting voices, both from within and outside the Christian community, usually stand beside the majority view during the three periods.

[9] Theologians and bishops of the early church are called "fathers" of the church, from which we get the term designating the age in which they wrote—the "patristic period." The patristic period extends beyond what I am calling the "prophetic period."

the premise that all rightful authority, including the Roman emperor's and his magistrates', was instituted by God (see Rom 13:1); and when justice was the guiding norm, the authorities were acting, perhaps unwittingly, as ministers of God, authorized to execute his justice within the community.

On the other hand, Christians—*all* Christians—as consecrated to Jesus through their baptism and commanded to seek first the interests of the kingdom (Matt 6:10, 33), were prohibited from all participation in all bloodshed, whether in the form of military service, or in the handing down or carrying out of lethal punishments. Although involvement with bloodshed in the interests of justice was not illicit for the pagans, the early Christians had a very lively sense that it was incompatible with the vocation to Christian discipleship. As the great Alexandrian theologian Origen (d. 254) argued in the third century, the imperial powers should view Christians as they do their own pagan priests, as persons consecrated to the service of God. Christians serve the temporal community through prayer and intercession on behalf of the just exploits of the emperor. Consequently, they should be exempted from all the sanguinary duties of the administration of temporal justice.[10]

Universal Catholic Acceptance (the Fourth to the Nineteenth Centuries)

The Post-Constantinian Patristic Consensus

Constantine's Edict of Milan (313) made Christianity a tolerated religion of the Roman Empire, and Theodosius's Edict of Thessalonica (380) declared it the official religion of the state. As a result, the Christianization of the Roman world greatly accelerated. This evangelical advantage posed a problem for the traditional bifurcated view that saw the exercise of bloody punishment legitimate for pagans but defiling to Christians. The highest earthly authority—the emperor—supereminently endowed with coercive power was now a Christian. Governors, magistrates, military commanders, palace guards, Roman legionaries, hired watchmen, even executioners, all became candidates for membership in the Christian community. How long was it even possible, practically speaking, for Christians to abstain from every office charged with the exercise of lethal authority? History illustrates that within a century of Constantine's conversion, the phenomenon of the "Christian magistrate" was already normative.

---

[10] *Contra Celsum*, bk. 7, chap. 26, in *Origen: Contra Celsum*, trans. H. Chadwick (Cambridge: Cambridge University Press, 1953), 509.

Should we conclude from this, as some have argued, that the church—because of political "necessity"—uncritically accepted Christian participation in the dirty business of handing down and inflicting capital sentences?[11] Although the influence upon political affairs of the historical contingencies resulting from the Christianization of the empire can hardly be denied, to charge that the church was uncritical in the moves it made would be simplistic. No father of the church before or after Constantine's conversion ever denied in principle the legitimacy of capital punishment. Common biblical interpretation, both of the Old and New Testaments, supported it. Moreover, a world split by violent heretics, ubiquitous brigandry, and barbarian invasions seemed to require it. Whether capital punishment was in fact (ever) necessary to maintain public order is by no means transparent. Nevertheless, its necessity in late antiquity went unquestioned.

Having said this, it should be noted that even during the later patristic period, when Christian hands were commonly the instruments of temporal justice, some of the most influential church fathers still exhibited a lively sense that Christian discipleship was somehow incompatible with the infliction of capital punishment. Saints Ambrose (d. 397), Augustine (d. 430), and John Chrysostom (d. 407), all bishops of large and powerful sees, despised the death penalty and vigorously opposed its infliction in their ecclesiastical jurisdictions. Their advice to Christian magistrates was consistent: *restrain malefactors, but do not kill them.*[12] Each was conspicuous for his outspoken interventions for clemency on behalf of condemned criminals, and harsh in his criticisms of magistrates who appeared to take no regard for Christian mercy. Pope Gregory the Great (d. 604) expressed well the sentiment of these fathers: "I shrink from having anything to do with the death of anyone."[13]

---

[11] Francesco Compagnoni, OP, "Capital Punishment and Torture in the Tradition of the Roman Catholic Church," *Concilium* 120 (1978): 41.

[12] Augustine's disposition is illustrated in a series of letters to Christian magistrates urging them not to carry out sentences of blood: see St. Augustine, Letters, Volume II, *Letter LXXXVI* (AD 405) to Caecilianus, in *Fathers of the Church (FOC)*, vol. 18, ed. Roy J. Deferrari, trans. Sister Wilfrid Parsons (New York: Fathers of the Church, 1953), 12; *Letter C* (ca. AD 409) to Donatus, *FOC*, vol. 18, 142; *Letter CIV* (AD 409) to Nectarius, *FOC*, vol. 18, 184; Letters, Volume III, *Letter CXXXIX* (AD 412) to Marcellinus, *FOC*, vol. 20, 54.

[13] Gregory the Great, "Epistle XLVII, to Sabinianus," *Nicene and Post-Nicene Fathers of the Church*, series 2, vol. 12, ed. Philip Schaff and Henry Wace (Peabody, MA: Hendrickson, 1995) 161.

The Death Penalty in the Middle Ages

The death penalty's legitimacy continues to be defended throughout the Middle Ages, and practical inhibitions against its exercise gradually decrease. Historians generally date the beginning of the period somewhere between the fifth and seventh centuries (with the fall of the Roman Empire) and ending around the fifteenth century (with the rise of the Renaissance). The one-thousand-year period was politically diverse. There were phases of (1) terrible political fracturing, as during the barbarian invasions; (2) grand attempts at European unification, as under Charlemagne (d. 814); (3) the decentralization of political authority during the feudal period; and (4) the rise of an independent and influential papacy capable of exercising both spiritual and temporal authority over much of Christian Europe.[14]

The patristic opposition to bloody punishment was not entirely absent.[15] But the dominant concern of lawyers and theologians from the eleventh to the thirteenth centuries was not so much to limit the exercise of bloody punishment as to articulate clear foundations for its lawful infliction. The greatest treatises on political authority of the twelfth century by jurists such as Gratian[16] and John of Salisbury[17] are systematizations of traditional principles aimed at contributing to the reestablishment of the rule of law over and against the arbitrary rule and political cronyism that infected both feudal church and society.

Thomas Aquinas (1225–1274)

Aquinas's defense of capital punishment is indisputably the most influential Catholic account from the medieval period, and arguably from Catholic intellectual history. His argument is philosophical. It rests upon a common premise of Aristotelian political philosophy that the good of some whole is more perfect than the good of its parts and consequently the part

---

[14] The rise of the papacy follows the church's victory in the investiture controversy in the twelfth century. The issue of investiture was whether bishops and abbots would be appointed by the pope or by kings and emperors.

[15] See, for example, the insistence of Pope Nicholas I (d. 867) that the church only employs the "spiritual sword," never the temporal; "Letter to Archbishop Albino," in the *Decretals of Gratian*, Causa XXXIII, q. II, c. VI (*Corpus Iuris Canonici*, vol. I, col. 1152).

[16] See Gratian's famous *Decretum Gratiani* (*Concordantia discordantium canonum*), *Causa 23, questions 5, 8*.

[17] John of Salisbury (ca. 1115–80), *Policraticus*, bk. 4, chap. 2, trans. *Cambridge Texts in the History of Political Thought*, ed. and trans. Cary J. Nederman (Cambridge, UK: Cambridge University Press, 1990), 28–31.

is subordinate to the whole.[18] It follows that if the health of some part, say, a man's leg, threatens the health of his whole body, perhaps because it has contracted gangrene, it is not only legitimate but also salubrious and praiseworthy to amputate the leg for the sake of the body's health. By analogy, the good of the whole community is more perfect than that of any individual member. When on account of grave evildoing a member threatens the welfare of the community, he may be cut off—put to death—for the sake of the community.[19] If carried out by properly constituted civil authority, his killing would not only be legitimate but also salubrious and praiseworthy.

Aquinas asserts what in my judgment is one of the most serious errors in Catholic moral tradition concerning the death penalty. He takes a wrong turn when confronted with an objection based on Christian love. According to the objection, the charity we owe to all people, even evildoers, makes killing malefactors intrinsically evil and therefore a bad means to a good end. In response, Aquinas writes,

> By sinning man departs from the order of reason, and therefore falls away from human dignity, in so far as man is naturally free and exists for his own sake, and falls somehow into the slavery of the beasts, so that he may be disposed of according to what is useful to others. . . . Therefore, although it be evil in itself to kill a man who preserves his human dignity, nevertheless to kill a man who is a sinner can be good, just as it can be good to kill a beast; for an evil man is worse than a beast.[20]

Aquinas' argument is vulnerable to several serious criticisms, which, as I have argued elsewhere, render his defense of capital punishment unsound.[21] The most serious is the assertion that any man or woman can fall from human dignity to the status of a beast.

Admittedly, the meaning of the term "dignity" is not always transparent and can be understood in different (although connected) ways. We might say, for example, without raising serious problems, that grave wrongdoers

---

[18] Aristotle, *Politics*, bk. 1, chap. 2, 1253a18-29, *The Complete Works of Aristotle*, vol. 2, ed. Jonathan Barnes (Princeton: Princeton University Press, 1984), 1988.

[19] *Summa Theologica*, II-II, q. 64, a. 2; see also *Summa Contra Gentiles*, bk. 3, pt. 2, chap. 146, no. 4.

[20] *Summa Theologica*, II-II, q. 64, art. 2, ad. 2.

[21] See E. Christian Brugger, *Capital Punishment and Roman Catholic Moral Tradition* (Notre Dame: University of Notre Dame Press, 2003), 109–11, 165–77; "Aquinas and Capital Punishment: The Plausibility of the Traditional Argument," *Notre Dame Journal of Law, Ethics & Public Policy* 18, no. 2 (April 2004): 357–72.

forfeit their "social dignity" (i.e., the right to a good name and a place of respectability in the community); or that they fall from their "moral dignity" when they freely choose to carry out grossly unjust kinds of behavior; or even that they forfeit their "dignity of self-determination," when, after justice is served, they lose their liberty to share fully in the benefits of life in society.

None of these clarifying phrases correspond to Aquinas's sense of the term "human dignity." He connects human dignity to the "order of reason." Now it is undoubtedly true that evil actions are, in the classical sense, inconsistent with right reasons and in this sense with the "order of reason." So we could say truthfully that every sinful *act* departs (to that extent) from the order of reason. However, Aquinas says something more radical. He says that the *sinner* departs from the order of reason. Now if he merely means "departs from the order of reason in choosing the bad act," there would be no problem. But we know he means more, since he follows with the statement, "and therefore falls away from human dignity" ("decidit a dignitate humana"). In traditions following Aristotle and Aquinas, the concept "human" is an ontological category and is synonymous with "rational animal." Humans, like other animals, are bodily, conscious, and sentient. What elevates them above the status of other animals (of the "beasts") is reason: they are animals governed by the order of reason.

When Aquinas says that by sinning, one falls from human dignity and consequently falls into the slavery of a beast, he evidently, but erroneously, means one forfeits one's status as human. In Aquinas's view, the sinner no longer exists for his own sake and may be treated according to norms governing the way beasts are treated. This view must be rejected. We must reject the idea that we can forfeit our humanity. No transgression, however severe, compromises human dignity. Sinners never fall to the status of subhuman animals. Each person always also exists for one's own sake, never exclusively for the sake of the community, even though the community possesses the right to defend itself against the wrongdoing of its members. No human community has an absolute claim on any of its members. The moral claims to which personal dignity give rise remain intact even in murders. John Paul II makes this point in his encyclical *Evangelium Vitae* when he speaks of "the paradoxical mystery of the merciful justice of God."[22]

Although rejected here, Aquinas's argument in defense of capital punishment has great merit. It is the only substantive argument in the tradition that addresses the most basic objection to capital punishment: notwithstanding

---

[22] John Paul II, *Evangelium Vitae* (Libreria Editrice Vaticana, 1995), 9.

the benefits of killing criminals, capital punishment is still wrong because intrinsic human dignity prohibits us from treating fellow human beings in this way. Aquinas replies, sinners fall from that dignity and so killing them is not the same as killing other human beings; it is morally akin to killing an animal. We have shown that this reply is unsound. Therefore the objection still holds that capital punishment is doing evil to achieve good.

The "Waldensian Oath"

If Aquinas's is the most influential theological treatise of the period, a statement made in 1210 by Pope Innocent III in an oath is the most influential ecclesiastical teaching. The oath was designed to facilitate the reconciliation of a group of heretics called the Waldensians. Certain Waldensians apparently held that capital punishment was evil and that civil authority sins gravely whenever it imposes a capital sentence on anyone. In the oath that Innocent III prescribed for their reconciliation, the pope included the following statement: "We declare that the secular power can without mortal sin impose a judgment of blood provided the punishment is carried out not in hatred but with good judgment, not inconsiderately but after mature deliberation."[23]

Two things should be noted about this statement. First, the proposition strictly asserts only that it is possible for civil authority to inflict capital punishment without committing a mortal sin. It does not assert that the infliction of capital punishment is not a mortal sin, is not sinful, or is not intrinsically evil. Second, even if we take the proposition as teaching that capital punishment is not intrinsically evil, because the oath in which it is included was directed to a particular group and not to the universal church, and since the oath's promulgation was by means of a personal letter to a leader of the heretical group (Durand of Huesca), and not by means of a formal and universally binding document, such as a papal bull or the canon of an ecumenical council, the statement *per se* does not constitute an inalterable doctrine of the church. Nevertheless, it does constitute a teaching of the ordinary magisterium of the papacy and thus holds authority commensurate with such a teaching.[24]

---

[23] *Patrologiae Cursus Completus*, Series Latina, ed. J.P. Migne, vol. 215, col. 1512a, translation supplied.

[24] See Vatican II, *Lumen Gentium*/Dogmatic Constitution on the Church (1964), 25, for an exposition of types of authoritative church teaching and the assent that each requires of Catholics.

What Happened to Christian Consecration?

The chapter began with what I called the bifurcated position of the early fathers of the church. This two-sided view proposed the rights of pagan authorities on the one hand and the role of Christians on the other. The bifurcated view provided Christians in the first three centuries both a theologically elegant and practically workable compromise for dealing with the problem of capital punishment. When the reality of the "pagan world" faded into the memory of history, the pagan-Christian bifurcation became unworkable. Christians became the authorities of the state. Yet, Christians still felt the tension between the exalted vocation to discipleship and the lawful shedding of human blood. By the beginning of the seventh century, the now obsolete pagan-Christian bifurcation found itself reconceived (regretfully) along the lines of laypeople and cleric: laypeople rightfully could administer the justice of this age ("secular authority") while clerics, concerned strictly with the exercise of spiritual authority, were prohibited from all participation in sentencing or inflicting the death penalty.

Conclusion

It might be tempting to impose upon this narrative a falling-from-purity motif. According to this narrative, the primitive Christian community and the patristic church saw capital punishment for what it was: incompatible with the exalted vocation to Christian discipleship and the dignity of the human person made in God's image and likeness. Burdened by the duties of overseeing the administration of temporal justice, Christians began to tolerate and then defend what they had once rejected. This narrative is too simplistic.

Conscientious theological reflection always found tension between Jesus' teaching and the severest duties carried out by temporal authority. In the first centuries of the Christian era this tension resolved itself in the two-part (bifurcated) ethics noted above. A change came in the centuries after Constantine's reign. There occurred an elevation of the sacred realm served by clerics and religious. However, there was not a commensurate elevation of the life of the laity. The elevation of priests and religious was organically and rightly the result of the clarification of Christ's will for the threefold hierarchal constitution of church governance: bishop, priest, and deacon. The failure of the elevation of the realm of the laity was a predictable result of two striking developments: (1) institutionalization of the Catholic Church on a gigantic scale and (2) the accruing of *de facto* secular authority to ecclesiastical leaders. The barbarian invasions of the fourth through the seventh centuries brought a fracturing of the political landscape. Amid the fragmentation of Europe, the only viable public authorities in parts of the former empire were popes, bishops, abbots, and abbesses.

Church leaders became *de facto* secular rulers. Ecclesiastical authority took on, in the mind of the faithful, something of a hybrid status, *politico-ecclesiastical* authority. Respect for the spiritual authority of the hierarchy mixed with the fear and docility that the populace rightly had toward political authority. Moreover, contemporaneous with the barbarian invasions arose the enormously influential turn toward living in monastic community, called the *cenobitic movement*. Living in community, certain Christians would flee "the world" in order to consecrate themselves completely to a strict living of the gospel. Common men and women in these centuries had few vocational choices before them. Already set in place, for most people, was where they lived, their livelihoods, faith, and the authorities to whom they owed allegiance. As the medieval feudal landscape took shape, society became organized into a matrix of hierarchically structured social roles; a person's place in that order was largely determined by birth.[25] As a result, the question of consecrating one's life uniquely to Christ and the gospel was effectively a question of whether or not one should become a priest or religious.

In the next chapter we will see that for many reasons the twentieth century brought a renewed concern for the common vocation of all baptized Christians called equally, though uniquely, to Christlike perfection and the sanctification of the social order through faithfulness to God's will. This renewed awareness carries with it a renewed scrutiny of the compatibility between the universal call to Christian holiness and the killing of criminals by public authority.

Review and Looking Forward

Editors

Throughout history, the issue of capital punishment tangled up with issues of power and authority. What are the rights and obligations of kings, emperors, and heads of state? What is the role of church in relationship to secular authority? Do authorities have the right and power over the life and death of their subjects? Christian Brugger has provided a sketch of how these questions have been asked from ancient times to the begin-

---

[25] For a balanced account of the arising of the elitist notion of the priesthood, see Germain Griesz and Russell Shaw, *Personal Vocation: God Calls Everyone by Name* (Huntington, IN: Our Sunday Visitor Press, 2003), 47–49.

ning of the modern period. He (in chap. 10) and Msgr. Stuart Swetland (in chaps. 11 and 12) will indicate that the answers to these questions gain greater clarity in the twentieth century.

As the story unfolds, both Christian and Msgr. Stuart will draw upon a constitution of the Second Vatican Council, *Lumen Gentium* (Dogmatic Constitution on the Church, 1964). The Constitution's chapter on the laity explains that all the baptized share Christ's office of priest, prophet, and king. Given that this chapter has focused on secular rule, we will highlight the kingly office here. The kingly office addresses the problem (noted by Christian) that the laity's role in the church was not articulated well in the late medieval and early modern periods. *Lumen Gentium* attends to this problem:

> It is the special vocation of the laity to seek the kingdom of God by engaging in temporal affairs and directing them according to God's will. . . . It is their special task to illuminate and order all temporal matters in which they are closely involved in such a way that these are always carried out and develop in Christ's way and to the praise of the Creator and Redeemer. (31)

As a people of God, the church—clergy and laity—is called to live out God's love, mercy, and communion in the world. This call to holiness and the kingly office of our baptism will be important to how the church rethinks capital punishment—"to the praise of the Creator and Redeemer."

Questions for Discussion

1. Blessed John Henry Newman (1801–90) is noted for his understanding of the development of doctrine. In his *Essay on the Development of Christian Doctrine* (1845), he shows that true development gives unity and expression to earlier expressions of faith. Development is not the same as evolution or the idea that basic truths change. Development means that later explanations of doctrine "fill out" and make explicit what is implicit in early stages or times. Can you see an implicit stance or pull against capital punishment in the earlier stages of Christian history?

2. Christian Brugger holds that the early "bifurcated" view of the use of capital punishment cannot be sustained in the Middle Ages. Why? Is there another option?

3. Discuss Christian's worries about oversimplification. What is the temptation to simplify this history (or history in general)? What are the dangers of giving way to the temptation?

Chapter 10

The Church Today

Editors

In 1961, on the eve of Vatican II, Pope John XXIII recalled his thinking in announcing a council of the whole church. He "felt at once the urgent duty to call our children together in order to give the Church the possibility to contribute more effectively to the solutions of the problems of the modern age."[1] The council is remembered for changes in the liturgy, the reestablishment of permanent deacons, a reinvigorated approach to Scripture, an ecumenical spirit, and a statement in support of the freedom of religion. In short, Vatican II is remembered for its reforms.

One of the minds behind Vatican II was Fr. Joseph Ratzinger, that is, Pope Benedict XVI, who was a professor of theology at the University of Bonn and a theological consultant to Cardinal Josef Frings. Father Ratzinger is known to have influenced the "style" of the council, moving away from a "textbook" approach and toward a pastoral, spiritual, and evangelical perspective. He and Cardinal Frings encouraged the council to use "the vital language of Scripture and the Church Fathers."[2] Looking back at the council, Pope Benedict notes that Vatican II "had to focus in particular on the theme of anthropology . . . [and] had to determine in a new way the relationship between the church and the modern era."[3]

"Anthropology," as Benedict uses the term, means an understanding of the human person in his or her relationship to God and God's creation. In other words, one main task of Vatican II was to clarify and deepen our

---

[1] John XXIII, *Humanae Salutis* (December 25, 1961), http://www.vatican.va/holy_father/john_xxiii. See the English translation by Rev. Joseph Komonchak at http://conciliaria.com/2011/12/john-xxiii-convokes-council/.

[2] John W. O'Malley, *What Happened at Vatican II* (Cambridge, MA: Belknap Press, 2008), 76.

[3] Pope Benedict XVI, "Interpreting Vatican II," *Origins* 35:32 (January 26, 2006): 537.

understanding of human life, the dignity of each person, and our fulfillment as God's creatures, and to do so in relationship to the "joys and
hopes, the grief and anguish of the people of our time."[4] From its first
convocation in 1962, the bywords for the council were *aggiornamento* and
ressourcement. *Aggiornamento* identified a need and desire to bring church
life and expressions of our faith up-to-date. *Ressourcement* expresses a need
and desire to return to ancient sources and conceptions of the church.

Often these two ideas were put in opposition: one going forward and
the other going back. Pope Benedict, however, notes that they need not be,
and indeed should not be, set in opposition. Moving forward and looking
back are joined together when we seek to transform contemporary life in
terms of the continuity of past and present. Moving forward and looking
back are united when we begin with the foundation of the faith and seek
the truth. He explains,

> The Second Vatican Council, with its new definition of the re-
> lationship between the faith of the church and certain essential
> elements of modern thought, has reviewed or even corrected cer-
> tain historical decisions, but in this apparent discontinuity it has
> actually preserved her inmost nature and true identity.[5]

Benedict's understanding of Vatican II summarizes Christian Brugger's
approach. Christian charts the changes in attitudes toward and practices
of capital punishment. But he explains that the church's recent stance
against capital punishment is, in a sense, a return to its foundations.

Christian has already emphasized the anthropological question in
chapter 9. Is human dignity essential? As given by God, can a human being
take it away? The questions will be taken up further in chapters 11 and 12.
In this chapter, Christian guides us through developments concerning the
death penalty that follow from the Second Vatican Council. Key to this
development is a statement made in 1976 by the Pontifical Commission
for Justice and Peace. The commission notes that the church's historical
view of capital punishment is changeable, that is, not required by divine
law and not a "definitive" teaching of the church. The Vatican Commission also suggests change, a more critical stance toward the death penalty,
which is put into full effect by Pope John Paul II in *Evangelium Vitae* and
the 1997 edition of the *Catechism of the Catholic Church*.

---

[4] Vatican II, *Gaudium et Spes*/Pastoral Constitution on the Church in the Modern
World (1965), 1.

[5] Benedict XVI, "Interpreting Vatican II," 538.

The Church and Capital Punishment in the Modern Period

E. Christian Brugger

In this chapter we consider the epochal shift in thinking about capital punishment that takes place in the modern period. The shift first expresses itself outside the Catholic Church, among Enlightenment intellectuals in eighteenth-century Europe. It gradually takes root in Catholic thinking in the twentieth century. The shift marks a return in the church—with certain notable differences—to the kind of widespread opposition to capital punishment that we found in the first three centuries of Christianity.

Consistency during Unsettled Times

Catholic thinking on capital punishment from the sixteenth century through the early twentieth remained relatively consistent. Theological treatises,[6] Catholic catechisms,[7] dictionaries,[8] moral manuals,[9] and textbooks in canon law[10] agreed that public authority may rightly inflict death on malefactors for the sake of the common good, and that the authority to inflict it derives from God and is witnessed to in Sacred Scripture. In those texts that philosophically elaborate the issue, the debt to Aquinas is enormous; his part-to-whole and putrid limb analogues are practically ubiquitous.

---

[6] See, for example, the commentaries of the influential Dominican theologian Thomas Cajetan on Aquinas's *Summa Theologica*, written between 1507 and 1522; see especially commentary on q. 64, a. 2, p. 69 from *Commentaries of Thomas Cajetan*, in Aquinas, *Opera Omnia*, tom. IX, Leonine ed. (1897).

[7] The two most influential were the Roman Catechism issued by Pope Pius V in 1566 at the conclusion of the Council of Trent (see *Catechism of the Council of Trent*, part III, chap. VI, par. 4, trans. McHugh and Callan, 421) and the Catechism of Robert Bellarmine, SJ, published in 1597 and in a simpler version in 1598 (see "An Ample Declaration of the Christian Doctrine," trans. Richard Hadock, facsimile in *English Recusant Literature 1558–1640*, ed. D.M. Rogers [London: Scholar Press, 1977]).

[8] See Benedict Ojetti, SJ, *Synopsis Rerum Moralium et Iuris Pontificii*, 3rd ed. (Rome: Polygraphica Editrice, 1911), vol. II, s.v., "Homicidium," col. 2090.

[9] For a small sample of the manualist treatments of capital punishment see Victor Cathrein, SJ, *Philosophia Moralis In Usum Scholarum*, 5th ed. (Freiburg: Herder, 1905), pars. II, lib. II, cap. III, thesis XCIX, nos. 638–41, pp. 467–72; Joanne Petro Gury, SJ, *Compendium Theologiae Moralis* (Regensburg: *Typis et Sumptibus Georgii Josephi Manz.*, 1868), *Tractatus De Praeceptis Decalogi*, 5th Praec., cap. 2, art. 1, nos. 392–93, pp. 176–77.

[10] See Marianus de Luca, *Institutiones Juris Ecclesiastici Publici* (Rome: J. Pustet, Libraria Pontificia, 1901).

Support for the death penalty, however, was not only a Catholic issue. There was no substantial difference in the thinking on the issue among the great Protestant Reformers.[11] With the dissolution of the fragile unity of Western Christianity in the sixteenth and seventeenth centuries, intra-Christian conflict accelerated greatly throughout Europe. The problem of heresy increased (i.e., various Christians obstinately denying accepted tenets of faith). Heresy was by no means new to the period, but the social chaos in Christian Europe precipitated by the Reformation was unprecedented. The "wars of religion" in the sixteenth and seventeenth centuries are a sorry testimony to the lengths that Christians (of all traditions) were willing to go to secure a failing political unity whose religious heart had been eaten out in the fourteenth and fifteenth centuries by the scandals of Christian leadership, principally, but not exclusively, of the papacy.

Be that as it may, heresy could not be ignored. Its threat to the stability of that world is hard for the contemporary mind to grasp. Christians of the period, especially the Catholic Church, are not infrequently reproached with cruelty and intolerance for their willingness to shed blood over issues of faith. But in a world in which the principal unifying factor among peoples was not ethnic, racial, national, or economic identity, but Christian identity, a rupture in the system of belief could and did result in grave social disorder: heresy was a disease in the civil organism "more malignant than treason."[12] Unfortunately, capital punishment became a widely accepted, defended, and sometimes abused means of dealing with heresy.[13]

Amid the turmoil of the era, the eighteenth century saw the rise of popular movements for abolition of the death penalty in Europe. At first, the Catholic Church (and mainline Protestant communions) had little role to play in their success. The earliest defenders of abolition were invariably bitter critics of the church and the Christian faith (e.g., Voltaire, Robespierre and Diderot in France, Fichte in Germany, and Hume and Bentham in Britain). This played as much a role in shaping initial Catholic opposition to the cause of abolition as did the church's centuries-old support for the

[11] More radical sixteenth-century reform movements, such as the Anabaptists, rejected offices of secular authority and so participation in capital punishment; their successors today (e.g., Amish and Mennonites) still practice pacifism to differing degrees.

[12] For an illustration of characteristic Catholic theological thinking on the issue at the turn of the twentieth century, see *Catholic Encyclopedia*, 1911 ed., s.v. "Heresy."

[13] See the defense of killing heretics by the influential Spanish Jesuit philosopher Francisco Suarez (d. 1617) in Suarez, *Opera Omnia* (1856), tom. 12, tract. I, disp. 23, sec.1, 577, disputation 23 titled "whether it is lawful for the Church to punish Heretics with death."

institution. Early Catholic voices for abolition were not entirely absent.[14] However, they were muted in comparison to the more common voices who repeated the traditional view.

The Twentieth-Century "Turn" toward Opposition

The dramatic realignment of religious-political loyalties on the continent of Europe between the seventeenth and nineteenth centuries witnessed swift and significant marginalization of the Catholic Church from the heart of secular affairs. With the dispossession of the final remnants of the Papal States by Italian nationalist forces in 1870, the church's thousand-year experiment in temporal rule was ended. The loss of the Papal States was seen as catastrophic. But in hindsight, we can see the benefit, for the church became free to dedicate all its energies to administering its rightful domain of authority over the spiritual lives of the faithful. By the time Pope Leo XIII published his great social encyclical *Rerum Novarum* in 1891, on the condition of the European working classes, the church's historic transition from powerful administrator of secular affairs to privileged commentator on the social realm was practically complete.

The death penalty was not a topic of significance in Catholic writings or church teachings in the first half of the twentieth century. Influential Catholic texts such as the English language *Catholic Encyclopedia* (1911) and the French *Dictionnaire de Théologie Catholique* (1929)[15] hand on traditional accounts, including the recent history of the rise of abolitionist efforts, but firmly conclude in defense of capital punishment. Certain popes of the period (e.g., Leo XIII, Pius XI, and Pius XII) make passing references to the death penalty's legitimacy when treating other topics, but do not turn their attention directly to assessing its morality.[16]

---

[14] The earliest Catholic abolitionist writing that I have been able to find is from 1786 by an Italian priest, Cesare Malanima, who argues that the New Testament annuls the Old Testament precepts prescribing death for crimes and therefore the death penalty should be repudiated by Christians; see C. Malanima, *Commento filologico critico sopra i delitti e le pene secondo il gius divino* (Livorno, 1786).

[15] *Dictionnaire de Théologie Catholique*, A. Vacant and E. Mangenot (1929), s.v. "Mort (Peine De)," tom. 10, col. 2504.

[16] Leo XIII notes its legitimacy indirectly in a pastoral letter on dueling in 1891 (*Acta Apostolica Sedis* 24, [1891/92] 204b); Pius XI in chap. 4 of his 1930 encyclical on Christian Marriage (*Casti Connubii*) and Pius XII in an address to Catholic jurists in 1955 (AAS 47, 1955) do something similar.

The early 1970s marked a significant turning point in regard to eccle-siastical teaching on the death penalty. The US bishops went public for the first time in opposition to the death penalty in 1974. As a body, they made the following terse statement: "the US Catholic Conference goes on record in opposition to capital punishment."[17] Brief gestures of opposi-tion were made again in 1977 and 1978. Finally, in 1980, the US bishops published their lengthy Statement on Capital Punishment. They outlined ten reasons supporting the conclusion that "in the conditions of contem-porary American society, the legitimate purposes of punishment do not justify the imposition of the death penalty."[18] The 1980 document stood at the head of a long line of subsequent statements by both the conference of US bishops and individual bishops opposing capital punishment.[19] In 2005, on the twenty-fifth anniversary of the 1980 Statement, the United States Conference of Catholic Bishops (USCCB) published a successor document, A Culture of Life and the Penalty of Death, which opens with these words: "Twenty-five years ago, our Conference of bishops first called for an end to the death penalty. We renew this call to seize a new moment and new momentum."[20]

The Vatican went on record against the death penalty for the first time in 1976. The US bishops, preparing ideas that would eventually be taught in their 1980 Statement, had petitioned Rome for clarity on the status of capital punishment's legitimacy in church teaching. The Pontifical Commission for

[17] Resolution passed by the USCC, Nov. 18, 1974, in *Pastoral Letters of the United States Catholic Bishops*, ed. Hugh J. Nolan (Washington, DC: USCCB, 1984), vol. 3, 464.

[18] United States Conference of Catholic Bishops, Statement on Capital Punishment (Washington, DC: USCCB, 1980), in Nolan, *Pastoral Letters*, vol. 4, 427–34.

[19] In 2000, the US bishops wrote, "It is time to abandon the death penalty—not just because of what it does to those who are executed, but because of how it diminishes all of us. . . . We ask all Catholics—pastors, catechists, educators and parishioners—to join us in rethinking this difficult issue and committing ourselves to pursuing justice without vengeance. With our Holy Father, we seek to build a society so committed to human life that it will not sanction the killing of any human person." USCCB, Respon-sibility, Rehabilitation, and Restoration: A Catholic Perspective on Crime and Criminal Justice (Washington, DC: USCCB, 2000); see also A Good Friday Appeal to End the Death Penalty, by the Administrative Board of the USCCB (1999): "We oppose capital punishment not just for what it does to those guilty of horrible crimes but for what it does to all of us as a society."

[20] United States Conference of Catholic Bishops, A Culture of Life and the Penalty of Death, (Washington, DC: USCCB, 2005). Both the 1980 and the 2005 statements can be accessed at the web site of the USCCB's Catholic Campaign to End the Use of the Death Penalty, www.usccb.org/deathpenalty.

Justice and Peace replied with the statement The Church and the Death Penalty.[21] The text offers several assertions by way of summarizing the contents of Catholic teaching over the centuries:

1. The state has the right to enforce capital punishment.
2. Capital punishment is neither contrary to nor required by divine law.
3. The church has never "directly addressed the question of the state's right" to kill malefactors.
4. The church has never condemned its use, but it has "condemned" a denial of the right to its use (viz., in Innocent's Oath to the Waldensians).
5. In recent years, the church has emphasized "the rights of the person and the medicinal role of punishment." The "medicinal role" refers to the capacity of punishment to exercise a morally restorative influence on the criminal.

The Vatican document ends with an unusually strong statement: "Therefore, without reference to the American constitutional question, it can be concluded that capital punishment is outside the realm of practicable just punishments."[22]

It is interesting to note that this Vatican statement was drafted during the pontificate of Paul VI, two years before the election of John Paul II. In effect, the universal turn toward opposition to the death penalty was already underway when Cardinal Wojtyla was elected to the papacy. The third proposition is also interesting: The church has never "directly addressed the question of the state's right" to kill malefactors. "Directly addressed," it seems to me, should be interpreted to mean "universally and definitively addressed." To say that the church has never "directly addressed" the question means it has never "definitively taught" a judgment on the state's right to kill malefactors, neither in the form of a definition by an ecumenical council, nor through an exercise of papal infallibility. The point seems to me perfectly true.[23] We can say, then, that the "traditional" Catholic defense of the death penalty has been authoritatively but not definitively taught.

---

[21] The Pontifical Commission for Justice and Peace, "The Church and the Death Penalty," *Origins* (December 9, 1976), 389, 391–92.

[22] Ibid., 391.

[23] For a more complete defense of this assertion, see E. Christian Brugger, *Capital Punishment and Roman Catholic Moral Tradition* (Notre Dame: University of Notre Dame Press, 2003), 142–52.

By the time John Paul II turned his critical pen to the problem in 1995, in his greatest of great encyclicals, *Evangelium Vitae* (56), the Catholic Church's decisive turn toward abolition was already twenty years old. This encyclical, The Gospel of Life, marks the strongest opposition to capital punishment of the ordinary magisterium in Christian history. Its teaching was codified in an even more authoritative form when its analysis, whole and entire, was incorporated into death penalty teaching of the 1997 typical edition of the *Catechism of the Catholic Church* (2262–65).

The teaching of the *Evangelium Vitae* and the *Catechism*, it must be said, is not a continuation of the classical defense of the state's right to kill criminals as formulated in the theological tradition. It departs from the traditional analysis. By reconceiving an act of legitimate penal killing in terms of self-defense, the papal analysis intentionally distances itself from the classical retributive paradigm set forth clearly at least since Trent. It now assesses the legitimacy of the death penalty in terms of norms traditionally used (at least since Aquinas) to assess the legitimacy of killing aggressors by private persons in cases of self-defense. *Nowhere in those two texts (encyclical or Catechism), nor anywhere in the entire corpus of papal teaching of Pope John Paul II (and, for that matter, of Benedict XVI[24]), does the pope either directly assert or even imply that the state has the "right" to kill malefactors for what they have done.* Until this is brought out clearly by Catholic theologians, John Paul II's epochal contribution to the centuries-old conversation will not be properly understood.

Conclusion

We might ask, what happened? What accounts for the dramatic return in the twentieth century to the widespread sentiments against capital punishment of the first three centuries? This question deserves more attention than I am able to give it here. But I will briefly propose seven reasons that seem to make sense of the turn:

1. As noted above, beginning at the end of the nineteenth century, the Catholic Church was forcibly freed from the responsibility for administrating secular justice. Those territories of central and southern Italy known as the Papal States under direct sovereign rule of the papacy since the early Middle Ages required the pope to exercise temporal

---

[24] See the new preface to the 2nd edition of Brugger, *Capital Punishment and Roman Catholic Moral Tradition* (forthcoming), treating the death penalty teaching of Pope Benedict XVI.

power, including the administration of criminal justice, in addition to ecclesiastical primacy. The dissolution of the Papal States provided the papacy once again with the salutary and ancient opportunity of exclusively administrating spiritual authority.

2. As suggested in the fifth point of the Pontifical Commission document, the church in the twentieth century began surveying the good of the human person in terms of the notion of subjective rights. I suggest this turned attention in a new way to moral claims arising from the intrinsic dignity of every person, including malefactors. It was only in the second half of the twentieth century that the right to life began to be affirmed as "inalienable" and "inviolable" in church teaching.[25] If those terms are taken seriously, it poses an ethical problem for the type of intentional killing that capital punishment entails.

3. The wanton disregard for human life in the twentieth century, the reckless use of civil authority, and the rise and dominance of avowedly atheistic states led to an erosion of confidence in the state's prerogative to exercise lethal punishment.

4. The gradual global legalization of the intentional killing of the unborn precipitated a reconsideration of the legitimacy of all forms of state-sanctioned killing. This is not to say that the two types of killing—of the innocent vs. of duly convicted criminals—are morally commensurate in all respects. They are not. Yet the church's rightful outspoken defense of innocent human life in the second half of the twentieth century corresponded tightly to its increasingly strong assertion of the "unconditional" respect due to all human life (see *Evangelium Vitae*, 28, 60, 75, 77).

5. Evolving attitudes toward religion and life after death over the past two hundred years influenced the valuation that people gave to temporal life. If the present life is all there is, then the prospect of death becomes menacingly final. Avery Dulles, SJ, writes, "When death came to be understood as the ultimate evil rather than as a stage on the way to eternal life, utilitarian philosophers such as Jeremy Bentham found it easy to dismiss capital punishment as 'useless annihilation.'"[26] Alone, this provides no reason for Christians to reassess issues of

---

[25] The first explicit assertion of human rights as "inalienable" and "inviolable" is by Bl. John XXIII, *Pacem in Terris* (Libreria Editrice Vaticana, 1963), 9, 27, 47, 60, 79, 145; see also John Paul II, *Evangelium Vitae*, 5, 20, 40, 53, 81, 87; cf. 89.

[26] Avery Cardinal Dulles, SJ, "The Death Penalty: A Right to Life Issue" (Laurence J. McGinley Lecture, Fordham University, Oct. 17, 2000), 9.

life and death. But if through the disbelief of non-Christians, greater global attention was drawn to the problem of state-sanctioned killing, that attention could very well, under the influence of the other reasons mentioned above, contribute to a reevaluation.

6. The expanding dialogue of the church with secular society offered opportunity to think sympathetically rather than polemically about issues, such as abolition of capital punishment, that occupied secular thinkers since the nineteenth century.[27]

7. We should not disregard the possibility that among the many reasons accounting for the church's "turn" toward abolition, the most significant is because of the prompting of the Holy Spirit. Is it possible that capital punishment has always been contrary to God's plan for humankind, but that Christians, shaped by a history in which it would have been unthinkable to seriously question the state's "right" to kill, took a long time to open to the Spirit's promptings? No one who reads the consistently and universally negative treatments on capital punishment of the Catholic hierarchy in the past forty years can discount this as a real possibility.

Review and Looking Forward

Editors

We introduced the chapter with Pope Benedict XVI's perspective on Vatican II. Benedict notes that a view of the human person (i.e., theological anthropology) was a key task of the council. Its understanding of the person, as God's image and made for love for God and neighbor, has been important for subsequent developments pertaining to the death penalty. At the beginning of the Pastoral Constitution on the Church in the Modern World, the council states its purpose of

> throwing the light of the Gospel on them [humankind] and supplying humanity with the saving resources which the church has received from its founder under the promptings of the holy Spirit. It is the human person that is to be saved, human society which must be renewed. It is the human person, therefore, which is the key to this discussion, each individual human person in her or his totality, body and soul, heart and conscience, mind and will. (3)

---

[27] It is interesting to note that death was prescribed under Vatican City law for killing a pope for much of the twentieth century. Pope Paul VI quietly retired the statute in 1969.

In chapter 11, Msgr. Stuart Swetland will focus on the relationship between the church's anthropology and the revision of the *Catechism*'s teaching on the death penalty. He will call the revision "a true development of the church's teaching" in the sense described by Pope Benedict in reference to Vatican II. In chapter 12, Msgr. Stuart will go further, echoing Vatican II, that the message of divine mercy and forgiveness is a resource of the church that she is called to offer to the world.

Questions for Discussion

1. In matters like capital punishment, the development of the church's teaching requires (at least) (a) that the issue is a matter that is "changeable," and (b) that the development brings greater consistency with and expression to changeless truth. A true development will not reject past teaching, but will offer an explanation of it as well as of the transition through time. Are these two elements present in relation to the death penalty?

2. In chapters 9 and 10, Christian Brugger has attempted to give a brief overview of a complicated history. It is a difficult task. Do you have any open questions? Were there gaps in the narrative? Keep them in mind as Msgr. Stuart recounts the catechetical tradition and this history of the *Catechism* that we have today.

Chapter 11

The *Catechism* in Historical Perspective

Editors

"*Gaudium et Spes*, the *Pastoral Constitution on the Church in the Modern World*, would retain a privileged place in the thinking and affections of Karol Wojtyla for the rest of his life." The statement is made by George Weigel in his *Witness to Hope: The Biography of John Paul II*. Weigel explains that Archbishop Wojtyla's "primary contribution to the Second Vatican Council involved what eventually became the *Pastoral Constitution on the Church in the Modern World*."[1] The archbishop was passionate about the church's pastoral and evangelical interaction with the world—sharing the anxieties, worries, joys, and hopes of modern men and women. To this degree, the Pastoral Constitution had a profound effect on the future pope as well. Weigel points specifically to "the Christ-centered anthropology" of *Gaudium et Spes* 22.

In January 1959, John XXIII announced the convocation of a Vatican council. Just seven months before, Karol Wojtyla was consecrated as a bishop. He was only thirty-eight years old. But he had seen a lot of life. His mother died when he was eight, his sister before he was born, his brother when he was twelve, his father when he was twenty-one. He had lived through Nazi occupation and Communist rule. He had been a laborer in a limestone quarry and chemical factory. At one point, he had to go into hiding from the Nazi police. Later, he lived the precarious life of a priest under Communism. He was a man of arts and letters who hoped

---

[1] George Weigel, *Witness to Hope: The Biography of Pope John Paul II* (New York: HarperCollins, 1999), 169, 166.

"to grasp 'God, inscrutable in the mystery of man's inmost life' through his poetry, plays, and his philosophical essays" (ibid., 160).

According to Weigel, Wojtyla experienced Vatican II as a profoundly spiritual gathering and with great intellectual excitement. In 1959, as soon as he was given the chance, then- Bishop Wojtyla sent an essay to the commission that was preparing documents for the council:

> Rather than beginning with what the Church needed to do to reform its own house, he adopted a quite different starting point. What, he asked, is the human condition today? What do the men and women of this age expect to hear from the Church? . . . What was Christian humanism and how was it different from the sundry other humanisms on offer in late modernity? What was the Church's answer to modernity's widespread "despair [about] any and all human existence"? (ibid., 159)

Given these questions, it makes sense that the archbishop of Krakow would be deeply involved in discussions of religious freedom, the vocation of the laity in the world, and, as noted, the Pastoral Constitution on the Church in the Modern World.

Weigel calls John Paul II "a son of the Council" (155) and points, in particular, to two themes of *Gaudium et Spes*: not only the Christ-centered view of human persons in section 22, but also the deeply social and relational nature of human beings in 24. The first theme is a "humanism enriched by the human encounter with Christ, who far from alienating humanity, reveals to it the full truth of its dignity and glorious destiny" (ibid., 169). The second follows from the revelation of our humanity in Christ. It is the truth that we are fulfilled as human beings through our self-giving. "'Love therefore is the fulfillment of the Law' (Rom. 13:9-10; cf. 1 John 4:20). . . . [M]an, who is the only creature on earth which God willed for itself, cannot fully find himself except through a sincere gift of himself" (*Gaudium et Spes* 24).

In this chapter and the next, these two themes (Christ-centered and relational anthropology) will be developed under the heading of personalism by Msgr. Stuart Swetland, a professor of moral philosophy and Christian ethics. Here, Msgr. Stuart will show the connections between Christian humanism and the church's engagement with the world. In the next chapter, he will show the deep connection between John Paul II's Christ-centered philosophy of the person and his development of the church's teaching on the death penalty. The history of development outlined by Msgr. Stuart parallels the outline offered by Christian Brugger in chapters 9 and 10. However, as Msgr. Stuart focuses on the catechetical tradition, he is able to describe the nuance and richness of the Catholic theology of the human person, particularly in the work of Pope John Paul II.

The Catechetical Tradition

Msgr. Stuart W. Swetland

The teaching on the death penalty in the catechetical tradition has developed significantly over time. Concerning the issue, revisions were made in the *Catechism of the Catholic Church* between its initial publication in 1992 in French and its official Latin version in 1997.[2] The revisions are noteworthy. A catechism is meant to be a compendium of the teaching of an ecclesial community. For Catholics, the *Catechism of the Catholic Church* is to be seen, according to Blessed John Paul II, as "a sure norm for teaching the faith."[3] In effect, the revisions on the death penalty reflect a true development of the church's teaching.

This chapter will review the development of this catechetical teaching. The modern catechetical tradition begins in the late medieval period. In chapter 10, Christian Brugger noted the effects of religious upheaval and fragmentation in the sixteenth century. During this time, the catechetical tradition takes a more definitive form in the writings of the Protestant reformer Martin Luther and the Catholic bishops and theologians associated with the Counter-Reformation.[4] Like Christian's approach in chapters 9 and 10, I will give a brief history and then emphasize twentieth-century developments. The main modern development is what I will call the "personalist" turn. Personalism focuses on the dignity of each person in relationship to God—as the image of God—and in relationship to others, as we are created for communion.

In short, the catechetical teaching on capital punishment is developed through a theology of the human person. The personalist turn is the basis for Christian Brugger's critique of Aquinas in chapter 9. Recall his claim that "the most serious [problem with Aquinas's view] is the assertion that any man or woman can fall from human dignity to the status of a beast."

[2] The initial English version was published in 1994, and the second, revised English edition was published in 1997 (at the same time as the Latin).

[3] John Paul II, apostolic letter, *Laetamur Magnopere* (Libreria Editrice Vaticana, 1997); cf. apostolic constitution, *Fidei Depositum*, 4.

[4] Gerard S. Sloyan, "Religious Education: From Early Christianity to Medieval Times," *Source Book for Modern Catholics*, ed. Michael Warren (Winona, MN: Saint Mary's Press, 1983), 110–11.

Persons have a status and dignity that we ourselves do not create and cannot destroy. Our dignity as God's image is God's gift of creation. In light of this theology of the person, capital punishment becomes an important pastoral and evangelical concern for Pope John Paul II. To proclaim the gospel of life and the reality of creation and redemption is the task of the church today.

Catechism of the Council of Trent

Before the advent of modern democratic procedures, very few Christians were affected by the question of the death penalty. Not surprisingly, therefore, it is not a major focus of the catechetical tradition. In the *Catechism of the Council of Trent*, capital punishment is discussed under the fifth commandment ("Thou shall not kill"). The discussion is in a section dedicated to "exceptions" to the prohibition. This section discusses why the killing of animals, the execution of criminals, killing in a just war, killing by accident, and killing in self-defense are not forbidden by the fifth commandment. The paragraph on the "execution of criminals" states,

> Another kind of lawful slaying belongs to the civil authorities, to whom is entrusted power of life and death, by the legal and judicious exercise of which they punish the guilty and protect the innocent. The just use of this power, far from involving the crime of murder, is an act of paramount obedience to this Commandment which prohibits murder. The end of the Commandment is the preservation and security of human life. Now the punishments inflicted by the civil authority, which is the legitimate avenger of crime, naturally tend to this end, since they give security to life by repressing outrage and violence. Hence these words of David: *In the morning I put to death all the wicked of the land, that I might cut off all the workers of iniquity from the city of the Lord* (Ps 101:8).[5]

As Christian Brugger has shown in chapter 9, this is rather typical of the teaching of Christian churches since the fourth century.

For example, Martin Luther's *Large Catechism* (1529) exempted the government from the commandment, "You shall not kill," because of its delegated authority to punish evildoers:

---

[5] *Catechism of the Council of Trent for Parish Priests: Issued by Order of Pope Pius V*, trans. John McHugh, OP, and Charles J. Callan, OP (New York: Wagner, 1923), 421

We have now dealt with both the spiritual and the civil government that is divine and paternal authority and obedience. In this commandment we leave our own house and go out among our neighbors to learn how we should conduct ourselves individually towards our fellow men. Therefore neither God nor the government is included in this commandment, yet their right to take human life is not abrogated. God has delegated his authority of punishing evil-doers to civil magistrates in place of parents; in early times, as we read in Moses, parents had to bring their own children to judgment and sentence them to death. Therefore what is forbidden here applies to private individuals, not to governments.[6]

Thus, the standard catechetical teaching in the early modern period of most Christian churches accepted the state's right to execute criminals. The only exceptions were to be found among small Anabaptist groups (forerunners to modern Mennonites, Amish, and Quakers) who adopted belief systems rooted in pacifism.

There was very little change in the catechetical traditions of the churches on the death penalty for the next several centuries. There is some evidence even that the question was not controversial at all despite movements to abolish the use of the death penalty by some early reformers in some secular jurisdictions. For example, Cardinal James Gibbons of Baltimore did not directly mention the death penalty in his controversial best-selling apologetic work of the late nineteenth century, *The Faith of Our Fathers: Being a Plain Exposition and Vindication of the Church Founded by Our Lord Jesus Christ*. Similarly, no direct mention of the death penalty is made in the more universal *Catechism of Christian Doctrine* published by order of Pope St. Pius X in 1908. In fact, no mention is made in this brief catechism of any "exceptions" to the fifth commandment; rather it teaches that "homicide, suicide, dueling, fighting, blows, injuries, curses and scandal" are prohibited.[7]

The Baltimore Catechism

The first official catechisms in the United States were commissioned by the American bishops when they gathered in the premier see of Baltimore. The first such catechism was published in the late nineteenth century

---

[6] Martin Luther, *Large Catechism*, trans. J.N. Lenker (Minneapolis: Augsburg, 1967), 389.
[7] *Catechism of the Council of Trent for Parish Priests*, McHugh and Callan.

(1884) and became known as the *Baltimore Catechism*. Revised many times and adapted to various age levels, this question-and-answer *Catechism* was the standard catechetical text in the United States up to the 1960s. Question 253 (of 499) deals with what is forbidden by the fifth commandment:

> The fifth commandment forbids murder and suicide, and also fighting, anger, hatred, revenge, drunkenness, reckless driving, and bad example. *Everyone who hates his brother is a murderer. And you know that no murderer has eternal life abiding in him. (I John 3:15)*

In contrast to Luther's writing, which exempts governments, the *Baltimore Catechism* states that "the direct intention to kill an innocent is never permissible, either by public or private authority" (164).

The key term "innocent" does allow for the "normal exceptions" of self-defense, killing in a just war, and capital punishment. In this sense, the opposite of "innocent" is "aggressor." The opposite is not "guilty" as some might suppose. Self-defense is used against an aggressor for the sake of the innocent (nonaggressors). The text reads,

> The life of another person may lawfully be taken: first, in order to protect one's own life or that of a neighbor, or a serious amount of possessions from an unjust aggressor, provided no other means of protection is effective; second by a soldier fighting a just war; third, by a duly appointed executioner of the state when he metes out a just punishment for a crime.[8]

Like the other catechetical texts cited here, the *Baltimore Catechism* treated these cases as "exceptions" to the moral law about refraining from killing. This approach was both legalistic and minimalistic and tended to encourage Catholics to be good at "keeping the rules" but not necessarily to know the reasons behind the law.

However, these texts make clear that in the catechetical tradition there was a twofold purpose to the use of the death penalty. As the *Catechism of the Council of Trent* puts it, these purposes are to "punish the guilty and protect the innocent." These reasons were universally accepted in the standard moral textbooks of the day as well. They may be further refined as the retributive, reformative, deterrent, and protective purposes of punishment.[9] It was assumed that the use of the death penalty fulfilled these purposes.

---

[8] John A. O'Brien, *Understanding the Catholic Faith* (South Bend: Ave Maria Press, 1959).

[9] Cf. Karl H. Peschke, SVD, *Christian Ethics (Volume II): Special Moral Theology* (Alchester, UK: C. Goodliffe Newl, 1985), 270–71.

This went without question. Even as late as the 1950s, Pope Pius XII was defending the use of the death penalty and the Vatican City State kept the death penalty as a possible punishment for an attempted or successful assassination of a pope until Paul VI repealed it in 1969.[10] By then many had begun to question whether the death penalty served any ethical purpose.

A Personalist Turn

Despite this long tradition, there were several movements occurring simultaneously that began to shift the church's magisterium (official teachers) on the death penalty. First, the patristic movement, led by French theologians such as Henri de Lubac, SJ, Yves Congar, OP, and Jean Daniélou, SJ, was rediscovering early texts that focused on the radicalism of Jesus' teaching on nonviolence and brought into question the use of the death penalty. For example, it is generally accepted that early martyrs such as St. Clement of Rome and St. Justin Martyr were absolutely opposed to Christian involvement in the application of the death penalty. Saint Clement put his opposition this way: "To witness a man's execution, regardless of the justice of his prosecution, is forbidden by the moral law of Christ, for to assist at the killing of a man is almost the same as killing him."

Second, the historical and biblical movement in the Catholic Church was reemphasizing the words and teaching of Jesus and examining the development of doctrine through space and time. In addition, the gross misuse of the death penalty by dictators of Fascist and Communist regimes brought it into disrepute with many. Positively, the widespread abuses of basic human rights led many to emphasize the importance of defending individuals against abusive governmental powers and actions.

In the secular world, the philosophical movement known as personalism with its emphasis on the dignity of each human person began growing in influence. Politically, the *General Character of the United Nations* (1945) and the subsequent *Universal Declaration of Human Rights* (1948) made human dignity a central tenet of moral thinking. These efforts were aided and inspired by the work of Catholic authors such as Jacques Maritain, Peter Maurin, Charles Péguy, and Étienne Gilson.

These intellectual, political, and historical movements help form the spiritual and intellectual milieu surrounding the pontificate of Blessed

---

[10] Michael A. Norko, "The Death Penalty in Catholic Teaching and Medicine: Intersections and Places for Dialogue," *Journal of the American Academy of Psychiatry and the Law* 36 (2008): 470–81.

John XXIII and the calling of the Second Vatican Council (1962–65). At this time, the church articulates a theological account of the human person. It is an account that gives a deeper sense of human dignity than even the modern human rights revolution. The dignity of the person is expressed in John XXIII's *Pacem in Terris* (1963) and the work of the council, in particular *Dignitatis Humanae* (1965) and *Gaudium et Spes* (1965). This "personalistic turn" is particularly important in the death penalty debate because it helped focus the argument on two elements previously underdeveloped: (1) the dignity of each and every human person, even one who has committed a grave crime; and (2) the remedial or medicinal element in punishment.

In *Pacem in Terris* (1963), John XXIII writes in a way that foreshadows the church's stance for life in what John Paul II will call a "culture of death":

> Any human society, if it is to be well-ordered and productive, must lay down as a foundation this principle, namely, that every human being is a person, that is, his nature is endowed with intelligence and free will. By virtue of this, he has rights and duties of his own, flowing directly and simultaneously from his very nature. These rights are therefore universal, inviolable and inalienable. (9)

Here one sees an emphasis on the inviolability of human rights. This understanding corrects a more ancient tradition, a view (as Christian Brugger has noted) that was even adopted by St. Thomas Aquinas at times. Pope John XXIII counters the view that one could lose one's status as a human person and be reduced to the level of a "beast" or be seen as a "diseased limb" that needed to be excised from the political body.

In addition, there were renewed efforts in the church and the secular world in the area of prison reform and increased interest in programs of restorative justice. Much of this interest was fueled by popular literature and movies such as *Cool Hand Luke* and *The Birdman of Alcatraz*. As Rutgers University English Professor H. Bruce Franklin notes, "The true nature and functions of the American prison started to become known through the tremendous surge of prison literature in the late 1960s and early 1970s. The river of prison literature poured into public culture in books, songs, journals, and movies, dramatically influencing the political movement of that period."[11] The desire to help prisoners reform brought into question

---

[11] H. Bruce Franklin, *"The American Prison and the Normalization of Torture,"* www
.historiansagainstwar.org/resources/torture/brucefranklin.html.

the effectiveness of a whole host of criminal justice practices, not the least was of which capital punishment.

By 1974, the United States Conference of Catholic Bishops went on record against the use of the death penalty. They continued to hold this position even after the Oklahoma City bombing (of a federal building) and the multiple terror attacks of September 11, 2001. In fact, Howard Bromberg has documented numerous major church statements against the death penalty:

> There have been hundreds of statements opposing capital pun-
> ishments from American conferences of bishops over the last few
> decades. For many reasons, including the fact that the United States
> is one of the few predominantly Christian or advanced nations to
> retain capital punishment, it is worthwhile to note the uniformity
> of its Catholic episcopacy in following Pope John Paul II in op-
> posing capital punishment. Not only has every state's conference
> of bishops called for the abolition of capital punishment, but they
> have done so explicitly quoting or following *Evangelium Vitae.* . . .
> Taken together, these statements document a shift in the major
> religious bodies of North America, in the period from 1956 to the
> 1980s, from supporting to opposing the death penalty—a "crusade
> against capital punishment."[12]

Bromberg emphasizes that the number and uniformity of these statements is worthy of note. There are "twenty-two statements from American
Catholic bishops and bishops' conferences on the issue of capital punishment dating from 1960 through 1989 . . . [as well as] official statements
on capital punishment by Canadian Catholic bishops, from Eastern Orthodox Churches, from Protestant communities, from Jewish groups, and
from other religious bodies" (ibid.).

From a Christian perspective, the modern emphasis on human dignity
is a reclaiming of the moral ramifications flowing from the theological
anthropology of creation. Each and every person is a being created in the
image and likeness of God. Even after the Fall, the book of Genesis (and
the entirety of the Hebrew and Christian Scriptures) makes clear that God
desires a real relationship with every person regardless of race, creed, or
social status. In fact, Jesus' life and teaching suggest a preferential option

---

[12] Howard Bromberg, "Pope John Paul II, Vatican II, and Capital Punishment," *Ave
Maria Law Review* 6:1 (Fall 2007): 125, n. 47. Bromberg cites J. Gordon Melton, *The
Churches Speak on Capital Punishment* (Farmington Hills, MI: Gale Group, 1989), 1–52.

for those most depraved and lost. He proclaims God's mercy in leaving the ninety-nine to seek the one who is lost (Matt 18:12-14).

Conclusion

Central to this chapter and to the teaching of capital punishment is what I have called the personalist turn. As we move forward to the next chapter, we will see this emphasis on the dignity of each and every person in the writings of John Paul II. As a young priest and scholar, the then-Karol Wojtyla attempted a philosophical and theological synthesis building on the ancient traditions of the Catholic faith but also utilizing insights gleaned from the modern philosophical methods of personalism and phenomenology. A major contributor to the reforms of the Second Vatican Council, John Paul II mined the council documents to emphasize the church's concern for the dignity of every human person.

For example, in *Redemptor Hominis* (1979), his very first encyclical as pope, John Paul II reminded the world that the church's mission is to be of service to the human person:

> This man is the way for the Church—a way that, in a sense, is the basis of all the other ways that the Church must walk—because man—every man without any exception whatever—has been redeemed by Christ, and because with man—with each man without any exception whatever—Christ is in a way united, even when man is unaware of it: "Christ, who died and was raised up for all, provides man"—each man and every man—"with the light and the strength to measure up to his supreme calling."
>
> Since this man is the way for the Church, the way for her daily life and experience, for her mission and toil, the Church of today must be aware in an always new manner of man's "situation." That means that she must be aware of his possibilities, which keep returning to their proper bearings and thus revealing themselves. She must likewise be aware of the threats to man and of all that seems to oppose the endeavor "to make human life ever more human" and make every element of this life correspond to man's true dignity—in a word, she must be aware of all that is opposed to that process. (14)

John Paul II's emphasis on the dignity of every human person will have significant ramifications for his teaching on the death penalty.

Review and Looking Forward

Editors

In 1985, an extraordinary synod of bishops met during the twentieth-year anniversary of the close of Vatican II. Among various affirmations and interpretations of the council, the synod proposed that a new catechism be prepared—a "compendium of all Catholic doctrine regarding both faith and morals."[13] In the next chapter, Msgr. Stuart will recount the development of the *Catechism's* teaching on capital punishment. At this point, we will point out the similarities between the *Catechism* and the style and concerns of Vatican II and the papacy of John Paul II. We wish to point out only that the changes in approach to the death penalty fit with an overall engagement of faith in our times and the church's expression of hope for the world.

The first point to make is that the *Catechism* is not structured on a question-and-answer format that is to be memorized by rote, but reads more like theological prose that provides understanding and an orientation to key elements of the Christian life. The first part reflects upon the nature of belief and then explains the Apostles' Creed. The second part develops a "sacramental" orientation to our faith and then reviews the seven sacraments. The third part draws on themes of the moral life in the context of our relational and social nature—in our relationships to God and one another. Then it develops the good of life and human fulfillment in the context of the Ten Commandments. The fourth part discusses the life of prayer, its struggles and fruits, and turns to an explication of the Lord's Prayer. Following the guidelines of Vatican II, the *Catechism* draws heavily on Scripture. Moreover, "the documents of the Second Vatican Council are cited almost 800 times. . . . *Lumen Gentium* [the Dogmatic Constitution on the Church] and *Gaudium et Spes* [the Pastoral Constitution on the Church in the Modern World] are the two most frequently quoted Vatican II texts."[14]

In short, the teaching on capital punishment, as it develops through the *Catechism*, is an encapsulation of the story of the church's evangelical and pastoral role in the contemporary world.

[13] Weigel, *Witness to Hope*, 505.
[14] Ibid., 662.

Questions for Discussion

1. Reread the quotation from John Paul II's *Redemptor Hominis* in Msgr. Stuart's conclusion to his chapter. What does the quotation suggest about how Christians ought to engage the world?

2. George Weigel's *Witness to Hope* records comments made by Karol Wojtyla at Vatican II, specifically during a discussion of the document that would become the Pastoral Constitution on the Church in the Modern World. Archbishop Wojtyla noted that the working document presented "problems and questions that have arisen from the new situation of the world . . . However, the contemporary world also gives some answers to the questions, and it is necessary for use to consider these answers as well, because they conflict with the Church's answers."[15] Consider that John Paul II's stance against capital punishment provides an alternative to what he sees as the world's answers to violence.

3. Discuss how the dialogue of the church with contemporary society, as discussed in this chapter, mirrors dialogue on other life issues.

[15] Ibid., 168.

Chapter 12

The Death Penalty
in the Catechetical Tradition

Editors

Marietta Jaeger offered this prayer: "I prayed to God and asked to have my heart changed from rage to forgiveness."[1] Throughout this book, we have witnessed the words and actions of people deeply affected by the murders of loved ones. For those who have turned to God's mercy, there has been a consistent theme. They saw mercy and forgiveness as a way of freedom and healing, but they were not capable of forgiving the murderers. Recall, for example, the struggles of Antoinette Bosco, Ron Carlson, SueZann Bosler, and Bill Pelke. They asked God for his mercy to move through them. They prayed for the capacity to forgive, and they received the grace of sharing in God's forgiveness.

Marietta lived through the same pain of loss, the struggle with hate, and the healing of God's mercy. In the summer of 1973, Marietta's daughter, seven-year-old Susie, was abducted from a campground in Montana; her kidnapper cut through the "kids" tent and stole her in the night (ibid., 11). Sometime later, Susie was murdered, but this fact was known only to the killer. With no leads, the police allowed Marietta to make a plea through the television news and in newspapers. She asked to talk to the abductor and gave her phone number. Often during the difficult days and weeks, she prayed that she might have a Christlike response to Susie's abductor. On the anniversary of the abduction, the man called, and a few months later, he called again.

---

[1] Rachel King, *Don't Kill in Our Names: Families of Murder Victims Speak Out Against the Death Penalty* (New Brunswick, NJ: Rutgers University Press, 2003), 14.

In a talk before our students at Mount St. Mary's, Marietta explained how her prayers were answered—she was able to say to Susie's abductor that she felt compassion for him, recognizing that to do such harm to such a beautiful child would have to bring suffering. Her growing compassion brought a sense of peace, and her sense of peace allowed her to keep a cool head when talking to her child's abductor. Marietta was able to learn enough about the kidnapper to be instrumental, indeed indispensable, in identifying where he lived and who he was. The plea for a conversation worked, perhaps, because Marietta's desire to talk with the abductor was sincere. Through her compassionate response, this murderer was willing to disclose the details of other murders and to give some solace to other grieving parents.

Throughout the ordeal, Marietta prayed for her daughter Susie. She prayed to be free from the hate that was tearing her apart. She prayed for her family. She prayed for a sign that Susie was alive. She remembers that the pain was sometimes unbearable:

> I also prayed for the kidnapper. That helped me a lot. I prayed for him even when I didn't want to. Even when I felt rage. I prayed. I know that the rage had the power to consume me, and I knew that no matter what happened I did not want to live my life under the constant torment of rage. It helped to think about the kidnapper. I wondered what forces could possibly lead a person to take a small child from her family. It might sound strange, but I knew that he must be suffering, too. I imagined what I would say to him if he called. I had conversations with him in my head. I asked God to help me understand and forgive him. (ibid., 15)

By the time Susie's killer was arrested, Marietta's stance against the death penalty was clear. But, he committed suicide shortly after he was jailed and before his arraignment (ibid., 25).

Like others in her situation (Vicki Schieber, for example), Marietta believes that activism against capital punishment is a way for her to honor Susie's life. "She had a sweet and gentle spirit. I don't want that spirit dishonored by having her death avenged with more violence" (ibid., 28). Through her faith-inspired prayers, Marietta came to respond compassionately and mercifully to the man who had taken Susie's precious life. The theme of compassionate mercy is central to this chapter by Msgr. Stuart Swetland.

The Gospel of Life

Msgr. Stuart W. Swetland

"We need a paradigm shift," said Sr. Helen Prejean.[2] Sister Helen was speaking before the revision of the *Catechism of the Catholic Church* in 1997. Before and since, strong statements against the death penalty have made the church's position clear. Yet, popular attitudes are sometimes slow to change. Despite theological and pastoral developments on the issue, especially in the latter half of the twentieth century, the attitudes of some laypeople and clergy reflect views of the late Middle Ages (described in Christian Brugger's chaps. 9 and 10). The death penalty is still seen by many as a means of retribution.

The outdated language of retribution is often used by Catholic politicians, prosecutors, and judges to justify unqualified support for the generous use of the death penalty (ibid., 115–21). Having experienced this phenomenon on several occasions, Sr. Helen took pen in hand on New Year's Day 1997 and wrote an eloquent letter to John Paul II. She urged a change in the way that the church's teaching was presented, in order to better reflect the genuine developments made in the church's theology and pastoral practice. By the end of January 1997, the Vatican announced that there would be adjustments to the *Catechism of the Catholic Church*'s section on the death penalty to better reflect "progress in doctrine."

How much Sr. Helen's letter influenced the revised language of the *Catechism* is, of course, a matter of speculation. But the timing is interesting, and there is a firsthand account from the pope's staff that Blessed John Paul II personally read the entirety of her letter soon after receiving it in mid-January of 1997. This letter, which is reprinted in an edited form in Sr. Helen's book *The Death of Innocents*, spoke directly to how the older *Catechism* gave "permission" for the death penalty in cases where the crime was of "extreme gravity." The rare case of extreme gravity was being used to justify frequent recourse to this ultimate punishment. It was precisely this language that was changed in the second edition of the *Catechism*.

This chapter will delve deeper into the thinking of John Paul II, the revised *Catechism*, and the transition in language on the death penalty. It will conclude with the theological heart of the matter: a renewed understanding that the Christian moral life is ordered to spiritual worship. In "spiritual" worship, the bodily gathering, praise, and thanksgiving of the

---

[2] Sr. Helen Prejean, *The Death of Innocents: An Eyewitness Account of Wrongful Executions* (New York: Vintage, 2006), 115.

Eucharist are extended into our everyday lives. In spiritual worship, our daily lives are offered to God and in service to Jesus' mission of healing and redemption. Our lives become rooted in a deeper appreciation of the revelation of God's love as mercy and a rediscovering of patristic teaching and the concept of the universal call to holiness. Within this pastoral and evangelical context, the church's teaching on capital punishment can be more fully understood.

John Paul II

The call for an updated catechism came early in John Paul II's pontificate. In 1985, the extraordinary synod of bishops was convened, marking the twentieth anniversary of the closing of the Second Vatican Council. The extraordinary synod called for an updated catechism. By 1992, this work had reached a state where a text was ready for publication. Unlike in the past, when Latin was the official language, the working language of this draft was French. Early in the drafting process, a decision was made to publish the catechism in the major modern languages first and to wait to publish an official Latin version later. This would allow time for the massive translation work needed. It would also afford the opportunity to improve any section or paragraph that caused confusion or was found to be an inadequate presentation of the faith.

As we have seen, it also provided an opportunity for the section on the death penalty to be significantly updated in light of the publication by John Paul II of *Evangelium Vitae* (The Gospel of Life) in 1995. Along with the "personalist turn" noted in chapter 11, John Paul II reaffirms the ancient teaching of the Catholic Church that there are negative moral norms that have absolutely no exceptions. Among these is the proposition that it is always and everywhere wrong to voluntarily and directly kill an innocent human being:

> Therefore, by the authority which Christ conferred upon Peter and his Successors, and in communion with the Bishops of the Catholic Church, I confirm that the direct and voluntary killing of an innocent human being is always and gravely immoral. This doctrine, based upon that unwritten law which man, in the light of reason, finds in his own heart (cf. Rom 2:14-15), is reaffirmed by Sacred Scripture, transmitted by the Tradition of the Church and taught by the ordinary and universal magisterium. (57)

John Paul II praises the many hopeful signs in the world of an increase in respect for the dignity of the human person, including the increased opposition to the death penalty:

Among the signs of hope we should also count the spread, at many levels of public opinion, of a new sensitivity ever more opposed to war as an instrument for the resolution of conflicts between peoples, and increasingly oriented to finding effective but "non-violent" means to counter the armed aggressor. In the same perspective there is evidence of a growing public opposition to the death penalty, even when such a penalty is seen as a kind of "legitimate defense" on the part of society. Modern society in fact has the means of effectively suppressing crime by rendering criminals harmless without definitively denying them the chance to reform. (*Evangelium Vitae* 27)

The section of the encyclical on the death penalty still allowed for its use but severely limited it to "cases of absolute necessity . . . when it would not be possible otherwise to defend society. Today however, as a result of steady improvements in the organization of the penal system, such cases are very rare, if not practically non-existent" (56).

The 1992 version of the *Catechism* did allow for the use of the death penalty in "cases of extreme gravity" (2266). Below, note the side by side comparison of the first and second editions of the *Catechism*. The 1992 *Catechism* argued that "bloodless means" *should* be used if they were "sufficient to defend" the innocent. In the 1997 edition, two significant changes were made: (1) the phrase "not excluding, in cases of extreme gravity, the death penalty" was dropped (2266); and (2) the word "should" (use bloodless means) was changed to "will."

These changes in the *Catechism*'s teaching on the death penalty were also reflected in John Paul II's pastoral ministry. He frequently intervened with leaders of states and nations who still executed prisoners. He called for mercy and stays of execution. For example, in 1999 when he visited St. Louis, he successfully appealed for clemency in the case of Darrell Mease, who was scheduled to be executed in Missouri during the pontiff's visit. In John Paul II's remarks in St. Louis he stated,

> The new evangelization calls for followers of Christ who are unconditionally pro-life: who will proclaim, celebrate and serve the Gospel of life in every situation. A sign of hope is the increasing recognition that the dignity of human life must never be taken away, even in the case of someone who has done great evil. Modern society has the means of protecting itself, without definitively denying criminals the chance to reform (cf. *Evangelium Vitae*, no. 27). I renew the appeal I made most recently at Christmas for a consensus to end the death penalty, which is both cruel and unnecessary.[3]

---

[3] John Paul II, Homily at the TransWorld Dome, St. Louis (July 27, 1999).

First Edition

2266   Preserving the common good of society requires rendering the aggressor unable to inflict harm. For this reason the traditional teaching of the Church has acknowledged as well-founded the right and duty of legitimate public authority to punish malefactors by means of penalties commensurate with the gravity of the crime, not excluding, in cases of extreme gravity, the death penalty. For not analogous reasons those holding authority have the right to repel by armed force aggressors against the community in their charge.

The primary effect of punishment is to redress the disorder caused by the offense. When his punishment is voluntarily accepted by the offender, it takes on the value of expiation. Moreover, punishment has the effect of preserving public order and the safety of persons. Finally punishment has a medicinal value; as far as possible it should contribute to the correction of the offender.

2267   If bloodless means are sufficient to defend human lives against an aggressor and to protect public order and the safety of persons, public authority should limit itself to such means, because they better correspond to the concrete conditions of the common good and are more in conformity to the dignity of the human person.

Second Edition

2266   The efforts of the state to curb the spread of behavior harmful to people's rights and to the basic rules of civil society correspond to the requirement of safeguarding the common good. Legitimate public authority has the right and the duty to inflict punishment proportionate to the gravity of the offense. Punishment has the primary aim of redressing the disorder introduced by the offense. When it is willingly accepted by the guilty party, it assumes the value of expiation. Punishment then, in addition to defending public order and protecting people's safety, has a medicinal purpose: as far as possible, it must contribute to the correction of the guilty party.

2267   Assuming that the guilty party's identity and responsibility have been fully determined, the traditional teaching of the Church does not exclude recourse to the death penalty, if this is the only possible way of effectively defending human lives against the unjust aggressor.

If, however, non-lethal means are sufficient to defend and protect people's safety from the aggressor, authority will limit itself to such means, as these are more in keeping with the concrete conditions of the common good and more in conformity with the dignity of the human person.

Today, in fact, as a consequence of the possibilities which the state has for effectively preventing crime, by rendering one who has committed an offense incapable of doing harm—without definitively taking away from him the possibility of redeeming himself—the cases in which the execution of the offender is an absolute necessity "are very rare, if not practically non-existent."

The pope could not be clearer about the connections between the mission of the church, the dignity of human life, and the stance against the death penalty.

Other church officials and documents have echoed John Paul II's teaching and followed his example. For instance, Pope Benedict XVI has said,

> I express my hope that your deliberations will encourage the political and legislative initiatives being promoted in a growing number of countries to eliminate the death penalty and to continue the substantive progress made in conforming penal law both to the human dignity of prisoners and the effective maintenance of public order.[4]

The occasion for the statement is also important. Pope Benedict was addressing the participants of an anti–death penalty conference called "No Justice Without Life," held at the Vatican in November 2010.

In another very important statement of the church's social teaching, the Compendium of the Social Doctrine of the Church published in 2004, the Pontifical Council for Justice and Peace states,

> *The Church sees as a sign of hope "a growing public opposition to the death penalty,* even when such a penalty is seen as a kind of 'legitimate defense' on the part of society. Modern society in fact has the means of effectively suppressing crime by rendering criminals harmless without definitively denying them the chance to reform." Whereas, presuming the full ascertainment of the identity and responsibility of the guilty party, the traditional teaching of the Church does not exclude the death penalty "when this is the only practicable way to defend the lives of human beings effectively against the aggressor." Bloodless methods of deterrence and punishment are preferred as "they better correspond to the concrete conditions of the common good and are more in conformity to the dignity of the human person." The growing number of countries adopting provisions to abolish the death penalty or suspend its application is also proof of the fact that cases in which it is absolutely necessary to execute the offender "are very rare, if not practically non-existent." The growing aversion of public opinion towards the death penalty and the various provisions aimed at abolishing

---

[4] "Pontiff Lauds Efforts to End Death Penalty: Notes Human Dignity of Prisoners," *Zenit* (November 30, 2011), http://www.zenit.org/article-33924?l=english.

it or suspending its application constitute visible manifestations of a heightened moral awareness.[5]

This Compendium is very important because it serves as a supplement to the *Catechism of the Catholic Church*, focusing on the church's rich social heritage and doctrine. This statement emphasizes the fact that the opposition to the death penalty is a more moral position and better in keeping with the dignity of the human person. According to the Pontifical Council for Justice and Peace, this opposition is also more in keeping with the common good as well. Thus, it is not surprising at all to read the statement from Dr. Tommaso Di Ruzza, an official at the Pontifical Council, given to Carol Glatz, a reporter from the Catholic News Service, in 2011. Dr. Di Ruzza holds that for Catholics "there is no room for supporting the death penalty in today's world."[6]

Living Divine Mercy

There is little doubt that the development of the church's teaching on the death penalty is due to a greater attention to human rights and the dignity of all human persons, including those who have committed grave offenses against justice. These reasons are moral and pertain to a theological understanding of the person. But there are liturgical reasons as well. This claim might strike the reader as odd. What does the death penalty (or any moral issue) have to do with the liturgy? Actually, the two are directly related.

I am an adult convert to the Catholic faith. During my initiation into the church, the catechism that was used was *The Teaching of Christ* (1978). Written and edited by several prominent theologians, this work made the important point that there is a certain primacy to the role of sanctifying in the church: "Teaching and ruling in the Church are each ordered to the important task of sanctifying. Sacred teaching is not aimed at satisfying curiosity, but at giving the saving truth, love of which is both a part of holiness and guide to doing the will of God in love." This sanctification is centered on our celebration of the Eucharist, which the Second Vatican Council called the "source and summit of the christian life" (*Lumen Gentium* 11).

---

[5] Pontifical Council for Justice and Peace, Compendium of the Social Doctrine of the Church (Washington DC: USCCB, 2004), 405 (italics original, notes omitted).

[6] Carol Glatz, "Dead wrong: Catholics must no longer support capital punishment," *Catholic News Service* (September 30, 2011), www.catholicnews.com/data/stories/cns/1103884.htm.

Another way of speaking about the moral life and the Eucharist is offered by Cardinal William Baum, former archbishop of Washington and prefect of the Pontifical Congregation for Education. Cardinal Baum states, "To put it bluntly: The magisterium teaches that which is necessary (in accordance with God's revelation) to make possible the efficacious celebration of the Eucharist."[7] Each Christian is baptized into Christ and shares with him his mission as priest, prophet, and king. But these offices are not equal. The prophetic and kingly offices are ordered toward the priestly office, where we offer to God our sacrifice of praise, worship, and life. As the *Catechism of the Catholic Church* states,

> *The moral life is spiritual worship.* We "present [our] bodies as a living sacrifice, holy and acceptable to God," within the Body of Christ that we form and in communion with the offering of his Eucharist. In the liturgy and the celebration of the sacraments, prayer and teaching are conjoined with the grace of Christ to enlighten and nourish Christian activity. As does the whole of the Christian life, the moral life finds its source and summit in the Eucharistic sacrifice. (2031)

In short, the church's moral teaching aids us in offering more fitting worship. Applied to capital punishment, the ongoing development of the church's teaching on the death penalty is to help us celebrate the Eucharist more worthily and efficaciously.

This connection between our call to holiness and worship is in keeping with the recent (re)discovery of Christ's teaching on mercy. Our understanding of Christ's mercy is facilitated in no small way by the mystical experiences and writing of St. Maria Faustina Kowalska. Saint Faustina reminded the church that the mission of Jesus' life was to reveal to the world the merciful love of the Father. This she called divine mercy. In a fallen world—a world full of sin—love, especially divine love (*agape*), takes the form of mercy. Jesus' mission was to make known the Father's merciful love for us and to embody that love in his life and teaching. By our baptisms we take on a share in the mission of Jesus. We, the church, carry it on through space and time.

Saint Faustina made known this message during the twentieth century— a centenary bloodied with wars, massacres, hatreds, false ideologies, the

---

[7] "Without communion with the Bishop of Rome, the episcopal magisterium does not exist . . . ," address of Cardinal Baum of Washington to the Federation of Catholic Scholars (April 28, 1978), http://www.ewtn.com/library/Theology/EPISCMAG.HTM.

gulags, the concentration camps, and the killing fields. It was a time in need of the message of mercy. But so is ours. Faustina wrote in her diaries what she believed God had revealed to her in her mystical experiences. These writings were carefully examined by the church, as was her life. The ultimate sign of the church's approval was given in St. Faustina's canonization in April 2000. In her diaries, she wrote the following words she heard from God: "The greater the misery of a soul, the greater its right to My mercy. . . . On the cross, the fountain of My mercy was opened wide by the lance for all souls—no one have I excluded!"[8]

Bishop Robert Finn of Kansas City-St. Joseph diocese has commented on the message of St. Faustina and the death penalty:

> God did not abolish justice. Rather, He intended by the offering of His Son to purge human justice of any sense of wrath or revenge. Time and again we see that violence begets violence in a seeming unending spiral. God told St. Faustina that "Mankind will not have peace until it turns with trust to My mercy." In the Divine Mercy, God receives and quenches human vengeance in Jesus' own wounded Heart. In this Heart, which is an abyss of love, mercy overcomes hatred. Mercy brings healing that is impossible on a merely human level. Divine Mercy can restore hope, because it flows from the heart of the Risen Christ who, once and for all, has vanquished the finality of death. The deep truth that faith teaches is that only in the context of mercy—God's mercy and our own forgiveness and mercy—can we, as wounded human men and women, find healing and hope. "Blessed are the merciful, for they will be shown mercy" (Mt 5:7).[9]

The teaching of Jesus is clear. When questioned by the religious leaders of his day why he would eat and drink in the company of tax collectors and other public sinners, Jesus' response was simple: "Those who are well do not need a physician, but the sick do. Go and learn the meaning of the words, 'I desire mercy, not sacrifice.' I did not come to call the righteous but sinners" (Matt 9:12-13).

---

[8] *Diary of St. Maria Faustina Kowalska: Divine Mercy in My Soul* (Stockbridge, MA: Marian of the Immaculate Conception, 2000), 1182.

[9] Most Rev. Robert W. Finn, "Divine Mercy and the Death Penalty," *The Catholic Key Blog,* http://catholickey.blogspot.com/2010/08/divine-mercy-and-death-penalty.html.

Conclusion

The church's evolving teaching on the death penalty is a stark reminder of Jesus' teaching on mercy. We are all sinners in need of God's grace and healing. No one should be excluded from our consideration or our mercy. We should even see in the convicted felon the presence of Jesus, who said in Mathew 25:36, "I was in prison and you visited me." If we fail to see him there, to love and serve him there; if we exclude him from our concern and even purge him from our midst, we fail to live divine mercy. And our community would be made less and our Eucharist would be less efficacious and full. This is why the catechetical tradition on the death penalty is in the midst of a genuine development—so that the world might see our witness to mercy.

Review and Looking Forward

Editors

On May 13, 1981, John Paul II was shot while greeting pilgrims in St. Peter's Square. Shot once in the stomach and once in the arm, he was rushed to the hospital and was on the operating table for hours.[10] The would-be assassin, Mehmet Ai Agca, had already assassinated the editor of the Turkish newspaper, *Milliyet*, in 1979. Before his trial was complete, he escaped from prison. "Three days later, he wrote a letter to *Milliyet* threatening to kill the Pope. . . . The threat was not carried out and Agca, a wanted man, disappeared into the dark underside of the modern world." Months later, in 1980, "a Turkish court convicted him *in absentia* and sentenced him to death" for the assassination of Adbi Ipeckci, the newspaper editor (ibid., 397).

So, when John Paul II visited Agca in an Italian prison in 1983, he was visiting a man who had nearly taken his life and also was guilty of murder and sentenced to death in Turkey. In *Witness to Hope*, George Weigel at first recounts the visit from afar. "Photos of their encounter showed the two men sitting on black plastic chairs, with Agca . . . listening intensely to John Paul, whose left hand was open and slightly raised in a characteristic gesture of explanation or instruction." It was learned later that the pope was reassuring Agca. He was telling him that he (Agca) ought not to worry about vengeance. Agca "had read in prison that the assassination attempt

---

[10] George Weigel, *Witness to Hope: The Biography of Pope John Paul II* (New York: HarperCollins, 1999), 413.

had taken place on the anniversary of the apparition at Fatima, and had concluded that the 'goddess of Fatima' who had saved the Pope was now going to do away with him. John Paul patiently explained that Mary . . . loved all people, and that Agca shouldn't be afraid" (ibid., 474). With these words, he put his call for mercy into clear relief—a call at the heart of his teachings on the death penalty.

Six months before the assassination attempt, John Paul II issued his second encyclical, titled *Dives in Misericordia* (Rich in Mercy, 1980). In it, the pope contemplates God's mercy and explains the need for us to show love and mercy to our neighbors. At the beginning of the encyclical he notes the challenges for our time:

> The present-day mentality, more perhaps than that of people in the past, seems opposed to a God of mercy, and in fact tends to exclude from life and to remove from the human heart the very idea of mercy. The word and the concept of "mercy" seem to cause uneasiness in man. (2)

The pope's words reflect his own response to the man who tried to kill him. To the man who wanted to dominate and destroy his life, he felt no desire for vengeance. His response, like Marietta's, powerfully focuses on mercy, as discussed in Msgr. Stuart Swetland's chapter. In bringing to light the vital importance of divine mercy, Msgr. Stuart turned, not only to John Paul II, but also to St. Faustina Kowalska, a Polish nun and mystic (1905–38) with whom the pope shared a "spiritual affinity."[11] In his homily on the canonization of Faustina, John Paul recalled words from his *Dives in Misericordia*: "Jesus Christ taught that man not only receives and experiences the mercy of God, but that he is also called 'to practice mercy' towards others: 'Blessed are the merciful, for they shall obtain mercy'" (14).[12] John Paul II's loving response to a killer presents this teaching to us.

---

[11] Weigel, *Witness to Hope*, 387.

[12] John Paul II, Homily for the Mass in St. Peter's Square for the Canonization of Sr. Mary Faustina Kowalska (April 30, 2000).

Questions for Discussion

1. Compare the first and second editions of the *Catechism* as presented in the chapter. What do you think is the most significant change?

2. Discuss St. Faustina and her witness to divine mercy. Is the witness to divine mercy applicable to capital punishment?

3. Discuss your responses to Pope John Paul II's response to his assassin and Marietta Jaeger's response to Susie's killer. Consider your responses in light of the church's teaching on capital punishment.

Part IV

The Least of These

Editors

The first section of this book discussed the endless rethinking of the death penalty throughout our American history. We keep rethinking—for what crimes, according to which procedures, why, how, where, and whom we execute. We keep narrowing the field of persons convicted of capital crimes who face execution. So who still runs the risk of being sentenced to death? And why is this question so important? The previous section on Catholic teaching on the death penalty addressed significant issues too often missing in reflections on capital punishment. The final section of this book focuses on aspects of the current practice of the death penalty that are morally troubling. While raising numerous moral concerns central to Catholic social teaching, these chapters bring us to face two important questions. Is it the case that the least of us—the powerless, marginalized, and most vulnerable—are most at risk of being executed? If so, what does this say about our society?

Chapter 13

Money Matters

Editors

As one begins to scratch the surface of the American death penalty, one fact becomes clear—money matters. In discussing our criminal justice system with our students at Mount St. Mary's University, Bryan Stevenson, founder and director of the Equal Justice Institute in Montgomery, Alabama, emphasized two related points:

1. A nation's greatness is shown in how it treats its weakest members.
2. The opposite of poverty is not wealth; the opposite of poverty is justice.

Stevenson often argues that if our nation does not commit in a complete way to justice for everybody, we risk perpetuating the dynamics that have harmed our progress as a nation.[1] He grew up in a poor, rural, segregated Alabama community. Stevenson early on recognized how a legacy of injustice tied to poverty and racism constrained the opportunities offered people and shaped the conditions of their lives. He became convinced that this legacy of injustice was most dramatic in the criminal justice system, and he committed his life's work to promoting equal justice. Much of his work focuses on ending the death penalty. He often calls young people to respond as he did—to stand when other people sit and to speak when other people are quiet.

Two people continue to stand and speak together on these issues: two brothers of condemned prisoners, one condemned to death and the other

---

[1] Eva Rodriguez, "A good day for society's 'most vulnerable kids,'" *Washington Post* (June 26, 2012): C2.

to life without parole. Their brothers' stories dramatically differ due to the impact of money and race. In her book *Capital Consequences: Families of the Condemned Tell Their Stories*, Rachel King tells how Bill Babbitt and David Kaczynski's lives intersected.[2]

In 1980, Manny Babbitt returned from Vietnam as a decorated war hero. Manny faced challenges in his youth after suffering a head injury in a car accident when he was twelve. Struggling in school, he dropped out in seventh grade. Although functionally illiterate, he passed the Marine entrance exam with the help of a recruiter. Manny suffered traumatic experiences in the Battle of Khe Sanh, one of the bloodiest battles of the war, and in subsequent tours. He returned home as a shattered man in 1969. Descending into drug and alcohol use, Manny suffered failed marriages and time in a psychiatric hospital and prison, and ended up living on the streets.

Evidencing signs of mental illness, including terrifying battlefield flashbacks and suicide attempts, Manny began roaming the streets at night patrolling for the enemy he once fought. After being acquitted on a rape charge, a state psychiatrist stressed Manny's need for psychiatric help. Knowing little then about post-traumatic disorders, his brother Bill moved Manny into his home and decided to turn to the Veterans Administration for assistance since his family lacked the financial means to support his care. But the plan came too late.

Leah Schendel, an elderly woman, died of a heart attack after an intruder entered her home and beat her. Finding objects identified as missing at the crime scene, Bill contacted the police about his suspicions and concerns that Manny was still lost on Vietnam battlefields. Bill believed the police when they assured him his brother would end up in a psychiatric hospital, not on death row. But soon Bill found himself witnessing a capital case unfolding. Devastated by this betrayal, he also witnessed the striking of all African Americans from the jury pool, the shocking inadequacy of Manny's public defender, and the limited resources available to match the prosecutor's efforts to convict Manny. Bill had to come to terms with what his cooperation with the police had set in motion—a guilty verdict and a death sentence for his mentally ill brother. Vets, especially from the Battle of Khe Sanh, rallied to support Manny.

Another man, who understood Bill's devastation all too well, also came to Manny's support. David Kaczynski contacted Bill. David is the brother of the "Unabomber," Ted Kaczynski, and director of New Yorkers Against

---

[2] Rachel King, *Capital Consequences: Families of the Condemned Tell Their Stories* (Piscataway, NJ: Rutgers University Press, 2004), 49–86.

the Death Penalty. Both their brothers had killed people, and both suffered serious mental illnesses. But one was white and had the support of a family of means, and one was black, facing an all-white jury, and had the support of a family, but lacked the means to support a strong defense. Bill describes the support he found in David: "He was one of the few people who understood how hard it was for me to turn in my brother. We both felt a responsibility to society to prevent further violence, but we also wanted help for our brothers. We both felt betrayed when the death penalty was pursued" (ibid., 69).

Race and money mattered. After killing three people and injuring others in seventeen bombings, Ted Kaczynski, child prodigy and university professor, was sentenced to life. Manny Babbitt, a decorated Marine, beat up a woman who died from a related heart attack, and was sentenced to death (ibid., 70). Manny, like many veterans of the Vietnam War, suffered from post-traumatic stress syndrome. Violent tendencies and disorientation are common effects. Vets gathered thousands of signatures on petitions asking for an act of clemency to commute his sentence to life without parole. After spending seventeen years on death row, Manny was executed by lethal injection at midnight on May 4, 1999, exactly one minute after his fiftieth birthday. Understanding the different treatment of their brothers, David and Bill continue to work with other murder victims' family members to end the death penalty. Like Bryan Stevenson, they stand up and speak out every chance they get about the role race and money play in the death penalty.

Manny's story—the connection between poverty and death row—represents a nationwide problem. However, current debate about the death penalty in the United States tends to focus on two issues related neither to the victim nor to the offender: method and cost. These issues are important. Executions have been halted due to complications with the drugs and skills required for lethal injection. In fiscally challenging times, legislatures worry about the exorbitant costs of the death penalty compared to the far less demanding process resulting in maximum sentences of life imprisonment. Costs have played a major role in recent State repeal decisions. In this chapter, Alejandro Cañadas and John Schwenkler, professors of economics and philosophy, lay out the cost-benefit analysis that drives many of these debates. But they also ask us to rethink how to consider and frame economic matters. They conclude that the discussion of the death penalty should not end with matters of cost, but with questions of human development. Catholic social teaching brings us to reflect far more deeply and broadly on issues bearing on the economics of the death penalty.

The Economics of the Death Penalty

Alejandro Cañadas and John Schwenkler

When they hear about "economics," many people think about costs and benefits. This is a good starting point, because cost-benefit analysis is an important tool that economists use in analyzing human decisions. However, it is important to realize that economics involves much more than simple cost-benefit analysis. From the perspective of the Catholic Church, economics is the science that explores the decisions made by human beings as they pursue integral human development. Therefore, this chapter will begin by exploring the "classical" conception of economics and contrasting it to the Catholic one, and then will analyze the effects of the death penalty in light of each.

What Is Economics About?

What do you want from life? Would you like some new clothes, a nicer car, better grades, more free time? How about to be a better person, to love and be loved, to know your vocation and follow it, or simply to be happy? As human beings, our desires are virtually unlimited. We may want all these things and more, but as individuals and members of societies we face a constraint called *scarcity* that prevents us from attaining everything we want. Scarcity is the fundamental concept in economics: it indicates that there is less of a good freely available than people would like. There are some things, like seawater and air, that seem not to be scarce, because nature has provided as much of them as people want. But almost everything else we can think of (even our time) is scarce. In economics we use the word "scarce" in a very specific way, such that even if large amounts of a good have been produced, it is still considered scarce as long as there is less of it available than some people would like.

The unlimited nature of our desires, coupled with scarcity of the goods and resources available to satisfy these desires, requires that we make choices. Should I spend the next hour studying or praying? Should I spend my last thirty dollars on a DVD or give that money to someone in need? Should I work on my laptop or play with my kids? Should I buy the house, go to graduate school, get married, or become a priest? *Choice*, or the act of selecting among incompatible alternatives, is the logical consequence of scarcity. It can be difficult to make the right choice when the alternatives are very important. We need information and careful discernment. When we make choices, we constantly face *trade-offs* between meeting one desire or another. To meet one need, we must let another go unmet. The concepts of scarcity, choice, and the trade-offs we face provide the foundation for economic analysis.

Integral Human Development

It is important to recognize that the dominant tradition in economics assumes an understanding of human nature and the human good that is different from that of the Catholic Church. The three main characteristics of the neoclassical framework are

- first, the belief that economic agents are rational when motivated by expected utility maximization and governed by purely selfish concerns (i.e., concerns that do not take into consideration the utility of others);[3]

- second, a reduction of the human being to material interests (as *homo economicus*) is the consequence of the theories created in economics in order to explain or fit existing observations and to make testable predictions;[4]

- finally, the disciplinary conception of economics as a value-free science without ethical implications. Thus, in pure neoclassical economics, human development is associated with material progress, and involves nothing more than maximizing gross domestic product (GDP).[5]

Carried out in this tradition, economics has revealed many important truths about human society. Nevertheless, it assumes an unrealistic view of human nature, as in the real world human beings pursue many goods other than material ones.

---

[3] These are theoretical assumptions created to construct economic models in order to make testable predictions that are often best represented in mathematical form. There are two reasons for this: first, mathematics allows the theory to be represented most concisely and unambiguously; second, it allows data to be collected and manipulated, resulting in precise predictions using the theoretical models created.

[4] This is a criterion chosen by scientists' attempt to abstract the information into the form that is the simplest while yielding the largest amount of information with the least amount of effort.

[5] A further analysis of this topic can be found in Alejandro A. Cañadas and Jim Giordano, "A Philosophically-based Biopsychosocial Model of Economics: Evolutionary Perspectives of Human Resource Utilization and the Need for an Integrative, Multi-disciplinary Approach to Economics," *The International Journal of Interdisciplinary Social Sciences* 5, no. 8 (December 2010).

The Catholic Church rejects the materialistic view of human nature, instead regarding the human person as both spiritual and bodily. Because of this, the church recognizes that each person has material necessities, such as "bodily integrity and to the means necessary for the proper development of life, particularly food, clothing, shelter, medical care, rest, and . . . the means of livelihood."[6] These material goods serve higher social and spiritual necessities, such as education that develops one's gifts and talents, participation in the development of culture, active engagement in social and political life, moral formation, prayer, and worship.[7] *Both* sets of necessities are important and have to be satisfied. However, from the Catholic point of view the spiritual necessities are higher and more fulfilling. Therefore, when there are trade-offs between spiritual goods and material ones, the tradition of Catholic social teaching holds that the latter should serve the former.

This is what Pope Benedict XVI is saying in his encyclical letter *Caritas in Veritate*, where he writes that "integral human development" concerns the whole person in every dimension, understood from the perspective of eternal life. Such development requires more than the accumulation of monetary wealth and satisfaction of material necessities. Without the perspective of eternal life, human progress risks being reduced to the mere accumulation of wealth and satisfaction of material needs. For this reason, integral human development can only be understood in terms of a transcendent vision of the human person in relation to God.

So there is disagreement between the Catholic Church and the dominant tradition in economics concerning the nature of the human person: the church regards human beings as spiritual and not just material, and as oriented to God rather than to merely material goods. In addition to this, the tradition of Catholic social teaching thinks of human *society*, and thus of social institutions, in a way that economists usually have not: for since integral human development is a spiritual concept rather than a purely material one, social institutions will promote true human development only insofar as they help people to attain these spiritual necessities.[8]

---

[6] John XXIII, *Pacem in Terris* (Libreria Editrice Vaticana, 1963), 11. For the list of higher goods below, see 12–38.

[7] Ibid., 11–27.

[8] See, for example, Pope Benedict XVI, *Caritas in Veritate* (Libreria Editrice Vaticana, 2009), 11.

Costs and Benefits of the Death Penalty

From the perspective of traditional economics, to talk about the "economics of the death penalty" means to conduct a cost-benefit analysis of it, in order to determine how the material costs of executing criminals compare to the social benefits of this practice. This section will summarize some data that show how poorly the death penalty fares in this regard: it is much more expensive than imprisonment or rehabilitation, and it has not been shown to reduce violent crime. In the next section, we supplement this analysis by thinking about the costs and benefits of the death penalty in light of the Catholic vision of the human person.

Costs

Many people believe that the death penalty is justifiable from a purely economic perspective: it should be less expensive to put a person to death than to keep him or her in prison for a life sentence. But this assumption is false. According to the Death Penalty Information Center, the average cost of defending a trial in a federal death penalty case is $620,932, or about eight times that of a federal murder case in which the death penalty is not sought.[9] There are many reasons for this, each having to do with the way our criminal justice system works—and has to work, if the power to execute is not going to be abused. For example,

- Death penalty trials are more complicated than ordinary criminal trials. The trial is bifurcated into two phases. In the first phase, the jury decides whether the defendant is guilty or innocent. If found guilty, the penalty phase requires the jury to consider additional information before determining if the defendant should be given a death sentence. Death penalty trials are also very expensive since they often rely heavily on expert testimony, jury selection takes longer, and all defendants sentenced to death are entitled to an automatic appeal of both guilt and sentence.

- Trials in cases where the death penalty is sought are also very lengthy: they can last up to four times longer than noncapital cases and are often followed by postconviction appeals. Due to the lengthy appeal process, death row inmates typically spend ten years awaiting execution, and some have spent over two decades uncertain about when

---

[9] "Financial Facts: Information on the Cost of the Death Penalty from DPIC," Death Penalty Information Center (2012), www.deathpenaltyinfo.org/costs-death-penalty.

they will be executed. In 2007 the average time between sentencing and execution was 12.7 years, according to the Death Penalty Information Center.[10]

- Especially given the enormous costs just described and number of poor people facing capital trials, most people facing the death penalty cannot afford their own attorneys, and so each must be provided with two public defenders by the state, which must also pay for the costs of the prosecution. Studies show that a defendant's representation costs are correlated with the likelihood of receiving a death sentence: the less money that is spent, the more likely the defendant is to be executed.

- Incarceration of prisoners on death row is also very expensive for the state: these prisoners are kept in highly restricted environments in special facilities requiring greater security and special accommodations, as most death row inmates are kept for twenty-three hours a day in their cells.

- Finally, in order to minimize mistakes risking wrongful executions, every inmate sentenced to death is entitled to a series of appeals, the costs of which are once again borne at the taxpayers' expense. These appeals are essential because some inmates have come within hours of execution before evidence was uncovered proving their wrongful conviction. The entire appeal process can take fifteen or twenty years before an execution.

Some might object that this shows only that we need to find ways to impose the death penalty more quickly and efficiently: after all, shouldn't it be *less* expensive to put someone to death than to keep him or her in prison for life?

But the requirement to treat capital cases in the ways described above is a matter of justice, not a mere historical accident—and despite all these safeguards there have still been 141 people exonerated and freed from death row since reinstatement of the death penalty in 1976. The exposure of these wrongful convictions shows either that the ideal of "heightened due process" in capital cases is actually not high enough, or that it is too often ignored. Richard C. Dieter of the Death Penalty Information Center

---

[10] "Death Penalty in 2008: Year End Report," Death Penalty Information Center (December 2008), www.deathpenaltyinfo.org/2008YearEnd.pdf.

states the point clearly: "The choice today is between a very expensive death penalty and one that risks falling below constitutional standards."[11]

Benefits

After all these costs, what does the use of the death penalty gain us? Many people assume that the execution of violent criminals leads to a reduction in the rate of crime. But there is no clear statistical evidence for this claim, and a growing number of law enforcement officials have concluded that the death penalty is not the most efficient way to reduce crime. A recent national poll of police chiefs asked them to identify what they believe to be the most effective ways of fighting crime, and how the death penalty fits into such crime-fighting methods. As leaders in law enforcement, they were also asked where the death penalty fits in their priorities. The poll found the following facts:

- When asked to name one area as "most important for reducing violent crime," greater use of the death penalty ranked last among the police chiefs, with only 1 percent listing it as the best way to reduce violence.

- Similarly, the death penalty was considered the least efficient use of taxpayers' money, with expanded training for police officers, community policing, programming to control drug and alcohol abuse, and neighborhood watch programs all seen as more cost-effective ways to combat crime.

- Of the respondents, 57 percent said that the death penalty does little to prevent violent crimes, because those who turn to violence rarely consider the consequences of their actions.

- Of various statements about the death penalty, the one with which the police chiefs most identified was, "Philosophically, I support the death penalty, but I don't think it is an effective law enforcement tool in practice."[12]

The leading criminologists in the country agree with the police chiefs about deterrence. A recent survey showed that 88 percent of the country's

---

[11] Richard C. Dieter, "Smart on Crime: Reconsidering the Death Penalty in a Time of Economic Crisis," *National Poll of Police Chiefs Puts Capital Punishment at Bottom of Law Enforcement Priorities: A Report from the Death Penalty Information Center* (October 2009): 20. See www.deathpenaltyinfo.org/documents/CostsRptFinal.pdf.

[12] Ibid., 9–11.

top criminologists do not believe the death penalty acts as a deterrent to homicide. Also, 87 percent believe abolition of the death penalty would have no significant effect on murder rates. The authors of this study conclude that "the vast majority of the world's top criminologists believe that the empirical research has revealed the deterrence hypothesis for a myth." That is, the claim that the death penalty deters would-be criminals from committing crimes is not supported by the evidence. "The consensus among criminologists is that the death penalty does not add any significant deterrent effect above that of long-term imprisonment."[13]

Opportunity Costs

It is a principle of economics that the use of scarce resources is costly, and so trade-offs must be made. Economists sometimes refer to this as the principle that "there is no such thing as a free lunch." Because resources are scarce, the use of resources to produce one good diverts those resources from the production of other goods. No option is free of cost; there is always some trade-off.

With this in mind, note that the enormous amount of money spent on the death penalty means that many other alternatives must be ruled out, such as employing more police officers, implementing more efficient law enforcement programs, spending more on education or poverty reduction, supporting crime victims, and so forth. The choice to pursue any of these options means the others must be sacrificed. This is particularly relevant during a financial crisis, when decisions are being made to eradicate government programs that do not work and to address deficits through layoffs, shorter hours for governmental services, and higher fees. Capital punishment uses huge resources on a few cases, with highly questionable results. Yet the same states that are spending millions of dollars on the death penalty are facing austere cutbacks in other areas.

Clearly, abolishing the death penalty would not solve all of these problems, but the savings would be significant. For example, a 2007 *Washington Post* article on the abolition of the death penalty in New Jersey notes that "the most compelling case for New Jersey lawmakers [to abolish capital punishment] was the economic one," as the state Corrections Department estimated that repeal could save the state as much as $1.3 million per

---

[13] Michael L. Radelet and Traci L. Lacock, "Do Executions Lower Homicide Rates?: The Views of Leading Criminologists," *The Journal of Criminal Law and Criminology* 99, no. 2 (2009): 489–508.

inmate.[14] If a new police officer (or teacher, or ambulance driver) is paid $40,000 per year, this money could be used to fund dozens of additional workers in each state to secure a better community. If it takes 1,000 hours of state-salaried work to arrive at a death sentence and only 100 hours to have the same person sentenced to life without parole, the 900-hour difference is a state asset. If the death penalty is eliminated, the county or the state can decide whether to direct those employee hours to other work that had been left uncompleted, or choose to keep fewer employees. There is a financial dimension to all aspects of death penalty cases, and proper cost studies take these "opportunity costs" into account. That means we should add all direct and indirect opportunity costs to all the direct and indirect costs of the death penalty to determine the real material costs of the practice.

More Than Money

This analysis of the material costs and benefits of the death penalty clearly undermines the idea that it is an efficient way to combat crime. But our discussion should not stop there. In light of the tradition of Catholic social teaching, the church invites us to reflect on the effects of capital punishment on human society in its spiritual dimension and to ask whether it forms us as people who see the divine image in one another.

As we have seen, such reflection shows us that reducing the economics of the death penalty to questions of material cost and benefit would be like thinking we can measure the quality of a person's life just by counting the calories that he or she consumes and burns off, without any attention to relationships to other human people or to God. Thus, as the US Conference of Catholic Bishops writes in the 2000 statement Responsibility, Rehabilitation, and Restoration, Catholics need to think about the death penalty by asking questions like, "How can we restore our respect for law and life? How can we protect and rebuild communities, confront crime without vengeance, and defend life without taking life?"[15] These traits—our level of respect for law and life, the health of our communities, and our capacity to avoid vengeance and refrain from killing one another—are

---

[14] Keith B. Richburg, "N.J. Approves Abolition of Death Penalty; Corzine to Sign," *Washington Post* (December 14, 2007).

[15] United States Conference of Catholic Bishops, Responsibility, Rehabilitation, and Restoration: A Catholic Perspective on Crime and Criminal Justice (Washington, DC: USCCB, 2000).

what determine whether we are fulfilling the vocation to integral human fulfillment; they reveal whether we stand in free solidarity with one another in light of our encounter with God.

Conclusion

In a way, this means that the economics of the death penalty is actually a topic of *all* the chapters of this book. If economic analysis is concerned with human beings not just as material creatures but also in their spiritual and social dimensions, then it will draw on questions traditionally assigned to the domains of theology (What is sin? How is it possible to encounter God?), philosophy (What is human nature? What is the good?), political science and sociology (What is human society? What brings us together, and what draws us apart?), and more. Such a multidisciplinary effort would be reflective of the nature of truth itself: as Pope Benedict writes in *Caritas in Veritate*, the church teaches that the truth is *"lógos* which creates *diá-logos"*—reason that creates dialogue—"and hence communication and communion" (4). For this reason, the truth is not the property of any particular discipline: in complex problems, all the relevant sciences must be drawn together, to seek the truth in the light of our encounter with God.

It is in this light that we should think about the concept of "restorative justice," which is central to Catholic social teaching. In promoting this concept in Responsibility, Rehabilitation, and Restoration, the bishops call on the faithful to "seek approaches that understand crime as a threat to community, not just a violation of law; that demand new efforts to rebuild lives, not just build more prisons; and that demonstrate a commitment to re-weave a broader social fabric of respect for life, civility, responsibility, and reconciliation" (27). Such a conception of the human person and society cannot be reduced to a metric of dollars and cents, but demands a vision of the human person that transcends the merely material. Only in the context of such a vision is a Catholic economics possible.

Review and Looking Forward

Editors

In her book *The Death of Innocents*, Sr. Helen Prejean notes how Pope John Paul II's encyclical *Evangelium Vitae* describes the increase in global opposition to the death penalty as a "sign of hope."[16] On January 1, 1997,

---

[16] Sr. Helen Prejean, *The Death of Innocents: An Eyewitness Account of Wrongful Executions* (New York: Vintage, 2006), 122. Subsequent references will be noted within the text.

she wrote to the pope, thanking him for raising his voice in opposition to the execution of Joseph O'Dell and helping to save his life (124–28). After recounting her experience of seeing "the suffering face of Christ in the 'least of these'" and being the face of Christ for these men as they went to their deaths, Sr. Helen addressed an important dimension of economics and the death penalty:

> The death penalty is very much a poor person's issue (99% of the 3,100 souls on death row in the U.S. are poor), and I have found that as a general rule those involved with justice for poor people readily oppose the death penalty, whereas those separated from poor people and their struggles readily support it. They are more prone to see poor people as the "enemy" and to be willing to inflict hard punishments to "control" them. (125)

In her journey through the death penalty system, Sr. Helen learned much about the economics of the death penalty. She began to understand all too well Justice Ruth Bader Ginsburg's statement that "people who are well represented at trial do not get the death penalty" (208).

Living with the poor in the St. Thomas housing projects in New Orleans gave her new eyes. For example, she began to notice how the murders of white people received front-page coverage, while the murders of poor black people barely merited a few lines of mention. Helen came to understand how "economic class . . . also plays a role in determining death sentences. District attorneys, who must calculate cost, court time, and personnel resources, must decide which murder cases are worth the expense of the death penalty. The murder of one minority by another may not help a DA's next election. When 'nobodies' are killed, law enforcement seems hardly to notice, much less vigorously prosecute the perpetrator" (203–4). Murders of poor persons often don't lead to investigations, let alone capital trials. Serving as spiritual adviser to men sentenced to death, she learned quickly of poor people's inability to get adequate defense (208). She witnessed the chilling effect of *Murray v. Giarratano*'s ruling that the Sixth Amendment's right to counsel did not extend to postconviction appeals (211).Working with the poor taught her that economic status definitely matters in the criminal justice system.

Working with the poor also brought Sr. Helen to read the gospels differently. Now she attended to how Jesus sought out the company of outcasts, took his meals with sinners, and responded to the downtrodden "least of these" (182). The gospels had clearly formed a new community that excluded no persons—even criminals who had done grievous harm to others. Sister Helen's journey with the poor in St. Thomas brought her to comprehend and passionately advocate the Catholic understanding of economics and death penalty. Alejandro and John's chapter helps us understand that from an economics perspective, the death penalty simply fails to combat crime efficiently. More importantly, it brings us to understand what Sr. Helen Prejean realized on her long journey. The real challenge we face is to shift our focus from endless tinkering with capital punishment to discovering effective ways in which we can begin to strengthen our communities, address crime without vengeance, and defend human life without destroying life. Her Catholic faith was the catalyst that inspired her journey. She remains confident that Catholic teaching on restorative justice can provide the catalyst needed to build the momentum toward national repeal of the death penalty. Now it is a matter of whether Catholics will join her in standing rather than sitting and speaking rather than remaining silent.

Questions for Discussion

1. Discuss the Catholic understanding of the human person that was developed in this chapter. How might this understanding of the person (as the image of God) transform our understanding of crime and society's response to it? Consult the US bishops' Responsibility, Rehabilitation, and Restoration: A Catholic Perspective on Crime and Criminal Justice as a rich resource. It is available on the USCCB web site.

2. Discuss how specific parts of the Lord's Prayer provide a lens for thinking about the Catholic understanding of economics explored in this chapter in relation to crime and punishment.

3. Over nine years New York spent approximately $170 million on death penalty cases and executed no one. Over twenty-five years, New Jersey spent $253 million and also executed no one. Discuss ways in which funds spent on the death penalty could be used to support crime victims and their families.

Chapter 14

A Legacy of Race

Editors

In 1994 an African American man named Michael Spikes was killed during a convenience store robbery in New York. Police delivered the news of Michael's murder to his wife, Bonnita. Michael's killers have never been caught. Bonnita and her four sons endured the immediate devastation of Michael's death. They also suffered continuing effects as Bonnita's then thirteen-year-old son attempted suicide, was hospitalized, and struggled with deep depression over the tragic loss of his father. Over time Bonnita came to see the disparity between funds directed to the pursuit of selective death sentences and funds directed to social services, such as counseling, that would support murder victim family members. She also became convinced that the time and funds wasted on pursuing death sentences would be better spent on solving murder cases, including cold cases. She knows all too well that identifying and convicting persons who commit violent crimes helps the healing process of grieving families and increases the safety of communities. Bonnita had no desire to seek a death sentence for her husband's killer; what she did desire was support for her family as it struggled through this tragic loss. Bonnita's experience brought her into contact with other African American families of murder victims who shared the same desire, and this motivated her to work with murder victim families in Maryland. Her work focuses on Baltimore City since it has the highest murder rate in the state.

In her 2008 testimony before the Maryland Commission on Capital Punishment, Bonnita described what she found to be the common reaction of African American families who dealt with the murder of a loved one:

> For most of these families, the notion of a death sentence for their loved one's murderer is not even a remote thought. They are

struggling to hold their households together, to help their families grieve, and to survive the trauma one day at a time. . . . We know that the death penalty costs millions of dollars more than a system of life without parole as a maximum sentence. Just a *fraction* of the savings from repealing the death penalty would impact thousands of our citizens in need of support and grief counseling and hundreds more who, as my son's experience demonstrates, need much more intense mental health care.[1]

In an attachment to her testimony, Bonnita cited polls taken by the Maryland Catholic Conference regarding attitudes toward the death penalty held by Maryland voters. Two polls conducted by Mason-Dixon Polling and Research, Inc. in 2005 and 2007 revealed that opposition to the death penalty had increased among African American voters from 45 percent to 51 percent in polls over this time span. Another 2007 poll conducted by Gonzales Research and Marketing Strategies of Annapolis for the Maryland Catholic Conference revealed that 61 percent of African Americans opposed the death penalty and 29 percent supported it. The Mason-Dixon polls also revealed an increase of support among African American voters for life without parole as a substitute for death sentences (an increase from 69 percent in 2005 to 77 percent in 2007). Bonnita stressed the importance of this statistic, given that close to eight out of ten murder victims in Maryland are African American. Bonnita Spikes now works to end the death penalty in the state of Maryland as a matter of heartfelt conviction but also because repeal of the death penalty will better serve all the families of murder victims and their communities.

The previous chapter considered the economics of the death penalty and made clear that money matters in numerous ways. Since poverty and race are so interrelated in the United States, a consideration of economics naturally leads into a consideration of race. Timothy Wolfe, a professor of sociology, provides a thorough analysis of the legacy of race in America and how it bears on the practice of the death penalty. Since the colonial period, our society has grappled with the moral dimensions of this legacy. A consideration of the current practice of the death penalty cannot avoid grappling with its troubling racial dimension.

The previous chapter's discussion of scarcity, choice, and trade-offs has bearing on the issue of race. When we choose among alternative courses

---

[1] "Testimony of Bonnita Spikes before the Maryland Commission on Capital Punishment" (August 5, 2008), www.goccp.maryland.gov/capital-punishment/documents /spikes-testimony.pdf.

of action, some alternatives are forgone. If we channel huge amounts of funding into capital cases, alternative use of those funds—for crime prevention and crime solving or social services for crime victims—will have to be sacrificed to some extent. Race has been shown to play a role in such funding decisions. A derivative problem of racial bias in the death penalty system is often found in police and prosecutors' efforts to solve murder cases. Personnel and funding resources are not unlimited; choices have to be made in pursuing criminal cases. Many family members of African American murder victims believe insufficient effort was put into solving the murders of their loved ones and removing dangerous killers from their communities. Many members of minority communities maintain that race plays a significant role in deciding whether or not local resources and workforces are used to apprehend violent criminals. The way that justice is pursued across the country shows that all people do not receive equal treatment; clearly race matters in the criminal justice system.

The Death Penalty and Race

Timothy W. Wolfe

On September 21, 2011, Troy Davis, a forty-two-year-old African American man, was executed by the state of Georgia. Troy was convicted in 1991 and executed twenty years later for the 1989 murder of an off-duty police officer, Mark MacPhail, who was gunned down one summer night as he was moonlighting as a security guard. Officer MacPhail was shot twice as he attempted to stop a man, later identified by witnesses as Troy Davis, from pistol-whipping a homeless man in the parking lot of a fast food restaurant. But there were questions about the witnesses' ability to recognize who killed Officer MacPhail. With slim and disputed evidence, Troy Davis was found guilty and sentenced to death in 1991.

Despite lingering questions about the credibility of the evidence used to convict Troy Davis, Georgia officials ultimately ignored pleas for clemency from people all around the world—including former president Jimmy Carter (D), Pope Benedict XVI, Archbishop Desmond Tutu, former FBI director William Sessions, and former US congressman from Georgia Bob Barr (R), among others. Even longtime supporters of the death penalty expressed their concerns about the Davis case, requesting that state officials spare Troy's life. Just eight days before the execution Bob Barr wrote,

> I am a longtime supporter of the death penalty. I make no judgment as to whether Davis is guilty or innocent. And surely the

citizens of Savannah and the state of Georgia want justice served on behalf of Officer MacPhail. But imposing an irreversible sentence of death on the skimpiest of evidence will not serve the interest of justice. By granting clemency, the Georgia Board of Pardons and Parole will adhere to the most sacred principles of American jurisprudence, and will keep a man from being executed when we cannot be assured of his guilt.[2]

Many, like Barr, believed it was unjust to execute Troy Davis when the evidence against him was so questionable.

The problems with the Troy Davis case are well documented: there was little physical and forensic evidence linking Troy to the murder, the murder weapon was never recovered, and eyewitnesses who initially testified they saw Troy commit the murder later recanted or substantially changed their testimony, even claiming in some cases that police coerced them into making false statements. It is easy to imagine the tremendous pressure police were under to find and arrest Officer MacPhail's killer. At least three of the jurors who found Troy guilty and sentenced him to death said they now have serious doubts about his guilt and agree with those who have called for Troy's execution to be commuted. Troy always maintained his innocence. He steadfastly refused to admit guilt regarding the murder, even though admitting so may have helped him avoid the death penalty.

Was an innocent man put to death for a crime he did not commit? Has the real killer never been brought to justice? Besides raising these troubling questions, the case of Troy Davis also renews questions and reinforces concerns about the death penalty and the role race plays in its application. Just three years earlier (2008), the same Georgia Board of Pardons and Parole that denied clemency to Troy granted it to convicted murderer Samuel David Crowe. Samuel, a white man, was convicted of the 1988 robbery and murder of Joseph Pala, a white manager of a lumber store near Atlanta, Georgia. Samuel was sentenced to death after pleading guilty to the bloody and brutal murder. Just hours before his scheduled execution on May 22, 2008, the Board of Pardons and Parole commuted Samuel's sentence to life in prison. Samuel, a confessed killer, was spared by the state of Georgia. Troy, who many believe was innocent, was put to death.

Was Troy Davis's case influenced by the fact that the murder was interracial (that is, between races)? Was Samuel David Crowe granted clemency

---

[2] Bob Barr, "Troy Davis Merits Clemency," *Savannah Morning News* (September 14, 2011), http://savannahnow.com/column/2011-09-14/barr-troy-davis-merits-clemency.

because his crime was intraracial (that is, within the same racial group)? It is impossible to answer these questions with certainty. It is clear that the biggest concerns raised by the Troy Davis execution have to do with the veracity of the case and the possibility of executing an innocent person, not so much with claims about racial inequality. Still, many observers believe it is crucial that we raise questions about the role of race in death penalty cases. Such questions about the role of race in death penalty cases are controversial, provocative, uncomfortable, and troubling, but they must be raised, especially when one considers the history of the American legal system, its often unfair and harsh treatment of minorities, and the disparate application of the death penalty. There are clearly alternative explanations for why Troy was denied clemency and Samuel was granted it. However, as long as the data show a racially disparate application of the death penalty, we must continue to ask such questions and press for answers. We must not ignore the problem or try to rationalize or justify it. We should seek the truth about the role of race in the application of the death penalty and confront the problem head-on.

Social Science Research Findings on the Death Penalty and Race

Social science research reveals a consistent link between the application of the death penalty and race. Not every peer-reviewed, published study finds racial disparity or imbalance, but most studies have found such a connection. Scores of studies spanning many decades find that the race of the defendant and, increasingly, the race of the victim matter in terms of who is charged with and tried for a capital crime, who is sentenced to death, and who is ultimately executed. Raymond Paternoster and his colleagues summarize what is objectively known about the death penalty. They have carefully reviewed and analyzed the research literature and social scientific evidence since the 1930s, and they find that there is, in fact, "a racial imbalance in the administration of the death penalty."

> [Before 1972] black offenders were treated more harshly in the criminal justice system than white offenders. In more recent decades this research has shown that the race of the offender is less important than the race of the victim: Those who kill whites are treated more harshly at virtually every stage of the process compared with those who kill nonwhites.[3]

---

[3] Raymond Paternoster, Robert Brame, and Sarah Bacon, *The Death Penalty: America's Experience with Capital Punishment* (New York: Oxford University Press, 2008), 212.

This link between race and the application of the death penalty is called "the race effect." To be sure that the race effect is real, researchers carefully account for and measure relevant legal factors and aggravating circumstances, such as the number of victims, presence of torture or rape, and criminal history of defendants.[4] Though it is beyond the scope of this chapter, it should be noted that the death penalty also disproportionately affects defendants with less income and less education.[5] In America, race and social class overlap.

Identifying "racial disparity" in the application of the death penalty is a relatively straightforward, statistical matter. Racial disparity exists whenever a racial group is overrepresented or underrepresented in some measurable way. For example, according to the most current population data, African Americans make up about 13 percent of the overall US population.[6] At the same time, they represent more than one-third (35 percent) of those executed in the United States between 1976 and 2011.[7] Therefore, African Americans are overrepresented in execution statistics by a factor of nearly three (35 percent of those executed versus 13 percent of the overall US population). White (non-Hispanic) Americans account for nearly two-thirds (64 percent) of the overall US population as of 2010, but they represent only 55 percent of those executed between 1976 and 2011. Whites are, therefore, somewhat underrepresented in execution statistics.

However, while these statistical findings show the existence of racial disparity, they do not necessarily show "racial discrimination," which is a more complicated issue. Racial discrimination refers to the direct, intentional, and differential treatment of a defendant because of race. Discrimination is much more difficult to isolate, to measure, and to "prove" in the legal system. US courts have ruled that statistical evidence of racial disparity alone is not sufficient to demonstrate racial discrimination. The landmark 1987 US Supreme Court case *McCleskey v. Kemp* ruled that intentional discrimination, not statistical disparity, is unconstitutional.

---

[4] See David C. Baldus and George C. Woodworth's "Race Discrimination in the Administration of the Death Penalty: An Overview of the Empirical Evidence with Special Emphasis on the Post-1990 Research," *Criminal Law Bulletin* 39 (2003): 194–227; Tushar Kansal, "Racial Disparity in Sentencing: A Review of the Literature" (Washington, DC: The Sentencing Project, 2005); and Paternoster, Brame, and Bacon, *The Death Penalty*.

[5] Howard A. Allen and Jerome M. Clubb, *Race, Class, and the Death Penalty: Capital Punishment in American History* (Albany: State University of New York, 2008).

[6] US Census Bureau, QuickFacts, http://quickfacts.census.gov/qfd/states/00000.html.

[7] Death Penalty Information Center, http://www.deathpenaltyinfo.org/race-and-death-penalty.

This ruling, as a number of observers have suggested, effectively inoculates jurisdictions from charges of racial discrimination unless evidence of blatant, intentional discrimination can be produced.

A recent ruling in North Carolina, however, opens the door for challenging death sentences that appear to be the result of racial bias. The Racial Justice Act was passed in North Carolina in 2009. The Act allows those on death row to challenge their sentences using statistical evidence of racial disparity. On April 20, 2012, Superior Court Judge Gregory Weeks converted inmate Marcus Robinson's death sentence to life without the possibility of parole. In his ruling Judge Weeks said, "race was a materially, practically and statistically significant factor" in Robinson's death sentence.[8] Judge Weeks's ruling is the first to uphold the state's Racial Justice Act. Prosecutors quickly indicated that they would appeal the ruling. Many observers think this ruling and the North Carolina Racial Justice Act will open the way for additional court challenges to death sentences that are the result of racial disparity and discrimination. The assumption was that it might, ultimately, lead to a reversal of the McCleskey ruling. Time will tell. But the debate about racial bias in sentencing is not over in North Carolina. On June 28, 2012, Governor Beverly Purdue vetoed Senate Bill 416 that repealed North Carolina's Racial Justice Act, explaining in her veto statement that it is "simply unacceptable for racial prejudice to play a role in the imposition of the death penalty in North Carolina."[9] On July 2, the North Carolina legislature overrode her veto.

The death penalty has a long history. We have been putting people to death for more than four hundred years. The first recorded execution was in 1608.[10] From 1608 to 1929 more than 10,500 people have been put to death. Since 1930 there have been another 5,136 recorded executions in the United States. Of these, 3,859 occurred between the years of 1930 and 1967, a period some scholars call the "premodern era" of capital punishment. Another 1,277 of these executions have occurred since 1976, a period scholars refer to as the "modern era," following two important Supreme Court cases addressing the constitutionality of the death penalty. As discussed in chapter 3, the cases are *Furman v. Georgia* (1972), which

---

[8] Anne Blythe, "Racial Justice Act spares 1st inmate from death sentence," *News and Observer* (April 21, 2012), http://www.newsobserver.com/2012/04/20/2013448/judge -sides-with-inmate-in-racial.html.

[9] Beverly Eaves Purdue, "Governors Objections and Veto Message: Senate Bill 416" (June 29, 2010), http://www.ncleg.net/sessions/2011/S416Veto/govobjections.pdf.

[10] Paternoster, Brame, and Bacon, *The Death Penalty*, 5.

invalidated the death penalty as it was being applied at that time, and *Gregg v. Georgia* (1976), which reestablished the constitutionality of the death penalty. There were no executions in the United States between 1967 and 1976, a period when there was a moratorium, effectively, on the death penalty.

In the modern era (since 1976) slightly more than half of all executions (55 percent) have been of whites and slightly less than half (45 percent) have been of minorities or nonwhites. During most of this same period of time (1976–2005), US Bureau of Justice statistics show that whites were the offenders in approximately 46 percent of all murders and nonwhites were the offenders in 54 percent of murders. Most murders in the United States are intraracial: between 1976 and 2005, approximately 86 percent of all white murder victims were killed by other whites; 94 percent of all black victims were killed by other blacks.[11]

As figure 1 reveals, about three-fourths (76 percent) of all executions in the modern era involve a white victim; about one-fourth (24 percent) of all executions involve a nonwhite victim. During most of this same period (1976–2005), 51 percent of all murder victims have been white, 49 percent nonwhite. Reflect for a moment on what these statistics suggest. Murder victims in modern times are split nearly 50-50 between white Americans and minority Americans, yet three-fourths of all executions involve a white victim, while only one-fourth involve a minority victim. As pointed out above, social science research studies show that case and background variables, like severity of crime and criminal history, do not account for or explain the disparate treatment between races.

The decision to seek the death penalty is made locally in the United States, typically at the county level. Most criminal cases, including capital crimes, are prosecuted at the state level by district attorneys (DAs) who work in a particular county (DAs are also known as states attorneys in some jurisdictions). Therefore, there is tremendous regional variation across the country and within a state as to who gets the death penalty. There are at least three key issues that need to be highlighted with regard to geography and the death penalty: For one, in our federated system states are allowed to design and implement their own laws (as long as they are constitutional). This is reflected in the fact that thirty-three states, plus the federal government and US military, currently have the death penalty, while seventeen states do not (Death Penalty Information Center). Secondly, even among

---

[11] Bureau of Justice statistics, http://bjs.ojp.usdoj.gov/content/homicide/race.cfm.

Figure 1:
State Executions in the Modern Era (1976–2011)
By Race of Murder Victim

Source: DPIC

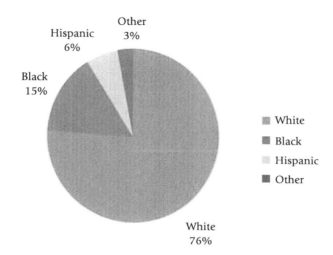

Other
3%

Hispanic
6%

Black
15%

White

Black

Hispanic

Other

White
76%

those states with the death penalty there is tremendous variation. Some states (e.g., Texas and Virginia) execute many more people than do other states. Thirdly and finally, there is tremendous variation within a single state. Some prosecutors aggressively apply the death penalty while others in that same state do not. A number of studies find that along with the race of the victim, location or jurisdiction is one of the most important predictors of who is sentenced to death.[12] One way to summarize these key points is to say that when it comes to the death penalty both race and place matter.

As figure 2 shows, executions are concentrated largely in the South. In fact, between 1976 and 2011, the overwhelming majority (82 percent) of the 1,277 executions in the United States have occurred in the South, 150

---

[12] See Raymond Paternoster's "Race of Victim and Location of Crime: The Decision to Seek the Death Penalty in South Carolina," *Journal of Criminal Law and Criminology* 74 (1983): 754–85; Raymond Paternoster, Robert Brame, Sarah Bacon, and Andrew Ditchfield, "Justice by Geography and Race: The Administration of the Death Penalty in Maryland, 1978–1999," *Margins: Maryland's Journal on Race, Religion, Gender, and Class* 4 (2004): 1–97; and Robert J. Smith, "The Geography of the Death Penalty and Its Ramifications," *Boston University Law Review* (2012).

Figure 2: Top 15 States Carrying Out Executions
State Number of Executions between 1976 and 2011

1. Texas 477

2. Virginia 109

3. Oklahoma 96

4. Florida 71

5. Missouri 68

6. Alabama 55

7. Georgia 52

8. Ohio 46

9. North Carolina 43

10. South Carolina 43

11. Louisiana 28

12. Arizona 28

13. Arkansas 27

14. Indiana 20

15. Mississippi 15

Note: 19 other states, the federal government and the U.S. military have executed 99 people during this same time period for a total of 1277 executions in the U.S. between 1976 and 2011. Source: Death Penalty Information Center

(12 percent) in the Midwest, 75 (6 percent) in the West, and 4 (less than 1 percent) in the Northeast (Death Penalty Information Center).

The rape of an adult was punishable by death until 1977, when the death penalty was ruled excessive, cruel, and unconstitutional in the US Supreme Court case *Coker v. Georgia*. A review of death penalty statistics for the crime of rape shows a particularly strong racial bias in the South. For example, there were 455 executions for rape in the United States between 1930 and 1967. Nearly all of these executions for rape (97 percent or 443 cases) occurred in the South. In 90 percent of these Southern executions for rape, the defendants were black.[13] Scholars have found a historical and cultural link between the racially disparate application of the death penalty, particularly in the South, and the lynchings of blacks in the South that occurred in earlier decades.[14] Retired US Supreme Court Justice John Paul

[13] Paternoster, Brame, and Bacon, *The Death Penalty*, 185.

[14] See Steven F. Messner, Robert D. Baller, and Matthew P. Zevenbergen, "The Legacy of Lynching and Southern Homicide," *American Sociological Review* 70 (2005): 633–55;

Stevens recently commented on the statistical evidence on race and the death penalty. He notes "that the murder of black victims is treated as less culpable than the murder of white victims provides a haunting reminder of once-prevalent Southern lynchings."[15]

Social science researchers continue to find that race matters. For example, one of the most recent studies on the death penalty and race examines data from the state of North Carolina and approximately fifteen thousand murder cases over twenty-seven years, from 1980 to 2007.[16] The data show that even after controlling for all legally relevant variables, those who killed white victims were three times more likely to receive a death sentence than those who killed black victims. There continues to be a pattern of racial disparity, especially in Southern jurisdictions. Where once the race of the defendant was a key factor in who was sentenced to death, today it is the race of the victim that makes a bigger difference. Those who kill whites pay a stiffer penalty.

A Brief History of the Legal System and Race in America

From its very inception, the United States has been a nation divided along racial lines. These racial divisions have been manifested in slaves versus slave holders, in states that legally recognized and enforced slavery and slave codes versus those states that did not, and in the myriad differences between how whites and nonwhites have been treated under the law. The very founding of the United States and the framing of our Constitution turned on compromises about the role of race and slavery. Delegates to the Constitutional Convention from Southern states where slavery existed and was vital to their economies (particularly Georgia, South Carolina, and North Carolina) made it clear that they would not form a union with those Northern states unless several compromises were made. These compromises, enshrined in the 1787 creation of the US Constitution, included the following: (1) the three-fifths clause, counting slaves as three-fifths of a person for purposes of representation and apportionment; (2) a twenty-year delay on ending the Atlantic slave trade, whereby

---

Richard E. Nisbett and Dov Cohen, *Culture of Honor: The Psychology of Violence in the South* (Boulder: Westview Press, 1996).

[15] John Paul Stevens, "On the Death Sentence," *The New York Review of Books* (December 23, 2010).

[16] Michael L. Radelet and Glenn L. Pierce, "Race and Death Sentencing in North Carolina, 1980–2007," *North Carolina Law Review* 89 (2011): 2119–59.

slaves from abroad could continue to be brought into the nation until at least 1808; and (3) the fugitive slave clause, guaranteeing that runaway slaves would be returned to their owners.[17] The conflicts and compromises over slavery were largely between the Southern and Northern states. As you saw above, this geographic and cultural divide is still present in the application of the death penalty today. This is a compelling example of how the past can be prologue.

It was no simple matter to end slavery as a legal, lucrative, brutal, and dehumanizing American social institution. It took a bloody civil war (1861–65), where approximately 625,000 soldiers from both sides died, the passage of the Thirteenth Amendment (1865) outlawing slavery, and the passage of the Fourteenth Amendment (1868) guaranteeing equal protection under the law. However, it would take at least another century of conflict, violence, and legal battles to end the set of laws and social policies known as Jim Crow. Jim Crow regulations, such as whites-only drinking fountains and restrictive voting law for blacks, were developed in the South after the Civil War. They made racial segregation legal and a fundamental aspect of everyday life. The legacy of slavery and Jim Crow are the background for the racially disparate application of the death penalty in the United States in modern times. Put another way, this legacy leads to a kind of "institutional racism" that continues to punish some offenders more harshly than others. When one studies the history of the legal system and race, it becomes clear that even in the absence of "personal" racism on the part of individuals in the criminal justice system—like police officers, prosecutors, judges, and jury members—it is not at all surprising to find that race still matters. Indeed, it would be very surprising to find no race effect.

Some scholars argue that our current criminal justice policies, especially the mass incarceration of minority males, represent a "new Jim Crow" or system of racial segregation and marginalization. As civil rights lawyer and author Michelle Alexander puts it, "Like Jim Crow (and slavery), mass incarceration operates as a tightly networked system of laws, policies, customs, and institutions that operate collectively to ensure the subordinate status of a group defined largely by race."[18] The mass incarceration of minorities (especially for nonviolent drug offenses), the disproportionate application of the death penalty for those who kill whites, and other

---

[17] S. Mintz, *Digital History (2007)*, http://www.digitalhistory.uh.edu.

[18] Michelle Alexander, *The New Jim Crow: Mass Incarceration in the Age of Color Blindness* (New York: The New Press, 2010), 13.

sentencing disparities all point to a legal system that continues to treat minorities more harshly than whites.[19]

As this section has shown, there is a long history of racial tension and discrimination in the US legal system, which includes slave codes that controlled blacks and allowed whites to treat slaves as property, Jim Crow laws that maintained the second-class status of minorities even after slavery was abolished, and the ongoing disparate treatment of minorities by our criminal justice system. There is a common thread connecting these historical periods and policies.

Summary and Conclusions

As the story of Troy Davis, the review of social science findings on the death penalty and race, and the brief discussion about the history of the legal system and race in America all show, there are problems with the way the death penalty is applied in the United States. Even those who believe that the death penalty is appropriate must be concerned with its racially biased application and the probability that innocent people have been executed.

What evidence is there of racial disparity in the application of the death penalty? How extensive is this racial disparity? Why does the disparity exist? Is it disparity only or is there reason to believe it is discrimination? What, if anything, can be done to reduce the racially disparate application of the death penalty? These are the sorts of questions we should be better able to begin exploring and discussing having now read this chapter.

I want to end with some personal reflections. As a social scientist and also a former employee in the criminal justice system, I have been aware of race problems within our criminal justice system for more than a quarter of a century now. It has only been in recent years, however, that I have come to the conclusion that reforming the death penalty so that it is applied in a just and reliable manner is nearly impossible. The historical legacy of racial discrimination and the ongoing problems of racial disparity are so vast that there is little hope, in my view, that we can maintain the death penalty and be assured it is applied fairly and accurately. I am in complete agreement with those, like former US Supreme Court Justice Harry A. Blackmun (1908–99), who argue that the death penalty must be abolished.

[19] Kansal, "Racial Disparity in Sentencing."

Justice Blackmun put it well when he came to this conclusion: "From this day forward, I no longer shall tinker with the machinery of death."[20] He went on to write, "It is virtually self-evident to me now that no combination of procedural rules or substantive regulations ever can save the death penalty from its inherent constitutional deficiencies." Justice Blackmun, once a supporter of the death penalty, arrived at these conclusions after spending twenty years on the court trying to make the death penalty fair and constitutional. A growing number of Americans are coming to the same view: the only way to eliminate the problems associated with the death penalty is to abolish it altogether.

Review and Looking Forward

Editors

June 29, 2012, marks the fortieth anniversary of the landmark *Furman v. Georgia* ruling, which suspended the death penalty in the United States and commuted the death sentences of death row inmates across the country. Reinstatement of the death penalty following the 1976 *Gregg v. Georgia* would require states to address the arbitrary application of the death penalty. In his concurring *Furman* opinion, Justice Thurgood Marshall stated that he judged it to be evident "that the burden of capital punishment falls upon the poor, the ignorant, and the underprivileged members of society. It is the poor, and the members of minority groups who are least able to voice their complaints against capital punishment. Their impotence leaves them victims of a sanction that the wealthier, better-represented, just-as-guilty person can escape."[21] Tim Wolfe's chapter shows how true the words of Justice Marshall ring forty years later.

As a sociologist, Tim has long been aware of the race problems pervading our justice system in general, and, in particular, the death penalty. The intense national and international coverage of the execution of Troy Davis in Georgia brought attention to what Tim already knew—the continuing arbitrariness and unfairness of the use of the death penalty in the United States. Given the serious questions about his guilt, people across the world were shocked when Troy was denied a last-minute stay of execution and

---

[20] Harry Blackmun, Opinion from the United States Supreme Court case *Callins v. Collins* (February 22, 1994).

[21] "U.S. Supreme Court: June 29 Marks 40th Anniversary of Furman v. Georgia," Death Penalty Information Center (June 29, 2012), http://www.deathpenaltyinfo.org /us-supreme-court-june-29-marks-40th-anniversary-furman-v-georgia.

an act of clemency. In a recent editorial, former president and governor of Georgia Jimmy Carter appealed to the state of Georgia and the United States to end the death penalty. After listing over eight major reasons why the death penalty should be ended, President Carter stated,

> Perhaps the strongest argument against the death penalty is extreme bias against the poor, minorities or those with diminished mental capacity. Although homicide victims are six times more likely to be black rather than white, 77 percent of death penalty cases involve white victims. Also, it is hard to imagine a rich white person going to the death chamber after being defended by expensive lawyers. This demonstrates a higher value placed on the lives of white Americans.[22]

Executions continue after all has quieted down after the execution of Troy Davis. We are left wondering how long it will be, after how many executions, until the American public reaches Tim Wolfe's conclusion.

Questions for Discussion

1. In addition to the racially disparate and discriminatory application of the death penalty, where else do you see racial inequality in contemporary American institutions? Do you think there are logical and historical connections between inequality in one institution (e.g., the legal system) and other institutions (e.g., education)?

2. Most people are not racist on a personal level. Yet, racism in the courts and other social institutions are well documented. Why? How do we respond?

3. Discuss the extent to which you think members of your local community are aware of the issues and facts explored in this chapter. What influences our awareness of the role of race in the criminal justice system?

[22] Jimmy Carter, "Show death penalty the door," *Atlanta Journal-Constitution* (April 25, 2012).

Chapter 15

Vulnerabilities and Risks

Editors

Very often things are not as they appear to be or as we assume them to be. Troubling images caught on film, such as in Selma and Birmingham during the civil rights era, bring us to question what we thought to be true of our society. Revelatory facts, such as the number of people unemployed or uninsured, bring us to question what we thought to be true about our local community. Unexpected statistics, such as the number of wrongfully convicted prisoners, bring us to question what we thought to be true about our judicial court system. The two previous chapters reveal that money and race matter in the death penalty system. Some persons know this to be obviously true; some of us find these disclosures deeply shocking.

In *The Death of Innocents*, Sr. Helen Prejean describes her movement from appearances and unexamined assumptions to realities and truths about our criminal justice system. Consistent with Tim Wolfe's discussion in the last chapter, she explains,

> I used to think that America had the best court system in the world. But now I know differently. Why is it that southern states are (and have always been) the most fervent practitioners of government killing, accounting for over 80 percent of U.S. executions? Why is it that Texas alone accounts for one third of the total number of U.S. executions . . . while the Northeast, supposedly guided by the same Constitution and Supreme Court guidelines, accounts for only 1 percent of executions? What explains the regional disparity in the way the death penalty is implemented?[1]

---

[1] Sr. Helen Prejean, *The Death of Innocents: An Eyewitness Account of Wrongful Executions* (New York: Vintage, 2006), xv–xvi.

Like Sr. Helen, many of us begin with the assumption that the death penalty is given consistently to persons proven beyond a reasonable doubt to be the "worst of the worst" criminals responsible for committing the most heinous crimes. We likely never thought that regional location, let alone money and race, matter. And we likely never thought that the most vulnerable among us—those who suffer from intellectual disabilities—are at risk of execution. We assume all persons on death row are culpable, proven guilty, and deserving of capital punishment.

This chapter takes us beyond assumptions and appearances and asks us to consider the truth about another dimension of the death penalty—the vulnerability of people with disabilities in our criminal justice system. The chapter opens with two contrasting stories among hundreds and goes on to explain how the Supreme Court's 2002 *Atkins* ruling attempted to address the risks faced by persons in such situations. But has the *Atkins* ruling eliminated the vulnerabilities and risks of persons with disabilities? Persons evaluated as being at or barely above the legal threshold for mental impairment continue to be executed. Standards and procedures for assessing disabilities vary from state to state. Numerous recent studies confirm the continuing vulnerabilities and risks of people with disabilities.

In March 2012 the Jesuit Social Research Institute of Loyola University published "Diminishing All of Us: The Death Penalty in Louisiana," a study by Alex Mikulich and Sophie Cull that focused on continuing problems in Louisiana's death penalty system. It concluded that the death penalty in Louisiana "has not been reserved for the 'worst of the worst' defendants but rather Louisiana's death row is overrepresented by individuals with serious childhood traumas, intellectual disabilities and mental disabilities."[2] We assume the *Atkins* ruling would prevent the execution of such persons. But Louisiana's legislature decided that "defendants have to prove their disability based on a preponderance of evidence, and that elected judges rather than mental health professionals are responsible for making that determination. The result is that unforgiving legal processes often result in offenders with very poor intellectual functioning remaining on death row" (ibid., 24).

Such problems continue in other states. For example, Georgia kept postponing the execution of Warren Hill, which was rescheduled for July 23, 2012. He tested at a sixth- to seventh-grade cognitive level, has an IQ level confirming intellectual disability, and suffered from neurological

---

[2] Alex Mikulich and Sophie Cull, "Diminishing All of Us: The Death Penalty in Louisiana," Jesuit Social Research Institute Loyola University New Orleans (2012), 5, www.loyno.edu/jsri/diminishing-all-us-death-penalty-louisiana.

impairment since birth. Nevertheless, Warren continues to face execution since the Georgia Supreme Court ruled that he failed to prove his intellectual disability beyond a reasonable doubt. Georgia has the highest standard for proving intellectual disability in the nation, placing a burden of proof that appears impossible to meet. On July 23rd after Warren was being processed for execution just two hours before his impending execution, he was granted a stay due to challenges regarding the state's lethal injection protocol. Warren's appeal on the basis of his intellectual disability will be heard next year, giving advocates for persons with intellectual disabilities time to persuade the state legislature to change the state's burden of proof standard.[3]

This chapter—collaboratively written by Thomas Powell, a former professor of education and current university president; Robert Perske, an author and advocate for persons with disabilities; and Mount St. Mary's students Tricia Lester and Dominique Nguyen—focuses on the situation of persons with intellectual disabilities in relation to capital sentencing. The chapter's opening story reveals the vulnerabilities and risks of persons with disabilities. The story is all too common; Joe Arridy's case repeats the story lines of many others. Prison personnel have reported that death row inmates with intellectual disabilities have asked whether they could eat the dessert of their last meal after the execution. Others describe such inmates turning to their executioners to thank them for the kindnesses of their treatment as they walk to their death. Given the challenges faced by persons with intellectual disabilities, it falls on us to determine whether the *Atkins* ruling merely gave the appearance of having addressed the important concerns of this chapter. Are persons with intellectual disabilities still vulnerable and at risk of being executed in our own states? It is our responsibility to find out the truth.

People with Disabilities and the Death Penalty

Thomas H. Powell, Robert Perske, Patricia A. Lester, and Dominique L. Nguyen

It only took seventy-two years for a basic sense of decency to prevail. On January 27, 2011, Governor Bill Ritter of Colorado granted a full and

---

[3] Bill Rankin, "Supreme Court Grants Stay of Execution to Killer," *Atlantic Journal-Constitution* (July 23, 2012), http://www.ajc.com/news/atlanta/state-supreme-court-grants-1483065.html.

unconditional pardon to Joe Arridy. Sadly, Joe had been executed on January 6, 1939, by the State of Colorado. The evidence was questionable, and Joe's intellectual disability was not allowed to be considered in his sentencing. Joe was a too willing defendant, and society was too quick to demand retribution, rather than seek justice. In this rare posthumous pardon, Governor Ritter noted the substantial body of evidence confirming that the twenty-three-year-old Joe Arridy was innocent. His confession was coerced, someone else admitted guilt, and his severe mental disability was never given due consideration. The governor said, "Pardoning Mr. Arridy cannot undo this tragic event in Colorado history. It is in the interests of justice and simple decency, however, to restore his good name."[4]

Joe Arridy's story is chronicled by Bob Perske in *Deadly Innocence*.[5] Joe grew up in Colorado at a time when services to people with intellectual disabilities were nonexistent. He was denied the opportunity to attend school. Joe was placed, for life, in an institution primarily intended to keep society safe rather than to provide education and treatment. One fateful night, Joe, along with a few other residents, escaped the confines of the institution and drifted from place to place, hopping freight trains. On August 15, 1936, in Pueblo, Colorado, fifteen-year-old Dorothy Drain was raped and murdered and her sister Barbara was brutally attacked in their home. At first the police investigation focused on Frank Aguilar since circumstantial evidence linked him to the crime, and the police later recovered the murder weapon from his home. Police in Wyoming, however, arrested Joe Arridy for loitering and assumed that he might be connected to Dorothy's murder. Frank Aguilar confessed to the murder, was convicted, and sentenced to death. In a separate trial Joe Arridy was also convicted and sentenced to death.

Joe's life on death row was anything but typical. Friendly to all, he liked to play simple games. The warden had a special relationship with Joe and arranged for this "happiest person on death row" to receive treats and toys. On January 6, 1937, Joe was led to the gas chamber and killed for a murder he did not commit. In granting this full and unconditional pardon, Governor Ritter drew on a basic standard of decency, demanding that we vigorously question the use of the death penalty for any person with intellectual, cognitive, or developmental disabilities.

---

[4] "Gov. Ritter Grants Posthumous Pardon in Case Dating Back to 1930s," Office of Gov. Bill Ritter Jr. (Jan 7, 2011), http://www.deathpenaltyinfo.org/documents /ArridyPardon.pdf.

[5] See Robert Perske, *Deadly Innocence* (Nashville: Abington Press, 1995).

An especially brutal murder was committed in 1976 in Billings, Montana. A man was beaten to death on a bitterly cold winter night, and his body was wrapped in another's coat and left in an alley. Despite extensive media coverage, the police had no leads, and the investigation came to a standstill. The outcome of this case stands in sharp contrast to the execution of Joe Arridy.

David (not his real name), a young man with an intellectual disability, experienced the first wave of deinstitutionalization in Montana. In 1974 he moved to a group home and later a supervised apartment, spending his days at a sheltered workshop doing odd tasks. He was known as a friendly person, eager to please and make friends with strangers. After hearing the report about the murder, David went directly to the police and confessed. Due to his intellectual disability and confusion, the police were initially skeptical and contacted his community support team. But David knew many details of the murder never released to the public. He told his community advocate that the man had propositioned him and when he persisted in touching him, David became enraged. Acting on impulse, he continued to hit the man. Unaware of the severity of the blows, he covered the man with his coat so he would not freeze to death. After extensive questioning, it was clear that David's blows had killed this man. In response, questions were raised: What is the decent response to such a murder? Was David morally culpable? How should his disability be considered in regard to the crime?

Instead of an extensive trial, the prosecuting attorneys, working with David's public defender, decided on a course of action based on the severity and circumstances of his crime and his intellectual disability. David knew what he did was wrong and felt deep remorse. Instead of a prison sentence judged to serve no purpose, David was sent to a treatment facility where he could continue to learn to deal with his challenges, effectively manage his responses, and develop skills, making possible community integration. David now thrives in a community program with extensive community support in another part of Montana.

In contrast to the case of Joe Arridy, a basic and wise standard of decency was applied in this case. There was no doubt that a serious capital crime had been committed by David. But both prosecutors and the defense team acknowledged the role David's intellectual disabilities played in this murder and sought restoration and rehabilitation rather than mere retribution.

The Need for Justice and Decency

While we have come a long way in our understanding of and response to people with intellectual disabilities who commit serious crimes, it is a fact that too many people with such disabilities are still in prison facing execution. As a nation we have a responsibility to understand the complex issues surrounding the death penalty as it bears on persons with intellectual disabilities. We have a responsibility for understanding cases such as that of Earl Washington, a man with intellectual disabilities who confessed to a crime he did not commit. In 1983 police persuaded Earl to make statements concerning a rape and murder of a woman in Virginia in 1982 that were used against him in his 1984 trial. The trial resulted in a death sentence. After moving to Virginia's death house, Earl had no legal representation. A fellow inmate fought to inform anyone who would listen about the injustice done to him. After years of struggle, DNA tests finally supported Earl's claims of innocence. In response to requests for a full pardon, Governor Wilder instead commuted his sentence to life with the right of parole. Later, after more extensive DNA testing reconfirmed his innocence, he was finally given a full pardon.

In 2008, Bob Perske chronicled fifty-three cases in which persons with intellectual disabilities falsely confessed to serious crimes, such as murder, rape, arson, and robbery.[6] In a follow-up study in 2011, Bob found that the new total number of people with intellectual disabilities falsely accused had risen to seventy-five. This number will likely grow in the future. As more people with disabilities live in local communities, they will increasingly confront a criminal justice system that is simply not responsive or prepared to accommodate their special needs.

Defining Intellectual Disability

Over the years, the terms with which we refer to people with intellectual disabilities have evolved in light of our understanding of these persons and their unique needs. The term *mental retardation* has been replaced over the past decade by the more accurate term *intellectual disability*. The American Association on Intellectual and Developmental Disabilities (AAIDD) has developed the most accurate and commonly used definition of intellectual disabilities. The AAIDD defines an intellectual disability as a disability characterized by significant limitations both in intellectual functioning and adaptive behavior, which covers many everyday social and practical skills.[7] This disability originates before the age of eighteen. Intellectual functioning—also called intelligence—refers to general mental capacity, such as learning, reasoning, and problem solving.

---

[6] Robert Perske, "False confessions from 53 persons with intellectual disabilities: the list keeps growing," *Intellectual and Developmental Disabilities* 46:6 (2008): 468–79.

There are various means to measure intellectual capacity. One criterion of measurement is an IQ test. Generally, an IQ test score of around 70 or as high as 75 indicates a limitation in intellectual functioning. Standardized tests can also determine limitations in adaptive behavior, which comprises three skill types: conceptual skills (such as language and literacy), social skills (such as interpersonal skills, social responsibility, problem solving, and ability to follow rules and avoid being victimized), and practical skills used in daily living. Such intellectual disability is typically manifested and diagnosed early in life. But in defining and assessing intellectual disability, professionals must take additional factors into account, such as community environment, linguistic diversity, and cultural differences, which influence the way people interact and typically affect standardized intelligence test scores. Finally, assessments must also assume that limitations in individuals often coexist with strengths, and that a person's level of life functioning will improve if appropriate education and supports are provided over a sustained period.

Vulnerability to Injustice

While no one argues that the presence of an intellectual disability in and of itself warrants an exemption from responsibility for one's actions, this disability requires special consideration to determine legal culpability. People with intellectual disabilities share a number of characteristics that put them in greater jeopardy in the legal system. While many people with intellectual disabilities know the difference between right and wrong, their intellectual deficits play a significant role in determining culpability for crimes that they may commit.

Intellectual deficits have significant consequences relevant to the criminal justice system. People with intellectual disabilities typically have significant communication problems. They have diminished capacities to understand and process information, especially complex information and proceedings in any legal venue. They have significant problems generalizing from past learning and experience. The ability to recognize subtle differences between social situations, which most of us take for granted, is a major aspect of their disability. While most of us are able to learn from past mistakes, people with intellectual disabilities are unable to abstract from mistakes to guide their actions in new situations. Additionally they lack reasoning skills needed to

---

[7] R. Luckasson, ed., *Mental Retardation: Definition, Classification, and Systems of Supports*, 10th ed. (American Association on Mental Retardation, 2002). (The organization is now the American Association on Intellectual and Developmental Disabilities.)

follow complex situations, such as dealing with the legal system. Eager to please others, especially authority figures, they can be easily coerced into admitting falsehoods. Given this, criminal confessions by them are highly questionable. Many people with intellectual disabilities have problems with impulse control and are quick to react and misunderstand the intentions of others. Due to problems of factual recall and distinguishing between reality and fantasy, they make poor witnesses. They also may not be able to communicate remorse for their actions.

Given these challenges, people with intellectual disabilities are unable to adequately assist their counsel in their defense. Their intellectual disabilities undermine the integrity and procedural protections of our legal system, especially capital jurisprudence safeguards. Failure to recognize the characteristics of this disability leads to the type of tragedy experienced by Joe Arridy.

Retribution and Deterrence

Common arguments used to justify capital punishment are that the death penalty imposes just retribution for capital crimes and serves as a deterrent to others. Such justifications, challengeable on their own terms, become highly problematic when applied to people with intellectual disabilities. Just retribution relies on the culpability of the offender, which becomes highly problematic in such circumstances. Did persons with intellectual disabilities know and intend what they were doing? Did they plan their actions or merely react on impulse? Did they understand the outcomes of their actions? When culpability is in question, there can be no justification for capital punishment on the basis of just retribution. The deterrent argument assumes that agents deliberate about their actions, weighing the anticipated consequences of their actions. Such premeditation and deliberation are less likely for persons with intellectual disabilities. The cognitive and behavioral impairments that make these defendants less culpable also diminish their capacity to process information related to the expectations of punishment for their actions.

The Supreme Court Weighs In

Over time, opposition to the execution of persons with intellectual disabilities has continued to build. Key professional and civic organizations have taken a strong public stand, including the American Bar Association, American Psychological Association, American Association on Intellectual and Developmental Disabilities (AAIDD), The Arc of the United States, the

American Civil Liberties Association, and the US Conference of Catholic Bishops (USCCB). Finally, the Supreme Court intervened. On June 2, 2002, the US Supreme Court in the landmark *Atkins v. Virginia* decision ruled, in a 6–3 vote, that executing death row inmates with intellectual disabilities violates the ban on cruel and unusual punishment. The justices concluded that the Eighth Amendment, in relationship to evolving standards of decency, implies that a death sentence for such persons is excessive and thus unconstitutional. The ruling claimed that people with intellectual disabilities should be held responsible for crimes they commit. However, it argued that "because of their reasoning, judgment and control of their impulses . . . They [persons with intellectual disabilities] do not act with the same moral culpability that characterizes the most serious adult criminal conduct" (536 US 2002). The court also recognized that such defendants face a very high risk of wrongful convictions.

The Atkins case set a new standard of decency, overruling the 1989 *Penry v. Lynaugh* ruling (492 US 302, 335). At the time of the *Penry* decision, only two states (Maryland and Georgia) had legislated against the execution of persons with intellectual disabilities. Arguing that there was insufficient evidence of a national consensus against such executions, *Penry* ruled that executing persons with intellectual disabilities did not constitute cruel and unusual punishment. The court did emphasize that such disabilities should be considered a mitigating factor during the sentencing trial phase. The landmark *Atkins* decision clearly set a new standard of human decency. While the *Atkins* decision only applies to people with intellectual disabilities, it opened the court to further considerations of the appropriateness of the death penalty for people with other types of disability, such as developmental disabilities and disabilities resulting from traumatic brain injury or dementia.

Post-Atkins Concerns

In his vehement dissent in the *Atkins* decision, Justice Anton in Scalia raised concerns about the possibility of the courts being flooded by an increased number of defendants claiming to have an intellectual disability. Furthermore, some argued that the *Atkins* decision would be applied inconsistently across the states due to the lack of a consistent definition of intellectual disabilities. To test these concerns, John H. Blume, Sheri Lynn Johnson, and Christopher Seeds completed an empirical analysis of all cases adjudicated since *Atkins* to determine if there was an increase in true or frivolous claims of intellectual disabilities in capital cases. They found at the time that only one-half of the cases filed in response to *Atkins* had been ruled upon. However their extensive review found that the *Atkins* decision has not led to a significant number of nonmeritorious claims of intellectual disability and that the success rates for defendants making claims of intellectual disabilities has varied greatly among states. Their analysis also showed that race played a complicated role in *Atkins* claims. Their study concluded that "Justice Scalia's concerns have gone unfounded, but . . . Atkins is not evenhandedly protecting those it was designed to protect."[8] Clearly *Atkins* has not sufficiently protected persons with intellectual disabilities.

Continuing Challenges

The *Atkins* decision did not identify measures for intellectual disabilities, and, as a result, it set the stage for specific legislative revisions in states with capital punishment. Challenges remain regarding the defining and identifying of such disabilities; refining of procedures for evaluation; access of indigent defendants to qualified professional evaluation; and educating of prosecutors, defense attorneys, and judges regarding intellectual disabilities. In addition, while the *Atkins* ruling argued that persons with disabilities have constitutional protection from death sentences in past and future cases, some states still need to develop procedures for addressing the situation of persons with intellectual disabilities who have already been convicted.

Clearly much work remains to be done on the state level to prevent the execution of persons with intellectual disabilities. In his detailed study of the need for state legislation, Professor James Ellis of the University of New Mexico School of Law concluded that, even given *Atkins* protections, "experience teaches that sometimes the machinery of the criminal justice system works imperfectly, and for any number of reasons, an individual with mental retardation might end up on Death Row, facing the prospect of execution."[9] In 2008, AAIDD and The Arc issued a joint statement addressing such challenges, arguing that people with intellectual and/or

[8] John H. Blume, Sheri Lynn Johnson, and Christopher Seeds, "An Empirical Look at *Atkins v. Virginia* and Its Application in Capital Cases," Cornell Law School Legal Studies Research Paper Series, Paper No. 09-021, http://www.deathpenaltyinfo.org/documents/EmpiricalAtkins.pdf.

[9] See James W. Ellis, "Mental Retardation and the Death Penalty: A Guide to State Legislative Issues," Death Penalty Information Center, http://www.deathpenaltyinfo.org/documents/MREllisLeg.pdf.

developmental disabilities who are victims, suspects, or witnesses "have a right to justice and fair treatment in all areas of the criminal justice system, including reasonable accommodations as necessary." The statement concluded that persons with intellectual disabilities continue to face "fear, prejudice, and lack of understanding" in the criminal justice system and still run the risk of execution as "a consequence of falling through the cracks in the system."[10]

Texas illustrates the continuing challenges after *Atkins* left it to the states to define intellectual disabilities and establish evaluation procedures. In 2001 the Texas legislature passed a law mandating life sentences for persons with intellectual disabilities convicted of capital crimes. The bill passed with bipartisan support, but was vetoed by Governor Rick Perry due to his concern that it was an indirect attempt to erode the death penalty. Without fair and clear evaluative guidelines, persons with disabilities continue to be at grave risk in Texas. Since the *Atkins* ruling, thirteen men have been removed from Texas's death row based on the judgment that their intellectual and emotional capacities were that of twelve-year-olds. Yet Texas has a 28 percent success rate for *Atkins* appeals, in sharp contrast to the 40 percent national success rate. Recent developments in Texas justify continuing concerns. Dr. George Denkowski, the psychologist who judged sixteen death row inmates qualified for execution (two of whom have been executed), was recently reprimanded and fined by the Texas State Board of Examiners of Psychologists for using methods challenged by professionals.[11] Clearly persons with intellectual disabilities remain at risk of execution.

A Call to Action

While the *Atkins* decision and a significant number of state legislatures have banned the death penalty for people with intellectual disabilities, still more work is needed to ensure that persons with intellectual disabilities are not put to death. The first step for anyone who wishes to help ensure this is to stay informed and take actions consistent with our obligations as citizens. Below are six recommended actions:

---

[10] "Criminal Justice: Joint Position Statement of AAIDD and The Arc" (2008), http://aaidd.org/content_158.cfm?navID=31.

[11] B. Grissom, "Psychologist Who Cleared Death Row Inmates Is Reprimanded," *New York Times* (April 14, 2011).

1. *Advocate* for state legislatures to enact legislation banning the death penalty for persons with intellectual disabilities. Such legislation should protect not only those accused in the future but also those already sentenced.

2. *Seek information* about death row inmates with intellectual disabilities. If the state and federal prisons do not have such data, requests may lead to a reporting of the magnitude of the problem.

3. *Visit* prisoners with intellectual disabilities. Without regard to innocence or guilt, people with intellectual disabilities need to have their humanity affirmed.

4. *Educate* those in the criminal justice system (police, attorneys, judges) about the problems people with intellectual disabilities face in the criminal justice system.

5. *Speak out* on this issue to educate the general public.

6. *Support and join* organizations dedicated to the abolition of the death penalty.

Catholics are strongly called to action on this issue. In 2004, Pope John Paul II made his advocacy clear:

> The starting point for every reflection on disability is rooted in the fundamental convictions of Christian anthropology: even when disabled persons are mentally impaired or when their sensory or intellectual capacity is damaged, they are fully human beings and possess the sacred and inalienable rights that belong to every human creature. Indeed, human beings, independently of the conditions in which they live or of what they are able to express, have a unique dignity and a special value from the very beginning of their life until the moment of natural death. . . . In fact . . . it is in the more difficult and disturbing situations that the dignity and grandeur of the human being emerges. The wounded humanity of the disabled challenges us to recognize, accept and promote in each one of these brothers and sisters of ours the incomparable value of the human being created by God.[12]

---

[12] See Pope John Paul's message to the International Symposium on the Dignity and Rights of the Mentally Disabled Person (January 5, 2004), as quoted in by the USCCB, Life Matters: Persons with Disabilities, http://usccb.org/about/pro-life-activities/respect -life-program/2011/upload/life-matters-persons-with-disabilities-bulletin-insert.pdf.

Unquestionably as a society we have made progress in affirming the worth of persons with disabilities, but significant challenges still remain in the criminal justice system, especially regarding the death penalty.

The US bishops, like John Paul II, do not stop at defending the human rights of disabled persons. They ask us to recognize ourselves in the disabled and to see their lives as gifts:

> Persons with disabilities challenge us to be more fully human and compassionate, to recognize the presence of God in each human being. This requires us to sacrifice, to "stretch our hearts," as Pope Benedict XVI has said. This requires us to gradually become more like Christ, which is after all the goal of every Christian life. In short, as persons with disabilities share their gifts and needs, they bring out the best in our mutual humanity. (ibid.)

The bishops call us to recognize that "every human person—no matter how vulnerable or helpless . . . no matter how healthy, handicapped or sick, no matter how useful or productive for society—is a being of inestimable worth created in the image and likeness of God."[13] Our reflections on basic decency and justice in relation to persons with disabilities bring us to clearly understand this vision of the person central to all Catholic social teaching as it bears on the practice of the death penalty.

Review and Looking Forward

This chapter focused on the vulnerabilities and risks of persons with intellectual disabilities and called us to action in response to what we have learned. Similar concerns focus on an additional group: persons with severe psychological problems remain equally vulnerable and at risk. The introduction to the previous chapter on race illustrated the inconsistencies in judicial responses to persons suffering from severe psychological disorders. A number of states currently struggle with complex issues posed by the executions of mentally ill inmates.

In 1991, Steven Staley was convicted of capital murder for the killing of Robert Read. Steven had been judged competent to stand trial. But he showed signs of suffering from mental illness. In Texas, where he still faces execution, the standard for such competence was set low: a defendant simply had to be able to comprehend the charges against him and consult

---

[13] Ibid. (quoting John Paul II, Remarks at departure ceremony at the Detroit Airport, September 19, 1987).

rationally with his lawyer so as to assist in his own defense. This standard for competency at execution was set by the 1986 *Ford v. Wainwright* ruling, which held that the Eighth Amendment's ban on cruel and unusual punishment forbid the execution of insane persons.

The *Atkins* ruling banned the execution of persons with intellectual disabilities. But it is still not unconstitutional to execute convicted persons who suffered from a serious mental illness when they committed their offense. The Eighth Amendment has been interpreted as forbidding the executing of persons who are unaware of their punishment and the reasons why they are being punished. Condemned death row inmates must have a rational understanding of what is occurring. Many mentally ill persons can meet this standard. In Steven Staley's case, the symptoms of his serious mental illnesses are traceable to childhood and possibly inherited from a mother who suffered from schizophrenia. Steven's mental illness has worsened during his imprisonment, resulting in extended hospitalizations.

Steven continues to display symptoms of serious mental illness: visual and auditory hallucinations, paranoia, grandiose delusions, extreme depression, and psychotic behaviors. His impending execution can proceed only if he is forcibly medicated to the point of temporary competence. This situation has raised the question of whether a death row inmate can be forcibly medicated so as to allow his execution to proceed. Similar to the concerns raised in Kim Hansen's chapter on lethal injection, health care professionals fear that it is a perversion of mental health treatment to forcibly medicate a person so that the state can then inject him with lethal drugs. As of May 15, 2012, a stay of execution has been issued as constitutional issues are explored.

Similarly Abdul Awhal was scheduled to be executed in Ohio on June 6, 2012, despite continuing evidence of his history of mental breakdowns, hallucinations, suicidal depression, and repeated diagnosis of schizoaffective disorder. He was sentenced to death for two murders despite his being mentally incompetent to assist in his own defense. On death row he is convinced his continuing incarceration is tied to CIA agent threats against him. A June 7, 2012, editorial in the *New York Times* titled "Failure to Account for Severe Mental Illness" called the courts to be much more attentive to such death row inmates suffering from severe mental illness. It argued that "the death penalty system fails to take adequate account of severe mental illness, whether at trial, at sentencing or in postconviction proceedings." The editorial praised the decision of Governor John Kasich of Ohio to grant a two-week reprieve to Abdul days before his scheduled execution. The editorial concluded, "This is yet another reason the death penalty should be abolished and further evidence of the grave injustices of the system."[14]

The Death Penalty Information Center continues to update the cases of mentally ill inmates who have been executed or have had their death sentences reduced to life without parole.[15] The US bishops emphasize the government's obligation to protect communities from violence committed by persons of diminished mental capacities or suffering from mental illnesses. But they also call our communities to diagnose and address the needs of these persons.[16] If each of us can help educate our local communities about the needs of persons who are most vulnerable, the tragedies discussed in these chapters can be avoided.

Questions for Discussion

1. The United States Conference of Catholic Bishops has a Respect Life Program. In it, the bishops ask us to stretch our hearts and become more Christlike. Discuss what they mean when they say, "Persons with disabilities challenge us to be more fully human and compassionate" (USCCB, Life Matters: Persons with Disabilities, Respect Life Program, 2011–12).

2. In order to respond to the vulnerabilities and risks of persons with intellectual disabilities, we need to be aware of the risks they continue to face in specific states. Often their situation goes unnoticed. Discuss how we might be better informed, and how we might be able to take action on their behalf.

3. In a February 9, 2004, article titled "Mentally Ill Prisoners," the editors of the Jesuit publication *America* wrote of the growing problems faced by mentally ill persons in our prison system. The article stated that "jails and prisons hold three times as many mentally ill people as mental health hospitals." Discuss how this situation has developed and concrete ways concerned persons might respond to the situation of the mentally ill in their communities.

[14] "A Stay of Execution," *New York Times* (June 6, 2012), http://www.nytimes.com/2012/06/07/opinion/a-stay-of-execution.html?_r=3&ref=opinion.

[15] "Examples of Mentally Ill Inmates Who Were Executed," Death Penalty Information Center (2012), http://deathpenaltyinfo.org/mental-illness-and-death-penalty#executions.

[16] United States Conference of Catholic Bishops, Responsibility, Rehabilitation, and Restoration: A Catholic Perspective on Crime and Criminal Justice (Washington, DC: USCCB, 2000), 42.

Chapter 16

A Matter of Discipleship

Editors

No one knew the challenges of living the gospel better than Dorothy Day. For almost fifty years, she served and lived with the poor. In the early 1930s, she founded, with Peter Maurin, houses of hospitality, which fed and housed the needy in New York City. They also started the *Catholic Worker* newspaper. Soon the *Catholic Worker* and its houses of hospitality were a nationwide movement. Through the newspaper, Dorothy told the stories of the people with whom she lived. She made known the names and lives, hopes and struggles of the anonymous poor. And she called all of us—rich, poor, and in-between—to a life of mutual service and discipleship. Her life serves as an example for us of living out the traditional works of mercy. In 2000, Dorothy has been named, by Pope John Paul II, as a Servant of God.[1]

The works of mercy are gleaned from Scripture (e.g., Matt 6:14; 18:15; 25:34-40) and divided according to the needs of the body (corporal works) and the needs of the soul (spiritual works).[2] The corporal works are to feed the hungry, give drink to the thirsty, clothe the naked, shelter the homeless, visit the sick, visit and ransom the prisoner, and bury the dead. Dorothy is known for these corporal works. But she emphasized the spiritual works equally as much: to admonish sinners, instruct the ignorant, counsel the doubtful, comfort the sorrowful, bear wrongs patiently, forgive willingly, and pray for the living and the dead. Dorothy notes from experience that the works of mercy are difficult because they are often thankless and appear foolish. When practicing the corporal

---

[1] The title Servant of God indicates that her case for sainthood has been accepted, and her life and work is in the process of examination by the church.

[2] Consult the entry on "Corporal and Spiritual Works of Mercy" in the Catholic Encyclopedia, http://www.newadvent.org/cathen/10198d.htm.

works, people may take advantage of our kindness. When practicing the spiritual works, like instructing the ignorant and admonishing sinners, people may be indifferent or get angry and take offense.

In Jim Forest's biography of Dorothy Day, *All Is Grace*, he includes his personal remembrance of her:

> Dorothy helped bring about a conversion of heart that greatly influenced many people in the Church, especially in America. . . . [Such conversion] is rooted in the sacredness of life. Dorothy helped us better understand one of the primary biblical truths: that each person, no matter how damaged or battered by events and circumstances of life, is a bearer of the image of God and deserves to be recognized as such. She has reminded us of the real presence of Christ in the least person. . . . Dorothy gave us an astonishing example of hospitality and mercy as a way of life. "We are here to celebrate Him," she said time and time again, "through the works of mercy."[3]

She once asked, Why else would anyone attend liturgy, receive Communion, and call oneself a Christian if one was not trying to live the gospel (ibid., 325)?

Dorothy Day never avoided any of the controversial parts of the church's social teaching, including the death penalty. In this chapter, Fr. Jim Donohue will emphasize that preaching about issues like the death penalty takes strength and courage. Such preaching brings disagreements and arguments to the surface, but it also can sow the seeds of discipleship. Dorothy understood the core of the church's teaching on the death penalty (as explained in chaps. 10, 11, and 12). Visiting prisoners, she often commented, is the most neglected of all the works of mercy. She had been jailed in 1917 for being part of a women's suffrage demonstration and in the 1950s for protesting the policies of nuclear armament and escalation. She knew the crushing, numbing realities of prisons.

During a month's imprisonment in 1957, she asked why Christians are so blind to Christ's presence in the people society locks away. She wrote, "Christ is with us today, not only in the Blessed Sacrament and where two or three are gathered together in His Name, but also in the poor. And who could be poorer and more destitute in body and soul than these companions of ours in prison?" She knew the reality of prison and her fellow inmates, and she wrote of the challenge of seeing Christ in them

---

[3] Jim Forest, *All Is Grace: A Biography of Dorothy Day* (Maryknoll, NY: Orbis Books, 2011), 336–37.

and loving them in their suffering. She emphasized that in loving them "we are not oblivious to their faults, their sins. This is true love because primarily we love them because Jesus loved them—He came to call sinners, to find the lost sheep" (ibid., 207–8).

Dorothy Day cared deeply and publicly about the death penalty. She joined Pope Pius XII in opposing the execution of Ethel and Julius Rosenberg and encouraged high-ranking clergy in the United States to have the courage and strength to speak out against the execution. She continued to persevere, even when her efforts were not successful. She describes how while bathing her grandchild Nickie, her heart was heavy as she thought of the yearning of Ethel's heart for her soon-to-be orphaned sons.[4] She prayed for the couple as they went to their execution in Sing Sing Prison (not far from where she lived): "'Lord Jesus Christ, Son of the Living God, have mercy on them.' But somehow, feeling close to their humanity, I prayed for fortitude for them. 'God let them be strong, take away all fear from them; let them be spared this suffering, at least, this suffering of fear and trembling.'"[5]

She understood the suffering they had already endured on death row. "What greater punishment can be inflicted on anyone than those two long years in a death house, watched without ceasing so that there is no chance of one taking one's life and so thwarting the vengeance of the state. They had already suffered the supreme penalty." Her hope for a reprieve turned her thoughts to Dostoevsky, whose death sentence had been commuted at the last moment, and to Albert Einstein and Harold Urey, prominent atomic scientists, who both proclaimed the Rosenbergs' innocence and argued their guilt had never been proven. But Dorothy opposed their execution, independent of guilt, innocence, or proof, knowing the Christian response could be only one of "love and yearning for salvation" (ibid.).

Dorothy focused on the Rosenbergs' last gestures. She learned that the Rosenbergs' rabbi had read them Psalms 15, 23, and 31 as they walked to the electrocution chairs. She responded, "How mixed up religion can become. How little our activities are shaped by the holy words we know by heart."[6] After professing their innocence, they expressed their love for their sons, one of whom would go on to work to end the death penalty.

---

[4] See Robert Ellsberg's *Dorothy Day, Selected Writings,* 6th ed. (Maryknoll, NY: Orbis Books, 2011) for Dorothy's reflections on the Rosenbergs' execution summarized here (274–77). Jim Forest also discusses her reflections that were published as "Meditation on the Death of the Rosenbergs," in the *Catholic Worker* issue that followed the execution (194–95).

[5] Ellsberg, *Dorothy Day,* 276.

[6] Forest, *All Is Grace,* 195.

Then Ethel warmly embraced her female guards in a final gesture of love. Not surprisingly, Dorothy focused on this gesture, consistent with her frequent quoting of the words of St. John of the Cross—"Love is the measure by which we will be judged." Years later in response to a New York University student's question about whether killing was ever justified, Dorothy responded immediately, going straight to the heart of the issue: "We are taught by our Lord to love our enemies," and then she left her listeners considering which of his enemies Christ had killed (ibid., 320).

In 1997 Cardinal John O'Connor, archbishop of New York, initiated Dorothy Day's canonization process. He asked, "Why does the Church canonize saints? In part, so that their person, their works and their lives will become that much better known, and that they will encourage others to follow in their footsteps—and so the Church may say, 'This is sanctity . . .'" He went on to emphasize that Dorothy believed each person is "a temple of God, sacred, made in the image and likeness of God, infinitely more important in its own way than any building. . . . To Dorothy Day, everyone was a cathedral" (ibid., 307–8).

Dorothy Day's life shows the challenge of hearing and living the gospel. In this chapter, Fr. Jim Donohue, a professor of theology, will begin with an account of the difficulties in preaching about "social" issues like labor unions and the death penalty. Dorothy Day would recognize all too well his description of the challenge and his experience of rejection. She understood all too well that the social teaching of the church is an essential, far from tangential, part of Catholic faith. She repeatedly called the church—both clergy and laity—to live out its own teaching, the teaching that had become the center of her daily living. It is fitting that a book titled *Where Justice and Mercy Meet: Catholic Opposition to the Death Penalty* ends with a chapter called "The Heart of Our Faith." Father Jim brings us into the heart of the matter: the challenge of following Jesus and living out the corporal and spiritual works of mercy.

The Heart of Our Faith

Fr. James Donohue, CR

One of the priest-professors in the seminary told our class on homiletics that if we were to be effective preachers, then we needed to have the Bible in one hand and the newspaper in the other. It was his way of saying what is stated more formally in the General Instruction of the Roman Missal about the homily:

> It should be an explanation of some aspect of the readings from
> Sacred Scripture or of another text from the Ordinary or the Proper
> of the Mass of the day and should take into account both the mys-
> tery being celebrated and the particular needs of the listeners. (65)

This statement made an impression upon me, although I have to admit
that one weekend, early in my priesthood, I wished that I had not been
paying such close attention in the homiletics class that day.

It was the fall of 1983 and a large Canadian department chain was
intimidating workers who were attempting to unionize. The Canadian
bishops had publicly stated that the workers had a right to unionize. I
remember watching this story unfold on the news and feeling some pride
that the bishops had taken a public stand on an issue that was controversial. What I heard articulated by the bishops was in complete conformity
with what I had been taught in another seminary class on Catholic social
teaching. What surprised me were the number of parishioners who called
the rectory that week to wonder or to complain—I remember more com-
plaining—about the bishops meddling in affairs of which they had no
right to speak. There was the church and there was the world. Who did
these bishops think they were anyway?

Young, energetic, convinced, and naïve, I leapt into the fray with a
Sunday homily that attempted to explain why the bishops had weighed
in on this issue, underlying the fundamental point that people had
certain rights that flowed from the dignity of the person: the right to
organize, the right to fair pay, the right to safe working conditions, and
so forth. Knowing that it was a controversial issue, I was careful not to
be strident and to present this message as gently as possible. To put it
mildly, everyone had a reaction to this homily. Some parishioners found
it very helpful, telling me that it assisted them to make sense of what
the bishops had said. They let me know that they appreciated hearing
about church teaching that helped them understand a problem that was
dominating the news.

Others, however, were—simply put—enraged. I will never forget one
man in particular. I had just baptized his infant daughter two weeks earlier.
I went to the celebratory barbeque on that Sunday afternoon, returning
to the rectory with a good feeling that this is what pastoral ministry is all
about. And now he was inches from me, his face scarlet, yelling at the top of
his lungs, *damning* me for "allowing this filth into our church." He wanted
to know who the "idiot" was who ordained me and promised to phone
the local bishop, which he did on Monday morning. The only humorous
relief came from my pastor, who, imitating his counterpart played by Jack

Lemmon in the movie *Mass Appeal,* leaned over to the servers and said, "We will take the short way out!"

Social Dimensions of the Gospel

This experience for me was an introduction to the reality that preaching the gospel and the social teaching of the church, while challenging for many parishioners, will also be a challenge to the preacher. But, this reminds me of a stark fact brought forward by that same homiletics teacher who also said, "If you preach Sunday after Sunday, and people always say, 'That was great, Father,' you are probably not preaching the Gospel." God's word, as we know, "is living and effective, sharper than any two-edged sword, penetrating even between soul and spirit, joints and marrow, and able to discern reflections and thoughts of the heart" (Heb 4:12). Like it was for St. Paul, the contemporary preaching of the gospel will entail some suffering, which the preacher may have to share on behalf of his Body, the church (Col 1:24).

In a pastoral letter, Sharing Catholic Social Teaching: Challenges and Directions (1998), the US Catholic bishops begin by describing the basic challenge:

> Far too many Catholics are not familiar with the basic content of Catholic social teaching. More fundamentally, many Catholics do not adequately understand that the social teaching of the Church is an essential part of Catholic faith. This poses a serious challenge for all Catholics, since it weakens our capacity to be a Church that is true to the demands of the Gospel.

In a more recent essay, Kelly S. Johnson raises the question as to why it is that more Catholics do not know and care about the social teachings of the church. Although the bishops have developed the rich tradition of Catholic social teaching into seven themes that have made it more accessible, Johnson maintains that the social gospel is still not part of "the devotional, emotional, personal faith of most Catholics." Johnson's view is that the "social teaching" is partitioned off as such, leading to the problem that it "is not just that people need to know about the teaching, but that the teaching needs to be more clearly integrated into the ordinary life of faith."[7]

---

[7] Kelly S. Johnson, "Catholic Social Teaching," *Gathered for the Journey: Moral Theology in Catholic Perspective,* ed. David Matzko McCarthy and M. Therese Lysaught (Grand Rapids, MI: Eerdmans, 2007), 232.

For the bishops, the way to this integration lies in the efforts of continued education. From their own findings, the bishops realize that there is a pressing need to educate all Catholics on the church's social teaching and to share the social demands of the gospel and Catholic tradition more clearly. But while the bishops support new initiatives to integrate the social teachings of the church more fully into educational and catechetical programs and institutions, they also encourage "continuing formation of priests so they can more effectively preach, teach, and share the Church's social tradition and its concrete implications for our time" (ibid.). Although the homily cannot bear the entire weight of assisting people to integrate the social dimensions of the gospel into their lives of faith, there is an important role for it, especially when we consider how few people are exposed to or take advantage of ongoing formation and education opportunities.

I would like to think about the role of the homily as part of the broader initiative to assist people to integrate Catholic social teaching, in general, and the issue of the death penalty, in particular, by reflecting upon four aspects that touch upon the lives of contemporary believers: the demand for ongoing conversion, the call to discipleship, the need for evangelization, and the prism through which we understand human dignity.

Demand for Ongoing Conversion

Whenever we really enjoy a novel, it is most likely because we have entered into the world of the characters and places we have visited. In a sense, we have entered the text and have become part of it in some way. What is most interesting is that when we return from the "world" of this text to our own "world," we are often not the same. The text has the power to change us, to alter our views, to challenge our perspectives, to refocus how we see. In this sense, we can say that we have undergone some type of change or conversion through our encounter with the text.

A good homilist immerses himself into the text of the gospel and invites his congregation to enter with him into this world. This gospel world is, of course, different from the one that we usually experience because it is a world of graciousness, forgiveness, love, and compassion. Its story unfolds in unpredictable and unlikely ways, filled with paradoxes about losing your life in order to save your life (Mark 8:35), parables about how "the last will be first, and the first will be last" (Matt 20:16), and hard sayings such as "love your enemies" (Luke 6:27) and forgive "not seven times but seventy-seven times" (Matt 18:22). The gospel stories reveal to us a new world, with a new way of seeing that challenges us to see not like human beings see, but like God sees (Mark 8:33).

The homilist understands that just like himself, each member of the congregation has his or her own story with its own views and perspectives, patterns and predictabilities, tried-and-true ways of dealing with the realities of the world. But, the degree to which the homilist can assist people to enter into the story of the gospel and to conform themselves more closely to the person of Christ in his words and deeds, he will help people to change and to return to their own "world" markedly different. To the degree that people—each with his or her own story—become taken up into the story of Jesus, they will undergo conversion.

Preaching about the death penalty may include significant factual information relevant to the issue, but most importantly it is about helping the congregation to understand and to enter more fully into God's reign. It is about embracing and living out the values of God's reign in a world that often views forgiveness, compassion, and reconciliation as impractical, naïve, and foolish. It is about allowing God to change our hearts so that we will not be like those with "hard hearts." It is about opening our eyes to see as God sees. Conversion into the reign of God is the ground of possibility for people to be open to changing their minds and hearts about the death penalty. For only those who begin to see as God sees, who conform themselves ever more closely to Christ and his ways, will be able to exchange what our world commonly values—power, revenge, violence, and retribution—for what is valued in the reign of God: peace, forgiveness, reconciliation, and compassion.

The Call of Discipleship

Preaching about the death penalty cannot happen in a vacuum. While conversion into the reign of God opens possibilities of seeing differently, the call of discipleship provides the context for living this new life faithfully, hopefully, and lovingly. Preaching God's word is an opportunity to invite a congregation to imitate the One they worship. It is also the opportunity to assist the gathered community to grow in the awareness that this task of imitating Jesus is impossible without the grace of God. The church's Lectionary, over the course of the three-year liturgical cycle, offers many openings to pursue this truth. By way of illustration, two particular examples of how preaching can underscore this call of discipleship occur in the gospels throughout the Lenten season and gospel readings from Mark in Year B. In the case of the Lenten weekday gospels, it is interesting

to note that at the beginning of Lent the selections are taken from the
Synoptic Gospels, while toward the end of the Lenten season the selections
are taken from John. The Synoptic selections expose the congregation to
the ethical demands of Jesus and the cost and paradoxes of discipleship:
beginning anew, conversion, mutual forgiveness, hardness of heart, love
of enemies, absolute claims of justice and love over ritual and cult, the
call to holiness, and so forth.[8] For its part, the christological passages from
John expose us to the realization that salvation comes from the crucified
one who has been raised, and not from ourselves. He is the Son of God
in whom all who believe will have eternal life.

Mark Searle reflects upon how these two sections of the Lectionary fit
together. He notes that it is "no accident" that there is a shift from the
social and ethical dimensions of discipleship to christological passages
about the identity and mission of Christ:

> The shift from the "ethical" to the "christological" is no accident.
> The purpose of the first part of Lent is to bring us to compunction.
> "Compunction" is etymologically related to the verb "to puncture"
> and suggests the deflation of our lives as disciples of Jesus. By hitting
> us again and again with demands which we not only fail to obey, but
> which we come to recognize as being quite beyond us, the Gospel
> passages are meant to trouble us, to confront our illusions about
> ourselves. "Remember you are dust . . . " From this perspective,
> Lenten penance may be more effective if we fail in our resolutions
> than if we succeed, for its purpose is not to confirm us in our sense
> of virtue but to bring us home to our radical need of salvation. It
> is in answer to this profound awareness of need that the lection-
> ary shifts from the synoptic gospels to John, from the demands of
> discipleship to the person of Jesus. John presents Jesus as Savior,
> but Jesus can only save those who know their need for salvation.[9]

Similarly, the readings from Mark's gospel in Year B provide provocative
instruction on discipleship. In particular, readings from chapters 8–10
over consecutive Sundays reveal a Jesus and a road of discipleship that
is challenging and exasperating, not only for the disciples in the gospel,
but also for the preacher and the congregation. It should not surprise us
that this arrangement of stories is framed at each end with stories of the
healing of blind men—suggesting to us that the call of discipleship is not
something that is self-evident or easily seen.

---

[8] Mark Searle, "The Spirit of Lent," *Assembly* 8:3 (1981): 198.
[9] Ibid.

In these series of readings, the pattern is repeated three different times wherein Jesus talks about his upcoming suffering and death and the disciples, in turn, show that they do not understand that discipleship entails service and sacrifice in the way of the cross: Peter rebukes Jesus and his plan to go to Jerusalem (Mark 8:32), the disciples reveal that they had been discussing who among them was the greatest (Mark 9:34), and James and John ask Jesus for seats at his right and left when he comes into glory (Mark 10:37). Jesus meets their obtuseness with paradoxical teachings about discipleship: "whoever loses his life for my sake and that of the gospel will save it" (Mark 8:35); "If anyone wishes to be first, he shall be the last of all and the servant of all" (Mark 9:35); and "whoever wishes to be great among you will be your servant; whoever wishes to be first among you will be the slave of all" (Mark 10:43-44).

Like the disciples in Mark's gospel, preacher and congregation alike continue to struggle along "the way," trying to understand and appropriate the life and demands of the One who is "the Way." We find ourselves coming face-to-face with our own inability to live out the gospel demands of forgiveness, reconciliation, and compassion, crying out, "Then who can be saved?" But like the disciples, we too hear the words of Jesus in response: "For human beings it is impossible, but not for God. All things are possible for God" (Mark 10:26-27).

The call of discipleship that unfolds throughout the Lectionary—in many more places than the examples given here from the Lenten season and from the Markan gospel readings in Year B—provides many opportunities for the preacher to ground any issue that makes demands on a person in the authentic call to live faithfully, hopefully, and lovingly. They are opportunities to help people to have faith that God will fill the space that remains when people let go of hatred, revenge, and retribution. They are opportunities to enable people to hope in the one who proclaims that he makes "all things new," bringing forth new life from the worst situations that we could imagine. They are opportunities to encourage people to imitate Jesus in love and compassion as we forgive those who have harmed us. But most importantly, they are reminders, again and again, that we live as disciples in faith, hope, and love, not through our own power, but through the grace of God in his Son and the power of the Holy Spirit.

The Need for Evangelization

It is important for Catholics to hear God's word illumine an issue such as the death penalty, not only for the sake of the parishioners themselves, but also for the sake of "the world." One of the great movements in the church since the Second Vatican Council is the growing awareness and appropriation that the laity have taken to be salt for the earth and light for the world. This service to the world is rooted in a person's baptism.

The Second Vatican Council continually speaks of baptism as the source of all Christian service, clerical and lay. For instance, the Dogmatic Constitution on the Church (*Lumen Gentium*) identifies baptism as the source of all Christians' participation in the threefold mission of Christ as priest, prophet, and king (10–13). This teaching states that, by baptism, the laity "have been made sharers in their own way in the priestly, prophetic and kingly office of Christ and play their part in carrying out the mission of the whole christian people in the church and in the world" (31).

This is indeed a lofty challenge, but it is the particular role of the layperson to be engaged in the world, providing other people with a new perspective that leads to changed hearts. Good preaching will form and enable parishioners to carry out this important task that is specific to their mission in the world. It is this new reality that encouraged Pope Paul VI, in his apostolic exhortation *Evangelii Nuntiandi* (1975), marking the tenth anniversary of the Second Vatican Council, to take up the theme of evangelization. Here he expressed his desire "to make the Church of the twentieth century ever better fitted for proclaiming the Gospel to the people of the twentieth century" (2). In particular, he explained that prominent among the elements of evangelization is the rejection of violence and the humane treatment of all people, all of which is dependent upon a conversion of heart. But Pope Paul also recognized that in order for this to happen the church needs good preaching and teaching. He called upon "especially those 'who are assiduous in preaching and teaching' (1 Tim 5:17), so that each one of them may follow 'a straight course in the message of the truth' (2 Tim 2:15), and may work as a preacher of the Gospel and acquit himself perfectly of his ministry" (5). In the process of evangelizing herself, the church, in turn, sends out evangelizers (15).

Human Dignity

Underlying any preaching, implicit or explicit, about the death penalty will be the church's teaching on the dignity of the human person. But this may prove to be more challenging than a preacher might first think. As Kelly Johnson notes in her essay on Catholic social teaching, "The value of human dignity as such is not contested. What is contested is who counts as a person, what 'dignity' requires, and how it is to be upheld when it costs something to others."[10] In his encyclical *Dives in Misericordia* (1980), Pope John Paul II takes up the issue of human dignity as it emerges through the relationship between justice and mercy. On the one hand, he stressed that "reparation for evil and scandal, compensation for injury, and satisfaction for insult are conditions for forgiveness." On the other hand, John Paul II contends that "mercy has the power to confer on justice a new content which is expressed most fully in forgiveness" (14). Situations that call for forgiveness are the very ones that challenge us to embody our belief in the dignity of the other:

> Society can become "ever more human" only when we introduce into all the mutual relationships which form its moral aspect the moment of forgiveness, which is so much of the essence of the Gospel. Forgiveness demonstrates the presence in the world of the love which is more powerful than sin. Forgiveness is also the fundamental condition for reconciliation, not only in the relationship of God with man, but also in relationships between people. A world from which forgiveness was eliminated would be nothing but a world of cold and unfeeling justice, in the name of which each person would claim his or her own rights vis-a-vis others; the various kinds of selfishness latent in man would transform life and human society into a system of oppression of the weak by the strong, or into an arena of permanent strife between one group and another. (14)

Assisting people to reflect upon other experiences of forgiveness in their lives will assist them to see that their choice to forgive is not a concession to weakness, but the path to happiness and long-term fulfillment.

Preaching about the death penalty will take conviction and courage. But it cannot be done in a vacuum nor can it bear the entire weight as the only place where the church's teaching is articulated. Whatever the difficulties, however, God's word of forgiveness, compassion, and reconciliation must be brought to bear on this issue for the sake of all involved. Archbishop Oscar Romero, martyred in 1980—shot at a chapel as he was finishing a homily—was a person who knew something about proclaiming God's word in the midst of controversy. Archbishop Romero reminds us, "We cannot segregate God's word from the historical reality in which it is proclaimed. It would not then be God's word. . . . It becomes God's word because it vivifies, enlightens, contrasts, repudiates, praises what is

---

[10] Johnson, "Catholic Social Teaching," 227.

going on today in this society."[11] The preacher will need to sow the seeds of discipleship and human dignity so that this social issue, like any other, will take root in the lives of parishioners, who are continually called to conversion and the commitment to give witness to the gospel in the world.

Review and Looking Forward

This final chapter emphasizes that Christian conversion entails seeing differently and living this new vision "faithfully, hopefully, and lovingly." Preaching offers an opportunity to invite persons of faith to become more Christlike and to bring them to recognize all that is made possible through God's grace. Thus faith, hope, and love are central to the call of discipleship. Dorothy Day strove to follow this call, and she did so humbly, recognizing all this entailed—the challenges, obstacles, and weaknesses, coupled with the triumphs, joys, and delights. Jim Forest, who knew her so well, spoke of his endless wonder that, despite all her challenges and trials, "she nonetheless retained her capacity for faith, hope and love down to the last day of her life. She occasionally spoke of 'the duty of hope.'"[12] Filled with hope, she spoke out against the death penalty long before many others—clergy and laity—would join her powerful witness.

Those who knew Dorothy often spoke of her amazing perseverance, a perseverance that could only be sustained through hope. In a September 1957 issue of the *Catholic Worker*, she explains that all we can do, really, are the little things and hope that God will provide:

> One of the greatest evils of the day is the sense of futility. Young people say, "What can one person do? What is the sense of our small effort?" They cannot see that we can only lay one brick at a time, take one step at a time; we can be responsible only for the one action of the present moment. But we can beg for an increase of love in our hearts that will vitalize and transform our actions, and know that God will take them and multiply them, as Jesus multiplied the loaves and the fishes.[13]

Her words in a 1946 *Catholic Worker* article underline the point: "What we would like to do is change the world. . . . We can throw our pebble in

---

[11] Archbishop Oscar Romero, in a homily given on November 27, 1977, in *Oscar Romero: The Violence of Love*, trans. and ed. James R. Brockman, SJ (Maryknoll, NY: Orbis Books, 1988), 11–12.

[12] Forest, *All Is Grace*, 330.

[13] Ibid., 209.

the pond and be confident that its ever-widening circle will reach around the world. We repeat, there is nothing that we can do but love, and dear God—please enlarge our hearts to love each other, to love our neighbor, to love our enemy as well as our friend."[14] Like Archbishop Romero, she knew the challenge of proclaiming God's words amidst controversy and shared his hope that God's word "vivifies, enlightens, contrasts, repudiates, praises what is going on today in this society." She would be joyful over the powerful gospel witness of the church's teaching to end the use of the death penalty. Faithfully, hopefully, and lovingly, she would call each of us to do all we can—as clergy and laity—to "look ahead" in spreading the good news of this gospel witness.

Questions for Discussion

1. For many years, members of the Catholic Worker Movement stood for one night a month outside death row in Baltimore, silently witnessing their opposition to the death penalty. Discuss the value and importance of such witness. Think about other forms of gospel witness, in regard to the death penalty, that we might perform as a matter of faith.

2. Jim Donohue speaks of how challenging it is to preach the social dimensions of the gospel. It is difficult for both parishioners and preachers. Discuss whether you have stories similar to Fr. Jim's homily about unions. Imagine what the responses might be if a homily were preached on the death penalty. Discuss ways in which parishioners can encourage their congregations to affirm what Cardinal Bernardin called "the seamless garment of life."

3. This book began with the current situation of the death penalty in the United States, considered the development of the Catholic Church's teaching on the death penalty, returned to the moral dimensions of the current practice of the death penalty, and ended with the call to witness the gospel in relation to this current practice. Reflecting back on the details of this lengthy exploration, discuss how you think the gospel, in the words of Oscar Romero, "vivifies, enlightens, contrasts, repudiates, praises what is going on today in this society" regarding the death penalty.

---

[14] Ibid., 180.

Conclusion

Vicki Schieber

As one of the coeditors, I sit here writing the conclusion to our book on the thirty-eighth anniversary of my daughter Shannon's birth. The past week has been filled with so many beautiful memories of her time with us. Gazing at Shannon for the first time minutes after her birth, my husband Syl and I could never have imagined the incredible gift she would become in our lives as well as in the lives of the hundreds of people she would touch in her short twenty-three years on this earth.

Shannon had a real passion for social justice from an early age. In her youth she began working with low-income families needing home repairs through Rebuilding Together in Washington, DC, and later during periods of employment and graduate school, she was a volunteer teacher in Junior Achievement programs in the poorest sections of New York City and Philadelphia. Often she would come home and tell us that we needed to be doing more to help solve the problems of discrimination, poverty, and lack of employment opportunities she witnessed in the inner-city areas where she served. She really wanted to make a difference through her life and truly believed that "to whom much is given, much is expected." In her final year of life Shannon was completing the first year of her graduate studies at the University of Pennsylvania and living in Philadelphia. In May of 1998 a serial rapist broke into her apartment, and raped and murdered her on the day before she was to return home for the summer. Her students in the West Philadelphia Catholic High School Junior Achievement program were planning an end-of-year party to thank her for her work. Shannon never attended that party, but now a plaque honoring her work hangs in our home, a gift of the nuns she taught with at the school.

At the time of Shannon's death my husband and I knew little about the criminal justice system, specifically about the death penalty and its

arbitrary application related to race, geography, defendar
conviction of innocents, inadequate legal defense funds, anc
soon became involved with organizations of victims' family n
began to understand the inequities in the use of the death ¢
well as the incredible toll the system takes on surviving family members.
By the time Shannon's assailant was captured four years later, we had
learned that pursuing the death penalty would not be the way we would
want to honor our daughter's life, nor would that decision have helped
us deal with the painful reminders of her unfulfilled hopes and dreams.

Shannon's murder also forced us to come to grips with the teachings
of our Catholic faith and the lessons learned from numerous years of
Catholic education. We were tested in ways that no religion course exams
ever covered. Our struggle to respond with forgiveness and compassion
when we felt such intense anger and desire for revenge was challenging,
to say the least. Facing the reality of her death made us realize that the sacredness of life was not an abstract concept. Ultimately we concluded that
if we couldn't stand by our principles when it was excruciatingly difficult,
then they were not our principles at all. We took the stand to oppose the
use of capital punishment for our daughter's murder. Her assailant now
serves a sentence of life without the possibility of parole in a maximum
security prison. We could almost hear Shannon whispering to us then,
"Okay, now that you have experienced this unfair and biased system, what
are you going to do about it?"

We continued on our path to finding peace by seeking ways to honor
Shannon's memory. In the early years we were invited to share our story
with fellow communities of faith, teach classes at high schools and uni-
versities, and testify before state legislators considering changes in the
criminal justice system. We have learned over these years the importance
that education plays in the declining support for the death penalty evi-
denced in nationwide polls, and began to actively work in several of the
growing number of states that have repealed this sentence in recent years.

Our goal to educate society has continued in recent years through our
work with the Catholic Mobilizing Network to End the Use of the Death
Penalty (CMN). The mission of this organization, based in Washington,
DC, is to proclaim the church's unconditional pro-life teaching and its
application to capital punishment and restorative justice. CMN's goal is
to prepare Catholics for informed involvement in campaigns to repeal
state death penalty laws and to expand or inaugurate restorative justice
programs. I encourage you to learn more about and become involved in
this organization (www.catholicsmobilizing.org).

In 2010 CMN was invited to set up a second office at Mount St. Mary's University in Emmitsburg, Maryland. Our work on this campus involves collaborating with faculty on course curriculum, student intern projects, conference planning, and the publishing of this death penalty book. I have deeply enjoyed working with my fellow editors and members of the Mount community on this book and these other initiatives.

The excellent content of the sixteen chapters of this book teaches what we personally learned on our journey. The readers gain a deeper understanding of the many flaws in the system and the pain it causes, not only for murder victims' families, but also for the families of the executed and all those who interact with death row inmates awaiting execution. Our hope is that delving into each of these chapters will strengthen readers' knowledge of Catholic social teaching on the sacredness of all life, and hopefully encourage their involvement in and support of CMN's mission.

Father Jim Donohue's ending chapter, "The Heart of Our Faith," describes beautifully the gifts of the Holy Spirit that my husband and I received in "allowing God to change our hearts so that we will not be like those with 'hard hearts.'" We learned to "exchange what our world commonly values—power, revenge, violence, and retribution—for what is valued in the reign of God: peace, forgiveness, reconciliation, and compassion." Just imagine the impact these values would have on making a difference in our society today. We know Shannon is smiling as we continue this work in her honor.